THE KOVELS'
ILLUSTRATED PRICE GUIDE
TO
DEPRESSION GLASS
AND
AMERICAN DINNERWARE

THE KOVELS'
ILLUSTRATED PRICE GUIDE
TO
DEPRESSION GLASS
AND
AMERICAN DINNERWARE

Ralph and Terry Kovel

CROWN PUBLISHERS, INC.   NEW YORK

Inquiries should be addressed to Crown Publishers, Inc., One Park Avenue, New York, New York 10016

Printed in the United States of America

Published simultaneously in Canada by General Publishing Company Limited

Library of Congress Cataloging in Publication Data

Kovel, Ralph M.
  The Kovels' illustrated price guide to depression
glass and American dinnerware.

  1. Depression glass—Catalogs. 2. Ceramic tableware
—United States—History—20th century—Catalogs.
I. Kovel, Terry H., joint author. II. Title. III. Ti-
tle: Illustrated price guide to depression glass and
American dinnerware.
NK5439.D44K68 1980   738.2'0973'0750973   80-23905
ISBN: 0-517-540231

10 9 8 7 6 5 4 3

Acknowledgments

Fred and Jean Bailey, Jacksonville, Illinois; Barnes Antiques, Washington, Illinois; Betty's Glass Shop, Kenton, Ohio; Betty Blair Antiques, Jackson, Ohio; The Bonacquistas; The Bosworths, Kansas City, Missouri; Don and Irma Brewer; Bric-A-Brac Shop, Kansas City, Missouri; Nancy Brock, Rock Island, Illinois; Buttsville Center, Buttsville, New Jersey; Virginia Hillway Buxton; N.Y.; Denny's Antiques, Williamsburg, Missouri; Gloria's Collectibles, Orefield, Pennsylvania; Jaunita Grimes, Elmore City, Oklahoma; Gschwends Glass, Perkin, Illinois; Halbea Antiques, Washington, Iowa; Arlene and Marty Harty, Barrington, New Hampshire; The Hudsons, Ft. Worth, Texas; Bob and Sharon Huxford, Covington, Indiana; Norma Jones, Louisville, Kentucky; Ina Kansler, New York, NY.; Ann Kerr, Sidney, Ohio; Harriet Kurshadt, Lansing Lynn Antiques, Springfield, Illinois; Larry Lafary, Springfield, Missouri; Laub's Loft, Kewanee, Illinois; Mary's Antiques, Oklahoma City, Oklahoma; Merry Go Round Antiques, Metuchen, New Jersey; Minnewaska Trading Post, St. Petersburg, Florida; John Moses; Maxine Nelson, Huntington Beach, California; Betty and Bill Newbound, Union Lake, Michigan; Northwest Mfg. & Display Inc., Samuels, Idaho; Norma Rehl, Milford, New Jersey; Bob Thayer Antiques, Chicago, Illinois; Tin Hen House Antiques, Arthur, Illinois; Wayside Antiques, Zanesville, Ohio.

Special thanks to Jo Cunningham and the staff of *The Glaze* for their assistance; the dealers of the Second Annual American Pottery Earthenware and China Show; Mr. and Mrs. Fred McMorrow and the Western Reserve Depression Glass Collectors for their help with photographs; and a extra thanks to Don Hall for the hundreds of photographs.

Collector Clubs and Publications

National Depression Glass Association
News & Views
721 Cambridge Dr.
Lees Summit, MO 64063
(write for local chapter)

Paden City Partyline
13325 Danvers Way
Westminister, CA 92683

*Fiesta Collectors & Dealers
 Newsletter*
P.O. Box 100582
Nashville, TN 37210

Fiesta Dispatch
P.O. Box 2625
Toledo, OH 43606

National Autumn Leaf Collectors
4002 35th St.
Rock Island, IL 61201

Depression Glass

Introduction

Pastel-colored glassware in matching sets became popular about 1925. The Fostoria Glass Company of Fostoria, Ohio, made the first of these glass sets, which included dinner plates, coffee cups, and other pieces to be used at a dinner table. The glassware was expensive and its popularity led to similar pieces being made by other companies that were able to produce a less expensive glass.

Inexpensive glass was made by a method called tank molding: Silica sand, soda ash, and limestone were heated, and the molten glass mixture was passed through pipes to the automated pressing mold. Patterns were acid etched or tooled into the mold so the finished glassware had some design. Because the pressing process made a glass that often had flaws or bubbles, patterns used as decoration were often lacy in appearance as this helped to hide the flaws.

During the late 1960s interest in the inexpensive pastel glass led to several books and the term "Depression glass" came into general use, even though the glassware was made before, during, and after the Depression. The name has gradually come to include other glassware made from 1925 through the 1970s. Our price list includes the lacy types—pseudo-Sandwich glass, and Hobnail patterns, as well as the colors cobalt blue, ruby red, and many types of opaque-colored glass that are similar to milk glass.

Depression-glass designs can be divided into groups. The etched designs—e.g., "Adam" or "Cherry Blossom"—were made first, from about 1925 to 1935. Pastel colors were used.

Raised designs, often with fruit and flower patterns—e.g., "Open Rose" and "Sharon"—were made in the mid-1930s. Strong colors like cobalt blue or royal ruby, opaque glass, pastels, and clear glass were popular.

Geometric wares—e.g., "Hobnail" and "Ribbon"—were made during the late 1920s and again in the late 1930s and early 1940s. Simple outlines and bold colors predominated. Art Deco-influenced geometric designs include "Imperial Octagon" or "United States Octagon."

Enameled or silk-screen patterns were developed during the 1940s. White enameled designs were added to the glass. Cobalt blue, royal ruby, and clear glass were

3

the most popular colors that were decorated this way. Shirley Temple glasswares and "Sailboats" are two such enameled patterns.

A few patterns, "Floral & Diamond Band" for example, were made to resemble the cut glass of the nineteenth century, particularly the "Lacy Sandwich" pattern made by the Sandwich, Massachusetts Glassworks. About ten such pseudo-Sandwich patterns were made, and most of them were referred to as "Sandwich" in the manufacturers' catalogs.

Depression glass utility wares were also made. The dishes were made for use in the kitchen and not on the table—e.g., ice-box dishes, lemon reamers, cannister sets.

Opaque glass was popular in the 1930s. Each of the colors was given a special name by the company that produced it—e.g., "Monax" or "Ivrene." (See Glossary for color names and descriptions.)

There are many reproductions being made. Some are reissues by companies that sell full sets in retail stores. Some are deliberate fakes meant to fool the collector.

This book is a price guide to the marketplace, not an in-depth study of Depression glass. For more information about patterns, manufacturers, collector groups, and how and where to buy, see the books and publications listed in the Bibliography.

Bibliography

BOOKS

Anderton, Johana Gast. *The Glass Rainbow.* Kansas City, MO: Trojan Press, 1969.
Brady, Ann. *1979 Western Depression Glass Price Guide.* Privately Printed: 4413 N.E. Fremont, Portland, OR, 1979.
Florence, Gene. *The Collectors Encyclopedia of Depression Glass,* 4th ed. Paducah, KY: Collector Books, 1979.
Klamkin, Marian. *The Collector's Guide to Depression Glass.* New York: Hawthorne Books, 1973.
————. *The Depression Glass Collector's Price Guide.* New York: Hawthorne Books, 1974.
McGrain, Pat. *1979 Price Survey.* Frederick, MD : McGrain Publications, 1978.
Stearns, Glenita. *The Depression Glass Dictionary.* Privately Printed: 5040 S. I Street, Tacoma, WA, 1971.
Stout, Sandra McPhee. *Depression Glass III.* Des Moines, IA: Wallace-Homestead, 1976.
Weatherman, Hazel. *Colored Glassware of the Depression Era 2.* Springfield, MO: Glassbooks, 1974.
————. *Colored Glassware of the Depression Era 2: Price Trends.* Springfield, MO: Glassbooks, 1977.

MAGAZINES AND NEWSPAPERS

Depression Glass Glaze. P.O. Box 57, Otisville, MI 48463.
Glass Review. P.O. Box 2315, Costa Mesa, CA 92626.
National Glass, Pottery & Collectables Journal. 361 E. Main St., Kutztown, PA 19530.
Obsession in Depression. 20415 Harvest Ave., Lakewood, CA 90715.
The Glaze. P.O. Box 4929, Springfield, MO 65804.
Depression Glass National Market Appraisal Report. 2943 Realty Court, Gastonia, NC 28016.

Color Chart

AMBER	Topaz, golden glow
BLUE GREEN	Ultra-marine
CLEAR	Crystal
CREAM OPAQUE	Cremax, clambroth, chinex
DEEP BLUE	Ritz blue, cobalt, dark blue, deep blue
GREEN	Springtime green, emerald, imperial green
IVORY	Ivrene
MEDIUM BLUE	Madonna
OPAQUE BLACK	Black
OPAQUE BLUE	Delphite
OPAQUE GREEN	Jadite
OPAQUE WHITE	Milk white, monax
PINK	Rose Marie, rose, rose pink, rose tint, rose glow, nu-rose, wild rose, flamingo
PURPLE	Burgundy, amythyst
RED	Royal ruby, ruby red

Adam

Adam was made by the Jeannette Glass Company of Jeannette, Pennsylvania, from 1932 to 1934. It is found in green or pink.

GREEN

Ashtray, 4 1/2 In.	10.00 to 15.00
Berry Bowl, 4 3/4 In.	8.00
Bowl, Covered, 9 In.	12.00 to 30.00
Bowl, Oval, 10 In.	12.00 to 15.00
Bowl, 5 3/4 In.	8.00 to 12.00
Bowl, 7 3/4 In.	8.50 to 14.00
Bowl, 9 In.	7.00
Butter, Bottom	50.00
Butter, Covered	168.00 to 270.00
Candlestick	22.50
Candlestick, 4 In., Pair	38.00 to 65.00
Candy Container, Covered	25.00
Candy Container, Covered, 2 1/2 In.	85.00
Coaster, 3 1/4 In.	4.00 to 12.50
Creamer	6.00 to 6.50
Cup	3.33 to 11.00
Cup & Saucer	11.00 to 14.95
Pitcher	23.00 to 26.00
Plate, Cake, Footed, 10 In.	10.00
Plate, Grill, 9 In.	5.00 to 9.50

Plate, Square, 7 3/4 In.	3.00 to 7.50
Plate, Square, 9 In.	6.00 to 11.00
Plate, 6 In.	2.25 to 3.00
Platter, 12 In.	7.00 to 16.50
Relish, Divided, 8 In.	7.50
Salt & Pepper, Footed, 4 In.	52.50
Saucer,	2.00 to 3.00
Sherbet, 3 In.	1.00 to 16.00
Sugar & Creamer, Covered	35.00
Sugar, Covered	17.50
Sugar, Open	7.00 to 10.00
Tumbler, Footed, 4 1/2 In.	5.00 to 12.50
Tumbler, Footed, 5 1/2 In.	13.00 to 22.50
Vase, 7 1/2 In.	19.50 to 24.00

PINK

Ashtray	12.00 to 20.00
Ashtray, 4 1/2 In.	6.50 to 20.00
Berry Bowl, 4 3/4 In.	4.25 to 7.00
Bowl, Covered, 9 In.	12.50 to 28.00
Bowl, Oval, 10 In.	5.00 to 12.00
Bowl, 5 3/4 In.	8.00 to 17.50
Bowl, 7 3/4 In.	7.50 to 9.75

Adam

Adam

Adam

Butter, Bottom .... 6.00 to 85.00
Butter, Covered ...... 52.50 to 225.00
Candlestick, 4 In. ..... 16.00 to 20.00
Candlestick, 4 In., Pair . 27.50 to 35.00
Candy Container, Covered 28.00
Candy Container, Lid, 2 1/2 In. 33.50
Coaster .... 5.00 to 12.00
Creamer .... 5.00 to 9.00
Cup .... 5.00 to 15.00
Cup & Saucer .... 10.00 to 14.50
Pitcher, Cone Shape, Square Base 26.00
Pitcher, Round Base 38.00
Plate, Cake, Footed, 10 In. 5.00 to 10.00
Plate, Grill, 9 In. .... 4.50 to 9.50
Plate, Square, 6 In. ...... 2.00 to 4.00
Plate, Square, 7 3/4 In. . 3.50 to 17.50
Plate, Square, 9 In. ..... 5.50 to 10.00

Platter, 11 3/4 In. ...... 5.00 to 15.00
Relish, Divided, 8 In. .... 3.50 to 9.50
Salt & Pepper, Footed, 4 In. ... 35.00
Saltshaker .... 8.00 to 12.50
Saucer, Square .... 1.50 to 3.00
Sherbet, 3 In. .... 2.00 to 12.50
Sugar & Creamer, Covered 27.50
Sugar, Covered .... 14.00 to 19.50
Tumbler, Footed, 4 1/2 In. 7.50 to 12.00
Tumbler, Footed, 5 1/2 In. 16.50 to 30.00
Vase, 7 1/2 In. .... 69.50 to 70.00

Akro Agate

Akro Agate was made by the Akro Agate Company of Clarksburg, West Virginia, from 1932 to 1951. It was found in many basic colors and shades.

AMBER
    Cup & Saucer, Child's, Interior Panel
    .... 9.00
    Plate, Child's 5.00
    Saucer, Child's 4.50
    Teapot, Child's 7.50

AZURE BLUE
    Cup & Saucer, Raised Daisy ... 25.00
BLUE
    Ashtray, Marbleized Leaf 4.50
    Ashtray, Marbleized Shell 5.00
    Bell 100.00

Creamer, Octagonal, 1 1/2 In. ...   8.00
Flowerpot, 3 In. 3.00
Match Holder 6.50
Planter, Oval, 6 In. 3.50
Planter, Ribbed, 6 X 3 1/2 In. ..   3.50
Plate, Child's, Opaque, 4 1/4 In.   10.00
Plate, Octagonal, 3 3/8 In. 5.50
Saucer, Child's, Opaque 9.00
Sugar, Disk & Panel, 1 5/8 In. .   15.00

DARK BLUE
Jar, Powder, Colonial Lady 50.00
Match Holder, 3 In. 6.00
Pitcher, Child's, 2 7/8 In. 10.00

GREEN
Bowl, Cereal 6.00
Creamer, Child's 20.00
Cup, Child's, 1 1/4 In. 16.00
Cup, Octagonal, 3 3/8 In. 7.00

Flowerpot, Ribbed Top, 2 3/4 In.   3.00
Jar, Powder, Concentric 19.50
Planter, Rectangular 6.00
Plate, Child's, 3 1/4 In. 8.00
Plate, Octagonal, 4 1/4 In. 5.00
Saucer, Child's, Chiquita, 3 1/8 In.   3.00
Saucer, Child's, Interior Panel ...   3.00

OXBLOOD
Ashtray, Square, 3 In. 5.00
Planter, Oval, 6 In. 4.00

PUMPKIN
Planter, Oval, 6 In. 8.00
Planter, Rectangular 6.00

RED
Ashtray, Rectangular, 4 In. 5.00

WHITE
Bowl, Octagonal 7.00
Saucer, Concentric Ring, 2 3/4 In.   3.50

Alice

Alice was made by the Anchor Hocking Glass Company of Lancaster, Ohio, in the 1940s. It is found in jade-ite and opaque white.

JADE-ITE
Cup 2.00
Cup & Saucer 1.00
Plate, 8 1/2 In. 1.00

OPAQUE WHITE
Cup 2.00
Plate, 10 In. 50

American Beauty, see English Hobnail

American Pioneer

American Pioneer was made by the Liberty Works of Egg Harbor, New Jersey, from 1931 to 1934. It is found in amber, crystal, green or pink.

CRYSTAL
Bowl, Footed, 8 1/2 In. 4.00
Coaster, 3 1/2 In. 1.00
Goblet, Enameled Grapes, 6 In. ..   6.00
Ice Bucket, Bark, Cambridge, 6 In.   8.00
Nappy, Fruit Center ...... .50 to 1.50
Nappy, 4 In. 4.50
Plate, Etched Grapes, 8 In. 1.25
Plate, 11 In. 8.00
Relish, Round, Fruit Decal, 8 In.   5.00

Relish, Silver Frame, 8 In. 20.00
Salt & Pepper 3.50
Stein, Beer, Child's 1.50
Tumbler, Juice, Etched, 4 In. ...   3.00
Tumbler, 10 Oz. 2.00
Vase, 7 In. 3.50
Whiskey, Etched Grapes, 2 1/4 In.   1.50

GREEN
Bowl, 2-Handled, 9 In. 7.00
Cup .... 2.50 to 5.00

Cup & Saucer .... 6.50 to 8.00
Ice Bucket With Tongs 39.50
Plate, Handled, 11 1/2 In. 9.00
Plate, 8 In. .... 3.00 to 4.50
Sugar, 2 3/4 In. 5.00
PINK
Cup 4.50
Cup & Saucer 5.50

Ice Bucket, 6 In. 22.50
Lamp, Round, 5 1/2 In. 37.50
Plate, Handled, 11 1/2 In. 8.50
Plate, 8 In. .... 2.75 to 4.00
Saucer .... .75
Tray, Vanity 6.00
Tumbler, 4 In. ....,........ 7.50
Whiskey, 2 1/4 In. .... 25.00 to 35.00

American Sweetheart

American Sweetheart was made by the MacBeth Evans Glass Company, a firm with factories in Indiana, Ohio and Pennsylvania, from 1930 to 1936. It is found in blue, cremax, crystal, green, monax (white), pink, red or smoke.

BLUE
Berry Bowl, 3 3/4 In. 12.00
Bowl, Console, 18 In. 1095.00
Bowl, 6 In. .... 3.95 to 5.00
Cup & Saucer 100.00
Plate, 8 In. 3.50
Server, 15 1/2 In. 250.00
CREMAX
Bowl, 9 In. 27.00
CRYSTAL
Sherbet, Metal Holder 4.50
MONAX
Bowl, Oval, 11 In. ..... 29.50 to 47.00
Bowl, 6 In. .... 4.00 to 10.00
Creamer, Footed .... 3.00 to 8.00
Cup .... 5.50 to 8.25
Cup & Saucer .... 7.00 to 12.00
Lamp Shade .... 650.00 to 1500.00
Plate, Center Design, 10 1/4 In.   12.50
Plate, Chop, Allover Pattern 9.50
Plate, 6 In. .... 2.50 to 3.90
Plate, 7 1/2 In. 5.00
Plate, 8 In. .... 2.75 to 8.00
Plate, 9 In. .... 4.00 to 8.75
Plate, 9 3/4 In. .... 9.00 to 12.00
Plate, 11 In. .... 6.50 to 14.50
Platter, Oval, 13 In. ... 25.00 to 40.00
Salt & Pepper, Footed 140.00 to 200.00
Salver, 12 In. .... 8.00 to 16.00
Salver, 15 1/2 In. ... 118.50 to 150.00
Saucer .... 1.25 to 3.50
Sherbet, Footed, 4 1/4 In. 12.00
Soup, Cream 29.50
Soup, Flat, 9 1/2 In. ... 10.50 to 31.50
Sugar & Creamer, Lid 135.00 to 139.50

Sugar & Creamer, Open . 6.00 to 12.00
Sugar, Open .... 3.00 to 8.00
PINK
Berry Bowl, Flat, 3 3/4 In. 14.00
Bowl, Oval, 11 In. ..... 11.00 to 18.50
Bowl, 6 In. .... 2.00 to 8.00
Bowl, 9 In. .... 8.00 to 16.00
Creamer, Footed .... 3.00 to 7.00
Cup .... 4.00 to 5.50
Cup & Saucer .... 6.95 to 8.95
Pitcher, 8 In. .... 175.00 to 265.00
Plate, 6 In. .... 1.25 to 3.50
Plate, 8 In. .... 2.00 to 5.75
Plate, 9 In. 4.50
Plate, 9 3/4 In. .... 1.70 to 10.00
Plate, 10 1/4 In. .... 7.00 to 8.95
Plate, 11 In. .... 6.00 to 6.50
Platter, Oval, 13 In. ... 10.00 to 27.50
Salt & Pepper, Footed 137.50 to 160.00
Saltshaker .... 75.00 to 100.00
Salver, 12 In. .... 5.50 to 9.00
Saucer .... 1.00 to 2.50
Sherbet, Footed 10.00
Sherbet, Footed, 4 In. .... 3.00 to 8.95
Sherbet, Metal Base 4.00
Soup, Cream, 4 1/2 In. .. 8.50 to 16.50
Soup, Flat, 9 1/2 In. ... 12.50 to 16.50
Sugar & Creamer, Open . 9.00 to 12.00
Sugar, Footed, Open 5.50
Tray, Tidbit, 2 Tier 65.00
Tumbler, 3 1/2 In. .... 18.95 to 22.00
Tumbler, 4 1/2 In. .... 22.00 to 23.00
RED
Bowl, Console, 18 In.   625.00 to 995.00
Cup .... 40.00 to 85.00

Cup & Saucer .... 52.50 to 175.00	Saucer 24.00
Plate, 8 In. .... 45.00 to 65.00	Sugar, Footed, Open 80.00
Salver, 12 In. .... 85.00 to 125.00	Tray, Tidbit, 2 Tier, 8 X 12 In. 200.00

Anniversary

Anniversary was made by the Jeannette Glass Company of Jeannette, Pennsylvania, from 1947 to 1949 in pink. It was later produced in crystal or iridescent glass from 1970 to 1972.

CRYSTAL

Berry Bowl, 4 7/8 In. .... 1.50 to 1.75
Bowl, 7 3/8 In. 1.75
Bowl, 9 In. 4.00
Butter, Covered .... 12.00 to 25.00
Candlestick, 4 7/8 In., Pair 4.00
Candy Container, Covered 12.00
Compote, Metal Base 4.00
Creamer .... 1.50 to 3.50
Cup .... 1.25 to 2.25
Cup & Saucer .... .37 to 3.00
Cup, Gold Rim 1.00
Plate, Cake, Covered ..... 6.00 to 8.00
Plate, Cake, Footed, 12 1/2 In. .. 5.00
Plate, Server, 2 Tier 10.00
Plate, 6 1/4 In. .... .75
Plate, 9 In. 2.00
Plate, 10 In. .... .40 to 3.00
Plate, 12 1/2 In. .... 3.00 to 5.00
Sugar .... 2.25 to 3.00
Sugar & Creamer .... 3.00 to 4.00
Sugar, Covered 4.00
Vase, 6 In. 2.99

Vase, 6 1/2 In. .... 3.00 to 4.00
Wine, 4 In. 4.00
IRIDESCENT
Bowl, 7 3/8 In. 3.00
Creamer 3.00
Cup .... 2.25 to 2.50
Cup & Saucer 3.50
Plate, 6 1/4 In. .... 1.00 to 2.20
Plate, 9 In. 2.50
Sugar & Creamer, Covered 10.00
PINK
Berry Bowl, 4 7/8 In. 1.50
Butter, Covered .... 19.00 to 32.00
Candy Container, Covered 16.00
Creamer .... 3.00 to 6.50
Dish, Candy, 3-Legged ... 3.00 to 3.50
Glass, Wine 6.00
Plate, 6 1/4 In. .... 1.00 to 1.75
Plate, 9 In. 4.50
Plate, 12 1/2 In. 4.00
Sherbet, Footed .... 1.50 to 3.00
Vase, Wall 12.00
Wine, 4 In. .... 6.00 to 7.50

Apple Blossom Border, see Blossoms &
Band
Apple Blossom, see Dogwood

Aunt Polly

Aunt Polly was made by the U. S. Glass Company, a firm with factories in Indiana, Ohio, Pennsylvania and West Virginia. It is found in blue, green or iridescent.

BLUE

Berry Bowl, 7 7/8 In. ... 9.50 to 22.50
Bowl, Oval, 8 3/8 In. 7.50
Bowl, 4 3/4 In. 6.00
Butter, Covered 95.00

Nappy, 4 3/8 In. 3.00
Pitcher, 8 In. 95.00
Plate, 6 In. .... 2.00 to 3.50
Plate, 8 In. .... 3.00 to 5.00
Sherbet .... 4.00 to 6.50

Tumbler, 3 5/8 In. 8.00
Vase, Footed, 6 1/2 In. 12.50
GREEN
Butter, Covered ..... 245.00 to 270.00
Creamer 10.00
Nappy, 4 3/8 In. 5.00

Plate, 6 In. 2.00
Plate, 8 In. 4.00
Sherbet .... 4.00 to 5.00
Vase, Footed, 6 1/2 In. 13.00
IRIDESCENT
Vase 13.00

Aurora, see Petalware

Avocado

Avocado was made by the Indiana Glass Company of Dunkirk, Indiana, from 1923 to 1933. It is found in crystal, green or pink. Reproduction pitchers and tumblers were made in 1973 in amethyst, blue, frosted pink, green, pink or yellow.

CRYSTAL
Bowl, 9 1/2 In. 15.00
Dish, Pickle, 2-Handled 6.00
Soup, Bowl 7.00
GREEN
Bowl, Footed, 6 In. 22.50
Bowl, Handle, 5 1/4 In. 18.00 to 20.00
Bowl, 3-Legged, 6 1/4 In. 25.00
Bowl, 7 1/2 In. .... 20.00 to 45.00
Bowl, 8 1/4 In. 30.00
Creamer, 4-Legged .... 23.75 to 32.50
Cup .... 18.50 to 25.00
Plate, 6 1/4 In. .... 7.50 to 8.95
Plate, 8 1/4 In. .... 10.00 to 19.50
Relish, 3-Footed 16.50
Saucer .... 16.00 to 22.50
Sherbet .... 35.00 to 48.00

Sugar & Creamer, 4-Legged 75.00
Sugar, 4-Legged .... 14.00 to 25.00
Tumbler, Footed, 5 1/4 In. ... 115.00
PINK
Bowl, Handle, 6 1/4 In. 12.50
Bowl, Handled, 5 1/4 In. 13.00 to 17.00
Bowl, 3-Legged, 6 1/4 In. 20.00
Cup & Saucer .... 25.00 to 42.50
Dish, Relish, Oval, Handled, 8 In. 15.00
Plate, Cake, Handled, 10 1/4 In. 37.00
Plate, 5 1/4 In. .... 6.00 to 7.00
Plate, 6 1/4 In. .... 6.00 to 7.95
Plate, 8 1/4 In. .... 9.00 to 10.00
Saucer .... 14.50 to 20.00
Sherbet .... 32.50 to 75.00
Sugar, 4-Legged 16.00
Water Set, Footed, 3 Piece ... 685.00

Ballerina, see Cameo
Banded Cherry, see Cherry Blossom
Banded Fine Rib, see Coronation
Banded Petalware, see Petalware
Banded Rainbow, see Ring
Banded Ribbon, see New Century
Banded Rings, see Ring
Basket, see No. 615

Beaded Block

Beaded Block was made by the Imperial Glass Company of Bellaire, Ohio, from 1927 to the 1930s. It is found in amber, crystal, green, ice blue, iridescent, opalescent, pink, red or vaseline.

AMBER
 Plate, Square, 7 3/4 In. 15.75
BLUE
 Creamer 20.00
 Parfait, 4 1/2 In. .... 6.50 to 12.50
 Soup, Cream, 4 1/2 In. 18.50
 Vase 14.00
CRYSTAL
 Pickle, 2-Handled, 6 1/4 In. ... 12.50
 Pitcher, 5 1/4 In. 69.50
 Vase, 6 In. 5.00
GREEN
 Bowl, Lily, Round, 4 1/2 In. 9.00
 Pitcher, 5 1/4 In. 117.50

 Plate, Square, 7 3/4 In. 4.00
 Sugar 17.50
IRIDESCENT
 Parfait, 4 1/2 In. 6.00
PINK
 Bowl, Lily, Round, 4 1/2 In. 8.00
 Parfait, 4 1/2 In. 4.00
 Plate, 7 3/4 In. 10.00
 Sugar 10.00
VASELINE
 Bowl, 6 1/2 In. 22.00
 Creamer 15.00
 Soup, Cream, 4 1/2 In. 29.50
 Sugar 15.00

Bee Hive

Bee Hive was made by the U. S. Glass Company, a firm with factories in Ohio, Pennsylvania and West Virginia, in 1926. It is found in crystal with an amber or green trim or pink.

Bee Hive, see also Queen Anne

CRYSTAL
 Butter 13.00

Sugar & Creamer, Open 5.50

Belmont, see Rose Cameo
Beverage with Sailboats, see White Ship

Block Optic

Block Optic was made by the Hocking Glass Company of Lancaster, Ohio, from 1929 to 1933. It is found in crystal, green, pink or yellow.

CRYSTAL
 Cup & Saucer 4.00
 Goblet, 5 In. .... 4.50 to 8.00
 Pitcher, 8 In. 12.50
 Plate, 6 In. .... 1.25 to 2.00
 Plate, 8 In. .... 1.75 to 2.50
 Plate, 10 1/4 In. 5.50
 Sherbet 2.00
 Sherbet, Footed, 4 3/4 In. 4.80
 Tumbler, Footed, 9 Oz. 8.00
 Tumbler, 3 1/2 In. 3.00
GREEN
 Berry Bowl, 4 1/4 In. .... 1.75 to 4.00

 Berry Bowl, 8 1/2 In. ... 7.00 to 12.50
 Bowl, 5 1/4 In. .... 2.25 to 5.50
 Butter 15.00
 Butter, Covered, 3 X 5 In. 23.00
 Candy Container, Lid, 6 1/4 In. 10.00
 Compote, 4 In. 9.50
 Creamer, Cone Shape, Footed ... 7.50
 Creamer, Flat .... 4.25 to 5.00
 Creamer, Frosted 2.75
 Cup & Saucer .... 3.50 to 6.50
 Cup, Flared 2.75
 Cup, Gold Rim 3.00
 Dish, Candy, Covered, 2 1/4 In. 16.50

Goblet, 4 1/2 In. 15.00
Goblet, 5 3/4 In. .... 6.00 to 9.00
Mug .... 15.00 to 22.50
Night Set, Bottle, Tumbler, 6 In.   23.00
Pitcher, Rope Design, 8 In. 19.00
Pitcher, 8 1/2 In. ..... 20.00 to 32.50
Plate, 6 In. .... 1.00 to 2.00
Plate, 8 In. .... 1.50 to 6.00
Plate, 9 In. .... 6.00 to 6.50
Plate, 10 1/4 In. 6.00
Salt & Pepper, Footed . 10.00 to 20.00
Saltshaker 6.50
Saucer 1.50
Saucer With Ring .... 2.00 to 2.50
Sherbet .... 1.75 to 4.00
Sherbet, Footed, 3 1/4 In. 3.50
Sherbet, Footed, 4 3/4 In. 6.50
Sugar & Creamer 7.50
Sugar & Creamer, Cone Shape ..   9.95
Sugar, Cone Shape ...... 2.50 to 5.00
Sugar, Flat .... 3.00 to 4.25
Sugar, Frosted 2.75
Tumbler, Flat, 3 1/2 In. 6.00
Tumbler, Flat, 5 In. 4.00
Tumbler, Footed, 6 In. .. 7.00 to 10.00
Tumbler, 4 In. 6.00
PINK
Creamer, Cone Shape 5.00
Cup & Saucer .... 3.25 to 4.25

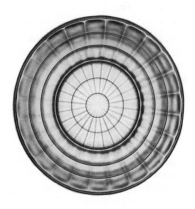

Block Optic

Block Optic

Goblet, 4 1/2 In. 7.00
Goblet, 5 3/4 In. .... 6.00 to 13.00
Plate, 6 In. .... 1.00 to 2.50
Plate, 8 In. .... 1.25 to 3.00
Plate, 9 In. 7.00
Plate, 10 1/4 In. .... 6.50 to 9.50
Salver, Center Handle, 13 1/2 In. 12.50
Sherbet 3.25
Sherbet, Footed, 3 1/4 In. 4.00
Sherbet, Footed, 4 3/4 In. 6.00
Sugar & Creamer, Cone Shape .. 7.00
Sugar & Creamer, Footed 9.00
Sugar, Cone Shape ...... 2.50 to 3.00
Tumbler, Flat, 5 In. ..... 5.00 to 8.00
Tumbler, Footed, 6 In. ... 6.00 to 7.00
YELLOW
Cup & Saucer 7.00
Dish, Candy, 2 1/4 In. 24.50
Goblet, 5 In. .... 9.00 to 11.00
Plate, 6 In. .... 1.50 to 2.25
Plate, 8 In. .... 1.50 to 4.00
Plate, 9 In. 9.50

Block Optic

Salt & Pepper, Footed 30.00
Sherbet, Footed, 3 1/4 In. 3.50
Sherbet, Footed, 4 3/4 In. 9.50
Sherbet, Low 4.00
Sugar & Creamer, Footed, Round 7.00
Tumbler, Footed, 6 In. 9.50

Block, see Block Optic

Blossoms & Band

Blossoms & Band was made by the Jenkins Glass Company of Kokomo, Indiana, in 1927. It is found in crystal, green, iridescent, marigold or pink.

PINK
    Bowl, Console, 11 In. 6.50

Boopie

Boopie was made by the Anchor Hocking Glass Company of Lancaster, Ohio, in the late 1940s and 1950s. It is found in crystal, Forest green and Royal ruby.

CRYSTAL
    Juice 1.50
    Sherbet 2.50
    Wine 2.00

FOREST GREEN
    Tumbler, Crystal Footed, 5 In. . 15.00

Bouquet & Lattice, see Normandie

Bowknot

Bowknot, manufacturer unknown, was made in the late 1920s. It is found in crystal or green.

GREEN
    Berry Bowl, 4 1/2 In. .... 2.00 to 3.50
    Cup .... 2.00 to 6.00
    Plate, 7 In. .... 2.00 to 6.00

Sherbet, Low, Footed 4.00
Tumbler, Footed, 4 In. ... 4.00 to 7.50
Tumbler, 5 In. .... 5.95 to 8.00

Bridle Bouquet, see No. 615

Bubble

Bubble was made by the Anchor Hocking Glass Company of Lancaster, Ohio, from 1934 to 1965. It is found in crystal, dark green, pale blue or pink. Ruby red and milk white were made in the 1960s.

BLUE
    Berry Bowl, 4 1/2 In. 4.50
    Berry Bowl, 8 3/8 In. .... 3.50 to 8.50
    Bowl, 4 1/2 In. .... .75 to 4.00
    Bowl, 5 1/4 In. .... 2.00 to 4.50

Bowl, 12 In. 27.00
Creamer .... 7.95 to 10.00
Cup .... 1.50 to 3.00
Cup & Saucer .... 2.00 to 5.00
Plate, Grill, 9 3/8 In. .... 2.00 to 6.00

Plate, 6 3/4 In. .... .50 to 1.75
Plate, 9 3/8 In. .... 2.00 to 3.50
Platter, Oval, 12 In. ..... 3.25 to 6.50
Saucer .... .95 to 2.50
Soup, Flat, 7 3/4 In. ..... 2.50 to 4.50
Sugar .... 2.00 to 8.00
Sugar & Creamer ..... 14.00 to 18.50

CRYSTAL
Berry Bowl, 4 In. .... 1.50 to 3.95
Berry Bowl, 8 3/8 In. .... 1.00 to 2.25
Bowl, 4 1/2 In. .... .75 to 2.50
Bowl, 5 1/4 In. 1.25
Candlestick, Footed ...... 1.50 to 4.00
Candlestick, Pair 10.00
Creamer 4.00
Cup .... 1.00 to 1.50
Cup & Saucer .... .37 to 2.00
Lamp, Pear Shape 30.00
Plate, 3 Gold Bands, 9 1/4 In. .. 1.00
Plate, 6 3/4 In. .... .50 to 1.00
Plate, 9 3/8 In. .... .58 to 3.00
Platter, Oval, 12 In. 2.75
Saucer .... .40 to 2.00
Sugar .... 1.25 to 1.50
Sugar & Creamer ...... 6.00 to 10.00
Sugar & Creamer, Red Trim 4.00
Tumbler, Flat, 12 Oz. 9.00

GREEN
Berry Bowl, 8 3/8 In. .... 2.00 to 3.00
Berry Set, 7 Piece 11.00
Bowl, 3-Legged, 4 1/2 In. 2.00
Bowl, 3-Legged, 8 1/2 In. 4.50
Bowl, 5 1/4 In. .... 2.50 to 5.00
Creamer .... 3.00 to 9.50
Cup 3.50
Cup & Saucer .... 3.75 to 4.50
Goblet, 4 1/2 In. 3.50
Goblet, 6 In. 5.00
Goblet, 6 3/4 In. 6.00
Nappy, 8 1/2 In. 3.50
Plate, 6 3/4 In. .... 1.50 to 3.00
Plate, 9 3/8 In. .... 3.75 to 12.00
Saucer .... 1.50 to 2.50
Sugar .... 2.50 to 7.50
Sugar & Creamer ...... 5.00 to 13.50
Wine Glass 3.00

PINK
Berry Bowl, 8 3/8 In. .... 2.25 to 7.00

RED
Bowl, 4 1/2 In. .... 1.75 to 2.25
Creamer, Footed 3.00
Cup .... 4.00 to 5.00

Bubble

Pitcher, Ice Lip 30.00
Saucer, Rolled Edge 1.25
Sherbet, Stemmed 4.00
Sugar & Creamer, Flat 5.00
Tumbler, 3 3/4 In. ...... 4.00 to 4.50
Tumbler, 4 1/2 In. ...... 4.50 to 6.50

Tumbler, 16 Oz. .... 5.50 to 8.00
WHITE
Creamer, 2 In. .... .75 to 1.25
Cup 1.25
Sugar, 2 In. 1.25

*Butterflies & Roses, see Flower Garden
with Butterflies*
Buttons & Bows, see Holiday
*Cabbage Rose with Single Arch, see
Rosemary*
*Cabbage Rose with Triple Arch, see
Mayfair, Federal*
Cabbage Rose, see Sharon

Cameo

Cameo was made by the Anchor Hocking Glass Company of Lancaster, Ohio, from 1930 to 1934. It is found in crystal with a platinum rim, green, pink or topaz.

CRYSTAL
Cup & Saucer 3.00
Cup With Platinum Rim 2.50
Pitcher, 5 3/4 In. 110.00
Plate, 7 In. 2.00
Tray 77.50
Tumbler, Footed, 5 In. ... 6.00 to 7.00
GREEN
Berry Bowl, 4 1/2 In. 3.00
Berry Bowl, 8 1/4 In. ... 8.50 to 20.00
Bowl, Console, 3-Legged 22.00
Bowl, Ice 67.50
Bowl, Oval, 10 In. .... 6.00 to 8.25
Bowl, Vegetable, Oval, 9 In. 6.50
Bowl, 5 1/2 In. .... 7.00 to 12.00
Bowl, 7 1/4 In. .... 18.00 to 20.00
Butter, Covered .... 75.00 to 120.00
Candlestick, 4 In., Pair . 52.50 to 54.00
Candy Container, Covered, 6 In. 79.50
Coaster 3.25
Compote .... 12.50 to 15.00
Cookie Jar, Covered ... 18.00 to 27.50
Creamer, 3 1/4 In. ..... 6.95 to 15.00
Creamer, 4 1/4 In. ..... 6.50 to 15.00
Cup & Saucer .... 6.00 to 9.50
Decanter & Stopper, 10 In. 52.00
Dish, Candy, Low, 4 In. 20.00 to 33.00
Goblet, 4 In. .... 32.00 to 39.50
Goblet, 6 In. .... 18.00 to 25.00

Ladle 10.95
Pitcher, Juice, 6 In. ... 12.00 to 27.00
Pitcher, Rope Trim, 8 1/2 In. .. 32.50
Pitcher, 8 1/2 In. ..... 26.00 to 26.75
Plate, Cake, 3-Legged, 10 In. ... 14.00
Plate, Grill, 10 1/2 In. ... 3.50 to 5.75
Plate, Handle, 10 1/2 In. . 5.00 to 8.00
Plate, Square, 7 In. 12.00
Plate, Square, 8 1/2 In. 16.50 to 19.50
Plate, 2-Handled, 11 1/2 In. 5.00
Plate, 6 In. .... 1.00 to 3.00
Plate, 7 In. 3.00
Plate, 8 In. .... 2.25 to 7.25
Plate, 9 1/2 In. .... 1.20 to 9.50
Plate, 10 In. .... 5.50 to 6.50
Platter, Oval, 12 In. ...... 6.00 to 9.00
Relish, 3 Part, 7 1/2 In. 7.95
Salt & Pepper, Footed . 23.50 to 50.00
Sherbet, 3 1/8 In. .... 5.00 to 6.75
Sherbet, 4 7/8 In. ..... 15.00 to 17.00
Soup, Cream, 4 3/4 In. . 32.00 to 34.00
Soup, Flat, 9 In. .... 9.00 to 22.00
Sugar & Creamer, 4 1/4 In.... 24.95
Sugar, 3 1/4 In. .... 4.75 to 9.50
Syrup, 5 3/4 In. ..... 84.50 to 120.00
Tray, Domino .... 40.00 to 50.00
Tumbler, Flat, 3 3/4 In. 12.50 to 17.00
Tumbler, Flat, 4 In. .... 8.50 to 11.00
Tumbler, Flat, 4 3/4 In. 11.50

Cameo

Tumbler, Flat, 5 In. ... 12.00 to 29.50
Tumbler, Footed, 3 Oz. 14.50 to 32.50
Tumbler, Footed, 5 In. . 10.00 to 19.00
Tumbler, Footed, 5 3/4 In. 13.50 to 19.50

Tumbler, Frosted, 5 In. 6.00
Vase, 5 3/4 In. .... 65.00 to 87.50
Vase, 8 In. .... 8.00 to 16.00
Wine Glass, 3 1/4 In. .. 27.50 to 35.00
PINK
Bowl, Console, 3-Legged, 11 In. 11.95
Cup 40.00
Plate, Square, 8 In. 15.00
Plate, 10 In. 15.00
Sugar & Creamer, 4 1/4 In. 80.00
Tumbler, 3 3/4 In. 59.50
TOPAZ
Bowl, Console, 3-Legged 26.50
Bowl, Oval, 10 In. ..... 12.50 to 18.50
Bowl, 5 1/2 In. 12.00
Creamer, 6 1/4 In. ..... 7.00 to 12.50
Cup & Saucer .... 4.50 to 10.00
Nappy, 5 1/2 In. 10.00
Plate, Grill, 10 1/2 In. ... 3.00 to 6.00
Plate, 6 In. .... 1.50 to 9.50
Plate, 9 In. .... 3.00 to 4.00
Plate, 10 In. 4.50
Platter, 12 In. .... 14.50 to 15.50
Sherbet, 3 1/8 In. 15.50
Sherbet, 4 7/8 In. ..... 19.95 to 21.50
Sugar & Creamer, 3 1/4 In. 16.00
Tumbler, Footed, 5 In. .. 7.50 to 12.50

Cape Cod

Cape Cod was made by the Imperial Glass Company of Bellaire, Ohio, in 1932. It is found mostly in crystal, but amber, blue or ruby were made.

CRYSTAL
Bowl, 6 1/2 In. 4.00
Candy Container, Footed, Tall .. 16.00
Goblet, 6 Oz. .... 2.50 to 6.50
Nappy, 6 In. 2.50
Parfait, 5 In. .... 2.25 to 5.00
Plate, 7 In. .... 1.50 to 2.00
Plate, 8 In. .... 2.50 to 3.50

Plate, 10 In. 3.00
Sherbet .... 1.50 to 3.50
Sugar 5.00
Sugar & Creamer, Footed 8.00
Tumbler, Flat, 5 Oz. 3.50
Tumbler, Flat, 12 Oz. 4.50
RUBY
Saucer 4.50

Caprice

Caprice was made by the Cambridge Glass Company of Cambridge, Ohio, in 1936. It is found in blue, crystal, pink or satin finish.

BLUE
Bowl, Crimped, 10 In. 42.00
Bowl, Crimped, 12 In. 46.00
Bowl, Footed, 13 In. 52.00
Bowl, Low, 13 In. 35.00
Candleholder, Tri-Level, Pair ... 45.00
Candlestick, Pair 65.00
Dish, Candy, Handle, 5 In. 10.00
Pitcher, 80 Oz. 75.00
Relish, 3 Part 22.00
Sherbet, Tall 14.00
Sugar 13.00

Sugar & Creamer 26.00
CRYSTAL
Bowl, Footed, Belled, 12 1/2 In. 12.00
Bowl, Handle, 8 1/2 In. 10.00
Candleholder, 2 5/8 In. 8.00
Cigarette Box, 3 1/2 X 2 1/4 In. 10.00
Dish, Candy 19.00
Plate, Handle, 6 1/2 In. 4.00
Sherbet, Footed, 7 Oz. 5.00
Sugar 5.00
Sugar & Creamer 15.00
Tumbler, Footed, 12 Oz. 7.00

Chain Daisy, see Adam

Cherry Blossom

Cherry Blossom was made by the Jeannette Glass Company of Jeannette, Pennsylvania, from 1930 to 1939. It is found in crystal, delphite, green, jadite, pink and red. Reproduction plates, cups and saucers, butter dishes and shakers were made in 1977 in blue, delphite, green or pink.

DELPHITE
Bowl, 2-Handled, 9 In. . 10.00 to 18.00
Bowl, 8 1/2 In. 25.00
Creamer .... 11.50 to 15.00
Creamer, Child's ...... 22.50 to 27.50

Cup .... 12.00 to 19.50
Cup & Saucer 15.00
Cup & Saucer, Child's . 18.00 to 25.00
Dinner Set, Child's, 14 Piece .. 189.00
Pitcher, Allover Design, 6 3/4 In. 95.00

Cherry Blossom

Pitcher, 8 In. .... 69.00 to 80.00
Plate, Child's, 6 In. ...... 5.00 to 8.50
Plate, 9 In. .... 9.00 to 12.00
Platter, Oval, 11 In. 27.50
Saucer .... 1.75 to 3.50
Saucer, Child's .... 2.50 to 8.50
Saucer, Ruffled 2.00
Sherbet .... 12.50 to 17.50
Sugar .... 11.00 to 15.00
Sugar & Creamer, Child's 40.00
Sugar & Creamer, Covered 21.00 to 27.00
Sugar, Child's 25.00
Tray, Handled, 10 1/2 In. 13.00
Tumbler, Round Foot, 4 1/2 In. 20.00
Tumbler, Scalloped Foot, 4 1/2 In. 20.00

GREEN
Bowl, Oval, 9 In. ...... 10.50 to 28.00
Bowl, 2-Handled, 9 In. . 12.50 to 14.00
Bowl, 3-Legged, 10 1/2 In. 30.00
Bowl, 4 3/4 In. .... 5.00 to 9.00
Bowl, 5 3/4 In. .... 13.50 to 18.00
Bowl, 8 1/2 In. .... 12.50 to 15.50
Butter, Covered .... 60.00 to 75.00
Coaster .... 6.00 to 9.00
Creamer .... 6.00 to 9.00
Cup .... 10.50 to 12.00
Cup & Saucer .... 13.50 to 16.00
Mug, 7 Oz. 125.00

Pitcher, Allover Design, 6 3/4 In. 24.00
Pitcher, Cone Shape, 8 In. 27.00
Pitcher, 6 3/4 In. 30.00

Cherry Blossom

Plate, Cake, 3-Legged, 10 1/4 In. 15.00
Plate, Grill, 9 In. .... 5.50 to 13.95
Plate, 6 In. .... 2.50 to 5.00
Plate, 7 In. .... 9.00 to 12.00

Plate, 9 In. .... 9.00 to 14.00
Platter, Divided, 13 In. . 20.00 to 32.50
Platter, Oval, 13 In. ... 13.00 to 32.50
Platter, 11 In. .... 16.50 to 17.50
Salt & Pepper 450.00
Saucer .... 2.25 to 3.00
Sherbet .... 5.50 to 10.00
Sherbet, Scalloped Base 7.00
Soup, Flat, 7 3/4 In. ... 20.00 to 32.50
Sugar & Creamer, Covered 20.00 to 26.00
Sugar, Covered .... 13.00 to 17.50
Sugar, Open .... 6.00 to 8.00
Tray, Handled, 10 1/2 In. 14.00
Tumbler, Flat, Design On Top, 5 In. 27.00
Tumbler, Flat, 3 1/2 In. 11.00
Tumbler, Flat, 4 1/4 In. 12.00
Tumbler, Round Foot, 3 3/4 In. 14.00
Tumbler, Round Foot, 4 1/2 In. 27.50
Tumbler, Scalloped Foot, 4 1/2 In. 22.00

PINK

Berry Bowl, 4 3/4 In. .... 5.25 to 7.50
Berry Bowl, 8 1/2 In. ... 7.50 to 15.00
Bowl, Cereal, 5 3/4 In. . 14.50 to 15.00
Bowl, Console, 3-Legged, 10 1/4 In. 36.50
Bowl, Oval, 9 In. ...... 10.50 to 15.00
Bowl, 2-Handled, 9 In. .. 8.50 to 12.00
Butter, Covered .... 42.00 to 80.00
Child's Set, 14 Piece 140.00
Coaster .... 6.50 to 12.00
Creamer .... 5.75 to 10.00
Creamer, Child's ...... 18.00 to 22.00
Cup 11.00
Cup & Saucer .... 7.35 to 25.00
Cup & Saucer, Child's . 19.00 to 23.00
Mug .... 125.00 to 129.50
Pitcher, Flat, Design On Top, 8 In. 24.50
Pitcher, Footed, 8 In. 30.00
Pitcher, Round Foot, 6 3/4 In. . 42.50
Pitcher, Scalloped Base, 6 3/4 In. 25.00
Plate, Cake, 3-Legged, 10 1/4 In. 14.50
Plate, Child's .... 1.00 to 8.50
Plate, Grill, 9 In. .... 8.95 to 12.95
Plate, 6 In. .... 1.25 to 5.50
Plate, 7 In. .... 8.00 to 11.00
Plate, 9 In. .... 8.00 to 10.00
Platter, Divided, 13 In. . 15.00 to 27.50
Platter, Oval, 11 In. 13.00
Platter, 11 In. 14.50
Platter, 13 In. 27.50

Platter, 2-Handled, 11 In. 10.50
Salt & Pepper 675.00
Saucer .... 1.75 to 7.00
Saucer, Child's .... 3.50 to 5.50
Sherbet .... 5.00 to 8.00
Soup, Flat, 7 3/4 In. ... 27.50 to 28.00
Sugar .... 5.00 to 6.75
Sugar & Creamer, Covered 20.00
Sugar, Covered .... 8.75 to 22.00
Tray, Handled, 10 1/2 In. 14.00

Cherry Blossom

Tumbler, Flat, 3 1/2 In. 9.50
Tumbler, Flat, 4 1/4 In. 11.00
Tumbler, Flat, 5 In. 27.50
Tumbler, Round Foot, 3 3/4 In. 11.50
Tumbler, Round Foot, 4 1/2 In. 18.00
Tumbler, Scalloped Foot, 3 3/4 In. 11.00
Tumbler, Scalloped Foot, 4 1/2 In. 18.00

Cherry, see Cherry Blossom

Chinex Classic

Chinex Classic was made by the MacBeth Evans Division of the Corning Glass Works, a firm with factories in Indiana, Ohio and Pennsylvania, from 1930 to 1940. It is found in ivory or ivory with decals.

IVORY WITH DECAL

Plate, Dinner, 9 3/4 In.	4.00
Saucer	2.50
Sherbet, Low Footed	7.00
Soup, 7 In.	7.50
Vegetable, 9 In.	11.00

IVORY

Bowl, Cereal, 5 3/4 In.	3.00
Butter	46.00
Creamer	4.00
Cup	3.50
Sugar	4.00

Christmas Candy Ribbon, see Christmas Candy

Christmas Candy

Christmas Candy was made by the Indiana Glass Company of Dunkirk, Indiana, in 1936. It is found in crystal and green.

CRYSTAL

Creamer	4.00
Cup	3.50
Saucer	1.00

Sugar	3.00

GREEN

Plate, Salad	4.50
Plate, 10 In.	5.50

Circle

Circle was made by the Hocking Glass Company of Lancaster, Ohio, in the 1930s. It is found in crystal, green or pink.

CRYSTAL

Salt & Pepper, Design, Red Band	8.50
Sherbet	1.50

GREEN

Berry Bowl, 4 3/4 In.	3.00 to 4.00
Bowl, 3-Footed, Ruffled, 6 1/4 In.	2.50
Cup	1.50 to 2.50
Cup & Saucer	2.75 to 4.00
Goblet, 4 1/2 In.	4.00
Pitcher	12.00 to 16.50
Pitcher, Rope Trim	10.00
Plate, 6 In.	1.00 to 1.50
Plate, 8 In.	1.25
Saucer	.75 to 1.00

Circle

Circle

Sherbet & Saucer, Footed 3.95
Sherbet, Stem, 3 1/4 In. .. 2.50 to 3.00
Sherbet, 4 3/4 In. .... 3.50 to 4.50
Sugar & Creamer 7.50
Tumbler, 5 In. 3.00
Whiskey 4.00

PINK
Creamer 2.50
Cup 1.75
Plate, 6 In. 1.00
Sherbet 1.50
Sugar, Cone Shape 2.50

Circular Ribs, see Circle

Cloverleaf

Cloverleaf was made by the Hazel Atlas Glass Company, a firm with factories in Ohio, Pennsylvania and West Virginia, from 1930 to 1936. It is found in black, crystal, green, pink or topaz.

BLACK
Ashtray, 5 3/4 In. 55.00
Creamer .... 6.50 to 12.00
Cup .... 7.00 to 10.00
Cup & Saucer .... 5.75 to 12.50
Plate, 6 In. .... 12.50 to 19.00
Plate, 8 In. .... 4.50 to 9.00
Salt & Pepper .... 32.00 to 60.00
Saucer .... .60 to 3.00
Sherbet, Footed, 3 In. ... 6.00 to 14.00
Sugar .... 6.00 to 9.50
Sugar & Creamer ...... 3.15 to 15.00

CRYSTAL
Creamer 6.00
Cup & Saucer .... 3.00 to 4.00
Saucer 1.25
Sherbet, Footed, 3 In. 1.25
GREEN
Bowl, 4 In. .... 5.90 to 8.50
Bowl, 7 In. .... 7.50 to 20.00
Creamer, Footed, 3 5/8 In. 5.00
Cup .... 2.00 to 3.50
Cup & Saucer .... 3.75 to 6.50
Dish, Candy, Covered .. 25.00 to 30.00

Cloverleaf

Pitcher, 8 In. 3.00
Plate, Grill, 10 1/4 In. .. 3.50 to 14.50
Plate, 6 In. .... 1.25 to 3.00
Plate, 8 In. .... 3.00 to 11.00
Salt & Pepper .... 14.00 to 25.75
Saltshaker .... 9.00 to 15.00
Saucer .... 1.00 to 2.50
Sherbet .... 2.50 to 5.00
Sherbet, Footed, 3 In. .... 3.50 to 4.50
Sugar 4.50
Sugar & Creamer ...... 7.50 to 12.00
Tumbler, Flat, 3 3/4 In. 12.50 to 17.50
Tumbler, Flat, 4 In. ... 14.00 to 15.00
Tumbler, Footed, 5 3/4 In. 14.00
Tumbler, 4 In. .... 11.00 to 13.50
PINK
Bowl, 4 In. .... 6.00 to 7.50
Cup .... 3.00 to 4.00
Cup & Saucer .... 3.50 to 6.50
Pitcher, 8 In. 3.00
Plate, 8 In. .... 2.00 to 4.00
Saucer .... 1.00 to 2.25
Sherbet, Footed, 3 In. .... 2.50 to 6.00
Tumbler, Flat, 4 In. 14.00
TOPAZ
Bowl, 7 In. 27.50
Creamer 9.50
Cup 5.00
Cup & Saucer 15.00

Cloverleaf

Dish, Candy, Covered 77.50
Plate, 6 In. 2.90
Plate, 8 In. .... 4.50 to 5.00
Saucer 2.50
Sherbet, Footed, 3 In. .... 5.00 to 8.00
Sugar 8.00
Sugar & Creamer ..... 10.00 to 20.00
Sugar, Footed, 3 5/8 In. 7.75

Colonial Fluted

Colonial Fluted was made by the Federal Glass Company of Columbus Ohio, from 1928 to 1933. It is found in crystal or green.

CRYSTAL
Berry Set 18.00
Plate, 8 1/2 In. 3.00
GREEN
Berry Bowl, 4 In. .... 2.00 to 2.50
Bowl, 6 In. .... 3.50 to 5.90
Bowl, 7 1/2 In. .... 4.50 to 5.50
Creamer .... 2.50 to 5.00
Cup .... 2.00 to 2.50

Cup & Saucer .... 3.25 to 3.50
Plate, 6 In. .... .75 to 2.00
Plate, 8 In. .... 1.50 to 4.00
Saucer 1.00
Sherbet 2.00
Sugar & Creamer ...... 6.75 to 10.00
Sugar, Covered 5.50
Sugar, Open 3.00

Colonial

Colonial was made by the Hocking Glass Company of Lancaster, Ohio from 1934 to 1936. It is found in crystal, green, opaque white or pink.

Colonial

CRYSTAL
Bowl, Flat Soup, 7 In. 8.50
Butter, Covered ...... 19.00 to 35.00
Celery, 5 1/2 In. 30.00
Creamer .... 2.00 to 5.00
Cup 4.00
Goblet, 4 In. .... 3.25 to 4.50
Pitcher, Water, 7 In. 27.50
Plate, 6 In. .... 1.00 to 1.50
Plate, 10 In. .... 7.00 to 9.00
Salt & Pepper 35.00
Soup, Flat, 7 In. 8.50
Sugar, Covered .... 6.50 to 12.00
Tumbler, Footed, 3 1/4 In. 2.50
Tumbler, Gold Trim, 5 1/4 In. .. 5.00
GREEN
Berry Bowl, 4 1/2 In. 5.95
Berry Bowl, 9 In. ...... 6.50 to 11.95
Bowl, Oval, 10 In. 7.00
Butter, Covered .... 35.00 to 45.00
Celery 27.50
Creamer, 5 In. .... 4.00 to 9.50
Cup 7.00
Cup & Saucer .... 35.00 to 45.00
Goblet, 3 3/4 In. ...... 17.50 to 19.95
Goblet, 4 In. 18.00

Goblet, 5 3/4 In. ...... 11.00 to 18.50
Pitcher, Ice Lip, 54 Oz. 22.50
Pitcher, Ice Lip, 68 Oz. 37.50 to 45.00
Plate, Grill, 10 In. ...... 9.00 to 14.50
Plate, 6 In. .... 1.50 to 4.00
Plate, 10 In. .... 12.50 to 22.00
Platter, Oval, 12 In. .... 7.95 to 11.95
Salt & Pepper .... 45.00 to 80.00

Colonial

Sherbet .... 5.50 to 7.50
Soup, Cream, 4 1/2 In. 22.50
Soup, Flat, 7 In. ...... 20.00 to 29.00
Sugar & Creamer, Covered 21.50
Sugar, Covered, 5 In. .. 12.00 to 15.00
Sugar, Open, 5 In. ...... 9.00 to 11.00
Tumbler, 4 In. 10.00
Whiskey, 2 1/2 In. ..... 5.00 to 12.00
PINK
Bowl, Oval, 10 In. ..... 10.00 to 12.50
Bowl, 4 1/2 In. 5.00
Celery .... 30.00 to 75.00
Creamer, 5 In. 9.50
Cup .... 4.00 to 4.50
Pitcher, Ice Lip, 54 Oz. 22.00 to 25.00
Plate, Grill, 10 In. .... 4.00 to 6.95
Plate, 6 In. .... 1.75 to 2.50
Plate, 8 1/2 In. 1.95
Plate, 10 In. .... 4.00 to 6.95
Platter, Oval, 12 In. 6.00
Salt & Pepper .... 39.50 to 89.00
Sherbet .... 4.75 to 6.00
Sherbet, Footed 4.25
Soup, Cream, 4 1/2 In. . 27.00 to 27.50
Soup, Flat, 7 In. 8.00
Sugar, Covered, 5 In. ... 4.00 to 25.00
Tumbler, Flat, 4 In. 7.50
Tumbler, Footed, 3 1/4 In. 5.00
Tumbler, Footed, 5 1/4 In. 7.75 to 9.00
Tumbler, 4 In. 5.00
WHITE
Cup & Saucer 10.00
Sugar 2.00

Colonial

Colony

Colony was made by the Hazel Atlas Glass Company, a firm with factories in Ohio, Pennsylvania and West Virginia, in the 1930s.

Colony, see also Raindrops

CRYSTAL
Candleholder, Double, Pair 12.50
Cocktail 6.75

Creamer, Footed, 3 7/8 In. 5.00
Saucer 1.00

Columbia

Columbia was made by the Federal Glass Company of Columbus, Ohio, from 1938 to 1942. It is found in crystal or pink.

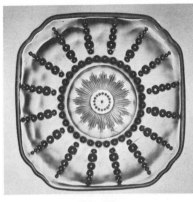

Columbia

CRYSTAL
Bowl, 5 In.	1.50 to 5.95
Bowl, 8 1/2 In.	2.00 to 6.00
Butter, Covered	7.50 to 25.00
Cordial, 1 Oz.	6.00
Creamer, Footed	4.00
Cup	1.50 to 5.00
Cup & Saucer	1.87 to 5.00
Goblet, 8 Oz.	7.00
Plate, Chop, 11 3/4 In.	3.50 to 5.00
Plate, 6 In.	.75 to 3.50
Plate, 8 1/2 In.	4.50
Plate, 9 1/2 In.	2.00 to 5.50
Salt Dip	3.50
Saucer	.75 to 4.00

PINK
Plate, 6 In.	3.75
Plate, 9 1/2 In.	7.00
Saucer	3.50

Columbia

Coronation

Coronation was made by the Anchor Hocking Glass Company of Lancaster, Ohio, from 1936 to 1940. It is found in crystal, pink or royal ruby.

CRYSTAL
Plate, 6 In. 1.80
Tumbler, Footed, 5 In. 5.00
PINK
Berry Bowl, 4 1/2 In. .... 2.00 to 2.50
Bowl, 2-Handled, 8 In. 6.50
Bowl, 6 1/2 In. 1.25
Bowl, 8 In. 3.00
Cup .... 2.00 to 4.00
Cup & Saucer .... 3.50 to 4.00
Plate, 6 In. .... 1.00 to 3.00
Plate, 8 1/2 In. .... 2.75 to 4.00
Plate, 9 1/2 In. 1.50

Saucer .... 1.25 to 1.50
Sherbet .... 2.00 to 3.00
Sherbet, Footed .... 1.50 to 3.00
Tumbler, Footed, 5 In. ... 5.00 to 6.00
ROYAL RUBY
Berry Bowl, 4 1/4 In. .... 1.50 to 3.00
Berry Bowl, 8 In. ...... 4.75 to 10.00
Berry Set, 5 Piece ..... 15.00 to 16.90
Bowl, 2-Handled, 4 1/4 In. 3.50
Bowl, 2-Handled, 8 In. ... 5.00 to 7.00
Bowl, 6 1/2 In. .... 2.50 to 6.00
Saucer 3.00

Cremax

Cremax was made by the MacBeth Evans Division of Corning Glass Works, a firm
with factories in Indiana, Ohio and Pennsylvania, from the late 1930s to the early
1940s. It is a white-colored ware with decals.

CREAM-COLORED
Bowl, Cereal, 5 3/4 In. 2.00

Creamer 2.25
Plate, Dinner, 9 3/4 In. 2.75

Criss Cross, see X Design Cube, see Cubist

Cubist

Cubist was made by the Jeannette Glass Company of Jeannette, Pennsylvania, from
1929 to 1933. It is found in crystal, green, pink or ultramarine. It has been reproduced in amber and avocado.

CRYSTAL
Bowl, 6 1/2 In. .... 2.00 to 3.00
Creamer, 2 In. .... .75 to 2.00
Jar, Powder 4.00
Plate, 6 In. .... .50 to 1.00
Saucer 1.50
Sherbet, Metal Foot 2.50
Sugar & Creamer, 2 In. $ 1.75 To 2.00
Sugar & Creamer, 7 1/2 In. 5.50
Sugar, 2 In. .... .85 to 2.00
Tray, 7 1/2 In. 3.00
GREEN
Bowl, Scalloped, 7 3/8 In. 6.00
Butter, Covered .... 18.50 to 42.50
Candy Container, Covered, 6 1/2 In.
.... 18.00

Cubist

Cubist

Coaster, 3 1/4 In. .... 2.50 to 2.95
Creamer, 3 In. .... 3.50 to 5.00
Cup 3.00
Cup & Saucer .... 3.50 to 6.00
Jar, Powder, Covered .. 10.00 to 13.00
Plate, 6 In. .... 1.25 to 2.00
Plate, 8 In. .... 2.00 to 3.50
Salt & Pepper .... 10.00 to 20.00
Saucer .... 1.25 to 1.95
Sherbet .... 2.00 to 3.75
Sherbet, Footed .... 4.00 to 4.50
Sugar & Creamer, Covered, 3 In. 19.00
Sugar, Covered, 3 In. .... 7.00 to 8.00
Sugar, Open, 3 In. 4.00
PINK
Bowl, 4 1/2 In. .... 1.75 to 4.50
Bowl, 6 1/2 In. .... 2.50 to 5.50
Butter, Covered ...... 27.50 to 42.00
Candy Container, Covered, 6 1/2 In.
.... 17.00
Coaster .... 2.25 to 3.50
Creamer, 2 In. .... 1.50 to 3.50
Creamer, 3 In. .... 2.75 to 3.50
Cup & Saucer .... 3.00 to 4.50
Jar, Powder, Covered ... 8.50 to 12.50
Plate, 6 In. .... .75 to 2.00
Plate, 8 In. .... 1.75 to 3.00
Salt & Pepper .... 7.00 to 12.00

Cubist

Saucer .... .75 to 1.95
Sherbet .... 2.50 to 4.00
Sugar & Creamer, Covered, 2 In. 12.00

Sugar, Covered, 3 In. 6.00
Sugar, Open, 3 In. 2.75
Sugar, 2 In. .... 1.50 to 2.00

Cupid

Cupid was made by the Paden City Glass Company of Paden City, West Virginia, in the late 1920s. It is found in green, light blue or pink.

GREEN
Bowl, Center Handle, 9 1/4 In. . 15.00
Candlestick, 5 In.Wide, Pair ... 16.00
Tray, Center Handle, 10 1/2 In. 12.50
LIGHT BLUE
Bowl, 11 In. 13.00
Compote, 6 1/4 In. 11.00

Plate, 10 In. .... 6.00 to 10.00
Vase, 8 1/9 In. 24.00
PINK
Bowl, Oval, Footed, 8 1/2 In. .. 15.00
Creamer, Footed, 4 1/2 In. 9.00 to 11.00
Sugar, Footed, 4 1/4 In. 10.00

Daisy Petals, see Petalware
Daisy, see No. 620
Dancing Girl, see Cameo
Danish Crystal, see Colony, Raindrops

Della Robbia

Della Robbia was made by the Westmoreland Glass Company of Grapeville, Pennsylvania, in the 1920s and 1930s. It is found in amber, crystal, green or pink.

CRYSTAL
Bowl, Console, 12 1/2 In. 10.00
Bowl, 4 3/4 In. 2.50
Champagne, 5 In. 6.00

Plate, 9 In. 3.00
Tumbler, Footed, 5 In. 5.00
Tumbler, 3 3/4 In. 4.00

Diamond Point, see Petalware

Diamond Quilted

Diamond Quilted was made by the Imperial Glass Company of Bellaire, Ohio, in the late 1920s to the early 1930s. It is found in black, blue, crystal, green or pink.

BLACK
Bowl, Ruffled, 7 In. 8.00
Cup & Saucer 25.00
Sugar & Creamer 22.50
BLUE
Bowl, 7 In. .... 7.00 to 9.00
Candleholder, Flat 7.50

Ice Bucket 39.75
Plate, 8 In. .... 1.75 to 6.00
Sherbet 6.00
Soup, Cream 7.00
Sugar .... 5.00 to 7.00
CRYSTAL
Compote, Covered, 11 1/2 In. .. 10.00

GREEN

Bowl, Fluted Edges, 12 In. 35.00
Bowl, 5 In. 4.00
Bowl, 7 In. 5.00
Candleholder, Pair ...... 9.00 to 10.00
Creamer 3.50
Cup 3.00
Nappy, 7 In. .... 5.00 to 8.00
Nappy, 10 In. 6.00
Plate, Cake, Footed, 10 In. 20.00
Plate, 6 In. 1.00
Plate, 8 In. .... 2.00 to 3.00
Saucer .... 1.00 to 1.50
Sherbet .... 2.25 to 3.15
Sherbet & Plate 3.50
Soup, Cream, 4 3/4 In. ... 2.50 to 4.60
Sugar .... 3.00 to 3.50
Sugar & Creamer 6.50

PINK

Bowl, 7 In. .... 4.00 to 4.50

Candleholder, Pair ...... 8.00 to 10.00
Candlestick, Pair .... 6.00 to 15.00
Compote, Mayonnaise 6.00
Console, Rolled Edge 12.00
Creamer .... 3.50 to 4.50
Cup 2.50
Dish, Candy, Covered 35.00
Goblet, Footed 4.50
Nappy 4.00
Nappy, 2-Handled, 5 1/2 In. 4.50
Plate, Grill, 8 In. 2.00
Plate, 6 In. .... 1.50 to 3.50
Plate, 8 In. .... 1.50 to 3.50
Sherbet .... 2.50 to 3.50
Soup, Cream, 4 3/4 In. 4.50
Sugar & Creamer .... 6.00 to 9.00
Sugar, Covered 4.50
Sugar, Open 2.75
Tumbler 6.50

Diamond, see Windsor

Diana

Diana was made by the Federal Glass Company of Columbus, Ohio, from 1937 to 1941. It is found in amber, crystal or pink.

AMBER

Bowl, 5 In. 3.50
Bowl, 11 In. .... 6.00 to 8.50
Creamer 4.50
Cup .... 3.50 to 5.00
Cup & Saucer .... 5.00 to 6.00
Dish, Candy, Covered ... 9.00 to 17.50
Plate, 6 In. .... .75 to 2.00
Plate, 9 1/2 In. .... 2.00 to 5.00
Plate, 11 3/4 In. .... 5.00 to 7.00
Platter, 12 In. .... 4.00 to 8.90
Salt & Pepper .... 20.00 to 69.50
Saucer .... .75 to 2.00
Soup, Cream, 5 1/2 In. ... 6.00 to 8.50
Sugar .... 4.00 to 4.50
Sugar & Creamer .... 5.00 to 7.00
Sugar, Open 3.50
Tumbler, 4 1/8 In. 5.50

CRYSTAL

Bowl, Scalloped, 12 In. ... 3.00 to 5.00
Bowl, 5 In. .... 2.50 to 3.50
Bowl, 9 In. 3.00

Bowl, 11 In. 4.00
Creamer 2.00
Cup 4.00
Cup & Saucer .... 3.00 to 4.00
Cup & Saucer, Demitasse . 3.00 to 6.00
Cup & Saucer, Demitasse, Gold Rim 3.00
Cup & Saucer, Demitasse, Silver Rim
.... 3.00
Cup, Demitasse .... 1.50 to 2.00
Dish, Candy, Covered 7.50
Goblet, 9 Oz. 7.50
Plate, Metal Handle, 11 3/4 In. . 3.00
Plate, 6 In. .... .75 to 3.00
Plate, 9 1/2 In. .... 2.00 to 3.00
Plate, 11 3/4 In. .... 2.50 to 4.00
Salt & Pepper 11.00
Saltshaker 6.00
Saucer .... .35 to 2.00
Saucer, Demitasse 1.00
Saucer, Demitasse, Gold Rim .... .50
Saucer, Gold Rim .... .40
Saucer, Platinum Rim .... .40

Soup, Cream, 5 1/2 In. ... 2.25 to 4.00
Sugar, Open 3.50
PINK
Ashtray, 3 1/2 In. ...,... 2.25 to 3.00
Bowl, 5 In. .... 1.50 to 3.00
Bowl, 9 In. 8.00
Bowl, 11 In. 8.00
Candy Container, 6 In. 15.00
Coaster, 3 1/2 In. .... 1.25 to 3.00
Cup & Saucer 8.00
Cup, Demitasse 2.00

Dish, Candy, Covered .. 12.00 to 21.00
Plate, 6 In. .... 1.00 to 2.00
Plate, 9 1/2 In. .... 2.00 to 5.00
Plate, 11 3/4 In. 7.00
Platter, 11 In. 8.90
Salt & Pepper .... 11.25 to 27.50
Saucer .... .60 to 2.00
Sherbet 3.25
Soup, Cream, 5 1/2 In. 2.00
Sugar & Creamer 6.00

Dogwood

Dogwood was made by the MacBeth Evans Glass Company, a firm with factories in Indiana, Ohio and Pennsylvania, from 1929 to 1932. It is found in cremax, crystal, green, monax, pink or yellow.

CREMAX
Plate, 12 In. 30.00
CRYSTAL
Cup & Saucer 6.00
Plate, 8 In. .... 1.50 to 2.00

Tumbler, Amber Footed, 5 1/2 In. 14.00
Tumbler, Flat, Etched, 4 In. 7.00
Tumbler, 4 In. 5.00
GREEN
Bowl, 5 1/2 In. 12.50

Dogwood

Dogwood

Bowl, 8 1/2 In. 50.00	Ice Bucket, Etched 10.00
Cake, Plate, 13 In. .... 35.00 to 40.00	Pitcher, Decorated, 8 In. 85.00
Cup 12.50	Plate, Cake, 13 In. .... 35.00 to 49.50
Cup & Saucer .... 15.00 to 17.50	Plate, Grill, 10 1/2 In. ... 5.95 to 9.00
Luncheon Set, 3 Piece 19.00	Plate, 6 In. .... 1.75 to 4.00
Plate, Grill, 10 1/2 In. ... 5.00 to 8.00	Plate, 8 In. .... 1.50 to 5.50
Plate, 6 In. .... 2.00 to 5.00	Plate, 9 1/4 In. .... 7.00 to 12.00
Plate, 8 In. .... 1.50 to 6.50	Plate, 12 In. .... 8.00 to 15.00
Saucer .... 2.25 to 2.50	Saucer .... 1.25 to 2.50
Sugar & Creamer, 2 1/2 In. 50.00	Sherbet .... 4.95 to 12.00
Sugar, 2 1/2 In. 25.00	Sugar & Creamer, Covered 19.95
Tumbler, 4 In. 10.00	Sugar & Creamer, Open, 2 1/2 In. 9.00
Whiskey 4.00	Sugar, Gold Rim 3.00
MONAX	Sugar, 2 1/4 In. 5.00
Plate, 12 In. .... 25.00 to 30.00	Sugar, 3 1/2 In. .... 2.50 to 7.50
PINK	Tray, 2 Tier, Metal Handle, 8 In. 52.50
Bowl, 5 1/2 In. .... 5.00 to 12.00	Tumbler, Decorated, 3 1/2 In. ... 3.00
Bowl, 8 1/2 In. .... 12.00 to 25.00	Tumbler, Decorated, 4 In. 15.00
Bowl, 10 1/4 In. 125.00	Tumbler, Decorated, 4 3/4 In. .. 22.50
Creamer, 2 1/2 In. ...... 3.50 to 8.00	Tumbler, Decorated, 5 In. 20.25
Cup .... .60 to 6.50	Tumbler, Etched, 4 3/4 In. 15.00
Cup & Saucer .... 4.00 to 8.50	Tumbler, Frosted, 3 1/2 In. 7.50

Doric & Pansy

Doric & Pansy was made by the Jeannette Glass Company of Jeannette, Pennsylvania, from 1937 to 1938. It is found in crystal, green, ultramarine or pink.

CRYSTAL	**PINK**
Cup 9.00	Bowl, 4 1/2 In. 4.00
Plate, 2-Handled 5.90	Bowl, 8 In. 10.00

Doric & Pansy

Creamer, Child's	20.00	Saucer, Child's	3.00 to 4.90
Cup & Saucer	6.00	Sugar & Creamer	40.00
Cup & Saucer, Child's	22.50	Sugar & Creamer, Child's	15.00
Dinner Set, Child's	115.00	Sugar, Child's	15.50 to 22.00
Plate, Child's	5.50 to 9.00	**ULTRAMARINE**	
Plate, 6 In.	3.50 to 7.00	Bowl, 2-Handled, 9 In.	15.00 to 30.00
Saucer	3.50	Bowl, 4 1/2 In.	5.00 to 7.50

Doric & Pansy

Child's Set 185.00
Creamer 75.00
Cup .... 6.00 to 12.00
Cup & Saucer .... 12.00 to 15.00
Cup & Saucer, Child's 18.75
Plate, Child's .... 7.00 to 9.00
Plate, 6 In. .... 5.40 to 12.00
Plate, 7 In. .... 22.50 to 25.00
Plate, 9 In. .... 11.50 to 14.00
Saucer .... 2.50 to 5.00
Saucer, Child's 5.00
Sugar, Child's 25.00
Tray, 2-Handled, 10 In. 36.50
Tumbler, 4 1/2 In. .... 29.50 to 35.00

Doric with Pansies, see Doric & Pansy
Doric with Pansy, see Doric

Doric & Pansy

Doric

Doric was made by the Jeannete Glass Company of Jeannette, Pennsylvania, from 1935 to 1938. It is found in crystal, delphite, green, pink or yellow.

CRYSTAL
Creamer 21.50
DELPHITE
Dish, Candy, 3 Part ..... 2.50 to 5.00
Sherbet .... 2.00 to 6.00
GREEN
Bowl, 2-Handled, 9 In. 6.00
Bowl, 8 1/4 In. .... 8.00 to 8.50
Butter, Covered .... 45.00 to 65.00
Candy Container, Lid, 8 In. 20.00
Coaster 10.00
Creamer .... 6.00 to 7.50
Cup .... 4.00 to 6.00
Cup & Saucer .... 5.00 to 7.50
Dish, Candy, 3 Part 3.75
Pitcher, Flat, 6 In. 22.00
Plate, Cake, Footed ...... 7.00 to 9.95
Plate, Grill, 9 In. .... 5.50 to 10.00
Plate, 6 In. .... 1.75 to 2.00
Plate, 9 In. .... 4.50 to 7.00
Platter, Oval, 12 In. .... 7.00 to 10.00
Relish, 4 Part 12.00
Relish, 4 X 4 In. .... 3.00 to 3.75
Relish, 4 X 8 In. 4.00
Salt & Pepper .... 20.00 to 23.00
Saucer .... 1.25 to 1.50
Shaker .... 22.50 to 23.00

Doric

Sherbet 7.00
Sugar & Creamer 12.50
Sugar, Covered .... 11.50 to 20.00
Tray, 2-Handled, 10 In. .. 2.75 to 9.00
Tray, 8 X 8 In. 5.00

Tumbler, 4 1/2 In. 54.50
Tumbler, 5 In. 35.00
PINK
Berry Bowl, 4 1/2 In. .... 1.25 to 3.50
Berry Bowl, 8 1/4 In. .... 7.00 to 8.00
Bowl, Oval, 9 In. 5.00
Bowl, 2-Handled, 9 In. 8.50
Bowl, 5 1/2 In. .... 3.00 to 8.00
Butter, Covered .... 35.00 to 59.00
Candy Container, Covered, 8 In.   32.50
Coaster .... 2.50 to 10.00
Cup .... 4.00 to 5.00
Cup & Saucer .... 4.50 to 6.50
Dish, Candy, 3 Part ..... 1.00 to 5.50
Pitcher, 6 In. .... 13.00 to 14.50
Plate, Cake, Footed, 10 In. 9.50
Plate, 6 In. .... 1.75 to 3.50
Plate, 7 In. 6.50
Plate, 9 In. .... 4.00 to 6.50
Platter, Oval, 12 In. 8.50
Relish, Metal Holder, Inserts .. 42.50
Salt & Pepper .... 15.00 to 28.00
Saltshaker 3.50
Saucer .... 1.35 to 2.50
Sherbet 3.25

Doric

Sugar & Creamer, Lid . 13.50 to 15.00	Tray, Handled, 10 In. .... 7.00 to 8.50
Sugar, Covered 12.50	Tray, 8 X 8 In. .... 3.50 to 8.00
Sugar, Open 4.50	Tumbler, Flat, 4 1/2 In. 15.00

Double Shield, see Mt. Pleasant
Double Swirl, see Swirl
Drape & Tassel, see Princess
Dutch Rose, see Rosemary
Dutch, see Windmill

Early American Hobnail

Early American Hobnail was made by the Imperial Glass Company of Bellaire, Ohio, in the 1930s. It is found in amber, black, blue crystal, green, pink or red.

Early American Hobnail, see also Hobnail

CRYSTAL
Bottle, Perfume 12.00

Bowl, Ivy, Footed 15.00
Jar, Powder 15.00

Early American Rock Crystal, see Rock Crystal
Early American, see Princess Feather

English Hobnail

English Hobnail was made by the Westmoreland Glass Company of Grapeville, Pennsylvania, from the 1920s to the 1970s. It is found in amber, blue, cobalt, crystal, green, pink or turquoise.

AMBER
Jar, Powder, Lid, 5 In. . 10.00 to 23.00
Sherbet 17.50
BLUE
Plate, 8 In. 5.00
CRYSTAL
Basket, 2-Handled, 5 In. 35.00
Berry Bowl, Ruffled, Large 15.00
Bowl, Crimped, 6 1/2 In. 4.00
Bowl, Oval, 9 In. 6.00
Bowl, 4 1/2 In. 4.00
Bowl, 6 In. 3.00
Candlestick 3.00
Candlestick, 12 In., Pair 25.00
Celery, 8 Salt Dips 40.00
Cup 3.00
Eggcup 15.00
Jar, Marmalade, Covered 12.00

English Hobnail

English Hobnail

Lamp For Candlesticks, 9 In. .. 25.00
Lamp, 6 1/2 In. .... 20.00 to 35.00
Plate, Round Or Square, 8 In. .. 4.50
Plate, Square, 7 1/4 In. .. 2.75 to 3.00
Plate, 5 1/2 In. 1.00
Plate, 6 1/2 In. .... 1.25 to 1.50
Plate, 7 1/4 In. .... 2.75 to 3.00
Plate, 8 In. .... 2.00 to 4.50
Salt & Pepper .... 12.00 to 25.00
Saltshaker .... 3.00 to 4.00
Saltshaker, Round Or Square Base 4.00
Sherbet, 3 1/2 In. 4.00
Tumbler, Footed, 7 Oz. 5.00
Tumbler, 6 In. .... 5.50 to 10.00
Vase, 7 1/2 In. 6.00
Wine, 4 1/2 In. 5.00
GREEN
Bowl, Round, 4 1/2 In. 9.50
Cup & Saucer 22.50
Goblet, 6 1/4 In. ...... 13.00 to 14.95
Jar, Powder, Round, 5 In. 10.00
Jar, Powder, Turquoise Bottom . 15.00
Lamp, Electric, 9 1/4 In. 95.00
Plate, Round Or Square, 8 In. .. 7.00

Plate, 6 1/2 In. 3.95
Plate, 7 1/4 In. 3.50
Saltshaker, Round Or Square Base 39.50
Sherbet 9.95
Sugar, Flat 8.00
Tumbler, Flat, 5 In. 14.95
Vase, 7 1/2 In. 27.50
PINK
Berry Bowl, Round, 4 1/2 In. ... 4.00
Bottle, Cologne, Stopper 22.50
Candy Container, Cone Shape .. 35.00
Cup & Saucer 15.00
Lamp, Electric, 9 1/4 In. 75.00
Lamp, 6 1/4 In. 40.00
Plate, Round Or Square, 8 In. .. 5.00
Plate, 6 1/2 In. 3.00
Plate, 10 In. 5.50
Sugar & Creamer, Footed 18.00
Tumbler, Flat, 5 In. 9.00
Tumbler, 3 3/4 In. 7.00
TURQUOISE
Bottle & Stopper, Cologne, Pair 55.00
WHITE
Candlestick, 4 1/4 In., Pair 4.00

Fan & Feather, see Adam

Fine Rib

Fine Rib was made by the Hazel Atlas Company, a firm with factories in Ohio, Pennsylvania and West Virginia, from 1936 to 1939. It is found in blue, crystal, green or pink.

Fine Rib, see also Homespun

BLUE
Pitcher, 42 Oz.	12.00 to 16.00
Pitcher, 80 Oz.	25.00
Pitcher, 96 Oz.	11.00
Salt & Pepper	7.50
Tumbler, 4 In.	3.00 to 6.00

CRYSTAL
Pitcher, 5 In.	5.00
Tumbler, 3 1/4 In.	2.50
Tumbler, 4 In.	2.80

PINK
Tumbler, 4 In.	3.00

Fire-King Dinnerware

Fire-King Dinnerware was made by the Anchor Hocking Glass Company of Lancaster, Ohio, from 1937 to 1938. It is found in blue, crystal, green or pink.

BLUE
Bowl, Oval, 10 In.	27.00
Creamer, Footed, 3 1/4 In.	26.00
Plate, Luncheon, 10 In.	18.00
Sugar, Footed, 3 1/4 In.	24.00

Fire-King

CRYSTAL
Cup 30.00
Platter, Closed Handles, 12 In. . 18.00
Tumbler, Water, Flat, 4 In., 9 Oz. 70.00
GREEN
Bowl, Cereal, 5 1/2 In. 15.00

Cookie Jar, Covered, 4 In. 72.00
Plate, Grill, 10 1/2 In. 13.50
PINK
Candy Jar, Covered 64.00
Pitcher, Footed, 3 1/4 In. 24.00
Tumbler, Footed, 6 1/2 In., 15 Oz. 20.00

Fire-King

Fire-King Oven Glass was made by the Anchor Hocking Glass Corporation of Lancaster, Ohio, from 1941 to 1950s. It is found in crystal or pale blue.

BLUE
Bottle, Infant's 3.75
Cake Pan, 8 3/4 In. ..... 5.00 to 7.00
Casserole, Covered, 4 1/2 In. 4.00
Casserole, Covered, 5 3/4 In. 5.25
Casserole, Covered, 8 3/4 In. 6.00
Casserole, Lid, Design, 4 1/2 In. . 5.00
Casserole, Open, Design, 4 1/2 In. 2.00
Casserole, Open, 8 3/4 In. 8.00
Casserole, Pie Cover, 8 3/4 In. .. 8.00

Custard, 5 Oz. .... 1.00 to 2.90
Custard, 6 Oz., 2 Styles .. 1.00 to 2.95
Hot Plate, 2-Handled ... 4.00 to 15.00
Jar, Refrigerator, Lid, 4 1/2 X 5 In. 4.00
Measuring Cup .... 5.50 to 9.00
Muffin, Flared, 5 Oz. 1.25
Pie Baker, Open, 1 Pt. 1.50
Pie Plate, 9 In. .... 3.50 to 6.00

Flat Diamond, see Diamond Quilted

Flora

Flora was made by the Imperial Glass Company of Bellaire, Ohio, c. 1925. It is found in amber, green, or Rose Marie (pink).

PINK
Bowl, 8 In. 10.00
Plate, 9 In. 6.50

Platter 6.75
Shaker, Footed 28.00

Floragold

Floragold was made by the Jeannette Glass Company of Jeannette, Pennsylvania, in the 1950s. It is found in blue, green, iridescent or pink.

BLUE
Salt & Pepper 25.00
GREEN
Cup & Saucer, Square 2.50
Pitcher, 40 Oz., 6 Tumblers 14.00
Plate, Square, 8 3/4 In. 2.00

Tumbler, 3 1/2 In. ...... 1.50 to 2.50
IRIDESCENT
Ashtray, 4 In. .... 2.75 to 4.50
Bowl, Handle, 5 In. 1.75
Bowl, Ruffled, 4 1/2 In. 3.75
Bowl, Ruffled, 5 1/2 In. 4.00

Bowl, Ruffled, 8 1/2 In. 7.00	Sugar, Covered 7.50
Bowl, Ruffled, 9 1/2 In. 5.50	Sugar, Open .... 2.50 to 2.95
Bowl, Ruffled, 12 In. .... 5.00 to 12.00	Tumbler, Footed, 10 Oz. 8.50
Bowl, Square, 4 1/2 In. 3.50	Tumbler, Footed, 11 Oz. 9.00
Bowl, Square, 8 1/2 In. 6.95	Tumbler, Footed, 15 Oz. 20.00
Bowl, 4 1/2 In. .... 2.25 to 3.00	Vase, Ruffled 85.00
Bowl, 5 1/2 In. 10.00	**PINK**
Bowl, 8 1/2 In. .... 3.00 to 6.50	Ashtray, 4 In. .... 3.50 to 4.50
Bowl, 9 1/2 In. .... 2.50 to 17.50	Bowl, Ruffled, 5 1/2 In. 2.50
Butter, Covered, Round 24.00 to 32.50	Bowl, Ruffled, 9 1/2 In. .. 5.00 to 8.00
Butter, Oblong .... 9.50 to 10.00	Bowl, Ruffled, 12 In. 6.00
Candlestick, Double, Pair 19.00	Bowl, 4 1/2 In. 2.50
Coaster .... 2.50 to 4.50	Bowl, 5 1/2 In. 2.00
Creamer .... 2.50 to 4.50	Bowl, 8 1/2 In. 6.00
Creamer, Footed 5.00	Bowl, 9 1/2 In. .... 11.00 to 18.00
Cup .... 2.00 to 5.00	Butter, Covered, Oblong 10.00
Cup & Saucer .... 5.00 to 7.50	Butter, Lid, Oblong 7.00
Dish, Candy, Handle 3.95	Butter, Open, Round ... 15.00 to 28.50
Dish, Candy, 4-Legged, 5 1/4 In. 8.00	Candlestick, Double 8.00
Plate, 8 1/2 In. .... 4.00 to 12.00	Candlestick, Double, Pair 20.00
Plate, 13 1/2 In. .... 6.50 to 10.00	Cup 2.00
Dish, Square, 4 1/2 In. 1.95	Cup & Saucer 5.00
Nut Cup, Footed 4.00	Dish, Candy, 4-Legged, 5 1/4 In. 5.00
Pitcher, 64 Oz. .... 12.00 to 17.00	Plate, 8 1/2 In. .... 8.00 to 10.00
Plate, 5 3/4 In. 4.00	Plate, 13 1/2 In. .... 6.00 to 10.00
Platter, Scalloped, 11 1/4 In. .. 10.50	Relish, 2-Handled, Round 3.50
Relish, Round, Handled .. 3.50 to 6.00	Sugar & Creamer, Lid .. 8.50 to 10.00
Salt & Pepper .... 22.00 to 30.00	Sugar & Creamer, Open 5.00
Salt & Pepper, Plastic Tops 25.00	Sugar, Open 2.50
Sherbet .... 5.00 to 5.50	Tumbler, 10 Oz. 7.50
Sherbet, Footed 5.00	Tumbler, 11 Oz. 7.50
Sugar & Creamer, Lid ... 5.00 to 9.00	Tumbler, 15 Oz. .... 9.50 to 11.00
Sugar & Creamer, Open .. 4.25 to 6.00	

Floral & Diamond Band

Floral & Diamond Band was made by the U. S. Glass Company, a firm with factories in Indiana, Ohio, Pennsylvania and West Virginia. It is found in black, green, iridescent or pink.

GREEN
Butter, Covered .... 49.00 to 50.00
Creamer 5.00
Pitcher, 8 In. 65.00
Sherbet .... 1.50 to 3.50
IRIDESCENT
Berry Bowl, 4 1/2 In. 2.50
Sherbet 2.50
Tumbler, 4 In. 5.90

PINK
Berry Set, 7 Piece 37.00

Floral

Floral was made by the Jeannette Glass Company of Jeannette, Pennsylvania, from 1931 to 1935. It is found in amber, crystal, delphite, green, jadite, pink, red or yellow.

CRYSTAL
Tumbler, 4 3/4 In. 6.00
GREEN
Berry Bowl, 4 In. 6.00
Bowl, Covered, 8 In. ... 10.00 to 27.50
Bowl, Oval, 9 In. .... 7.00 to 9.00
Bowl, Round, 7 1/2 In. 9.75
Butter, Covered .... 45.00 to 60.00
Candlestick, Pair ...... 19.95 to 28.00
Candy Container, Lid .. 18.00 to 22.00
Coaster, 3 1/4 In., Set Of 4 .... 7.00
Creamer .... 6.50 to 7.95
Cup .... 5.00 to 7.00
Cup & Saucer .... 7.50 to 10.00
Pitcher, Cone Shape, Footed, 7 In. 16.00
Pitcher, Cone Shape, 10 1/4 In. 150.00
Plate, 6 In. .... 1.50 to 3.00

Plate, 8 In. .... 3.95 to 7.50
Plate, 9 In. .... 3.00 to 9.00
Platter, Oval, 10 3/4 In. 8.00
Relish, Oval, 2 Part ..... 5.00 to 9.00
Salt & Pepper, Footed, 4 In. ... 27.50
Saltshaker, Footed 17.75
Saucer 3.50
Sherbet .... 5.00 to 8.00
Sugar & Creamer, Lid . 12.50 to 18.00
Sugar, Covered .... 7.50 to 14.50
Sugar, Open .... 4.00 to 6.00
Tray, 2-Handled, Square, 6 In. .. 8.00
Tumbler, Footed, 3 1/2 In. 12.00
Tumbler, Footed, 4 In. ... 7.00 to 8.75
Tumbler, Footed, 4 3/4 In. 9.00
Tumbler, Footed, 5 1/4 In. 22.50
Vase, 8 Sided 475.00

Floral

Floral

PINK

Berry Bowl, 4 In.	4.25 to 8.00
Bowl, Covered, 8 In. ...	15.00 to 18.50
Bowl, Oval, 9 In.	7.00 to 8.50
Bowl, 7 1/2 In.	5.00 to 10.00
Butter, Covered	48.00 to 90.00
Candlestick, 4 In., Pair	40.00
Candy Container, Covered	18.00
Coaster, 3 1/4 In.	3.75 to 7.00
Creamer	3.25 to 4.50
Cup	5.00 to 5.50
Cup & Saucer	6.50 to 9.00
Gravy Boat & Underplate	50.00
Pitcher, Cone Shape, Footed, 8 In.	25.00

Pitcher, 10 1/4 In. ..	100.00 to 110.00
Plate, 6 In.	1.50 to 3.00
Plate, 8 In.	1.35 to 6.50
Plate, 9 In.	5.00 to 8.50
Platter, Oval, 10 3/4 In.	7.00
Relish, Oval, 2 Part	4.50 to 6.50
Salt & Pepper, Flat, 6 In.	30.00
Salt & Pepper, Footed, 4 In. ...	27.50
Saltshaker, Flat, 6 In.	13.75
Saltshaker, Footed, 4 In.	17.50
Saucer	1.25 to 1.75
Sherbet	5.50 to 7.50
Sugar & Creamer, Lid .	14.50 to 17.00
Sugar & Creamer, Open	11.50
Sugar, Covered	4.00 to 12.00
Tray, Closed Handles, Square, 6 In.	8.50
Tumbler, Footed, 4 In. ...	7.50 to 9.00
Tumbler, Footed, 4 3/4 In.	9.50
Tumbler, Footed, 5 1/4 In.	17.50

Florentine No. 1

Florentine No. 1 was made by the Hazel Atlas Glass Company, a firm with factories in Ohio, Pennsylvania and West Virginia, from 1932 to 1935. It is found in cobalt, crystal, green, pink or yellow.

COBALT

Bowl, 5 In.	10.00
Sugar	30.00 to 34.50

CRYSTAL

Candleholder	8.00
Coaster, 3 3/4 In.	3.00

Compote, Ruffled	4.50
Creamer	2.25 to 4.00
Creamer, Ruffled	8.00
Cup	2.50 to 4.00
Cup & Saucer	3.50 to 5.50
Pitcher, Footed, 6 1/2 In.	20.00

Plate, Gold Rim, 8 1/2 In. 1.25
Plate, 6 In. .... .90
Plate, 8 1/2 In. .... 1.25 to 3.50
Plate, 10 In. 2.50
Salt & Pepper .... 15.00 to 20.00
Saucer .... .50
Sherbet, Footed .... 3.00 to 3.50
Sugar & Creamer, Covered 14.95
Sugar & Creamer, Open 6.00
Sugar, Open 3.50
Tumbler, Footed, 3 3/4 In. 4.00
Tumbler, Footed, 4 3/4 In. 6.00

GREEN
Berry Bowl, 5 In. 6.50
Berry Bowl, 8 1/2 In. 12.50
Bowl, Oval, 9 1/2 In. ... 7.00 to 15.00
Butter, Covered .... 55.00 to 85.00
Creamer .... 4.50 to 6.50
Cup .... 2.00 to 4.00
Cup & Saucer .... 6.00 to 7.00
Pitcher, Footed, 6 1/2 In. 27.00
Plate, Grill, 10 In. .... 3.75 to 5.50
Plate, 6 In. 1.50
Plate, 8 1/2 In. .... 3.75 to 5.00
Plate, 10 In. .... 3.00 to 7.00
Platter, Oval, 11 1/2 In. 9.50
Salt & Pepper .... 17.50 to 20.00
Saltshaker .... 8.00 to 12.00
Saucer 1.50
Sherbet .... 2.50 to 4.50
Sugar & Creamer, Covered 14.00
Sugar & Creamer, Open 8.75
Sugar, Covered .... 10.00 to 20.00
Sugar, Open .... 4.00 to 5.00
Tumbler, Footed, 3 3/4 In. 8.00
Tumbler, Footed, 4 3/4 In. 10.00

PINK
Bowl, 5 In. .... 6.25 to 7.00
Butter, Covered 125.00
Creamer .... 4.50 to 6.50
Creamer, Ruffled 15.00
Cup .... 2.00 to 4.00
Cup & Saucer .... 5.50 to 7.00
Pitcher, Footed, 6 1/2 In. 33.00
Plate, 8 1/2 In. .... 2.50 to 4.00
Salt & Pepper .... 27.50 to 37.50
Saucer .... 1.25 to 1.35
Sherbet .... 2.75 to 6.00
Soup, Cream 5.95
Sugar .... 4.50 to 7.00
Sugar & Creamer 11.00
Sugar & Creamer, Ruffled 25.00
Sugar, Open 4.50

Florentine No. 1

Sugar, Open, Ruffled ... 10.00 to 12.00
Tumbler, 4 3/4 In. 12.50

YELLOW
Ashtray, 5 1/2 In. 18.50
Berry Bowl, 8 1/2 In. 16.00
Bowl, Oval, Covered, 9 1/2 In. . 22.00
Butter, Covered 150.00
Coaster, 3 3/4 In. 12.00
Creamer 6.95
Plate, Grill, 10 In. .... 6.50 to 7.50
Plate, 10 In. 8.95

Florentine No. 1

Saucer	1.50	Sugar & Creamer, Open	12.00
Sherbet	5.50 to 9.50	Sugar, Covered	19.00
Sugar & Creamer, Covered	29.50	Tumbler, Footed, 3 3/4 In.	7.50

Florentine No. 2

Florentine No. 2 was made by the Hazel Atlas Glass Company, a firm with factories in Ohio, Pennsylvania and West Virginia, from 1934 to 1937. It is found in amber, cobalt, crystal, green, ice blue, pink or yellow.

AMBER
Plate, Grill, 10 In. 4.00
COBALT
Soup, Cream 25.00
Tumbler, Flat, 9 Oz., 4 1/2 In. . 46.50
CRYSTAL
Bowl, 4 1/2 In. .... 2.00 to 2.50
Candlestick, 2 3/4 In., Pair 25.00
Compote, Ruffled, 3 1/2 In. 7.50
Creamer .... 3.00 to 3.25
Cup .... 1.50 to 5.00
Cup & Saucer .... 2.50 to 5.25
Custard 9.00
Pitcher, Cone Shape, 7 1/2 In. . 18.00
Pitcher, Straight Sided, 48 Oz. . 30.00
Plate, 6 In. .... .80 to 1.50
Plate, 8 1/2 In. .... 2.00 to 2.50
Plate, 10 In. .... 2.50 to 3.50

Platter, 11 1/2 In. 3.50
Saltshaker 10.00
Saucer .... .80 to 1.00
Sherbet 2.50
Soup, Cream .... 3.00 to 4.50
Sugar 2.50
Sugar & Creamer .... 5.00 to 8.00
Tumbler, Flat, 4 In. ..... 3.00 to 7.75
Tumbler, Footed, 3 1/4 In. 6.00
Tumbler, Ribbed, 4 1/2 In. 6.00
GREEN
Ashtray, 5 1/2 In. ..... 13.50 to 19.95
Berry Bowl, 4 1/2 In. .... 4.00 to 5.50
Bowl, Round, 9 In. 9.00
Bowl, 8 In. 8.50
Butter, Covered 60.00
Celery 4.00
Coaster, 3 1/4 In. 7.50

Creamer 7.50
Cup .... 2.50 to 3.50
Cup & Saucer .... 3.50 to 10.00
Custard 6.50
Pitcher, Cone Shape, Footed, 28 Oz.
.... 16.00
Pitcher, 50 Oz. 40.00
Plate, Grill, 10 1/4 In. 4.50
Plate, 6 In. .... 2.00 to 5.00
Plate, 8 1/2 In. .... 2.25 to 4.50
Plate, 10 In. .... 4.50 to 7.00
Platter, Oval, 11 In. 6.50
Relish, 3 Section, 10 In. 11.00
Salt & Pepper .... 16.50 to 27.50
Saltshaker 8.00
Saucer .... .75 to 2.25
Sherbet, Footed .... 4.00 to 5.00
Soup, Cream, 5 In. 15.00
Sugar & Creamer, Open 8.00
Sugar, Open .... 3.00 to 5.00
Tumbler, Flat, 3 1/2 In. 9.00
Tumbler, Flat, 4 In. ..... 6.95 to 8.00
Tumbler, Footed, 3 1/4 In. 9.50
Tumbler, Footed, 4 1/2 In. 7.95
Tumbler, Footed, 5 In. .. 7.50 to 12.50

PINK

Bowl, 4 1/2 In. 6.00
Candy Container, Lid . 70.00 to 125.00
Coaster 8.00
Plate, 6 In. 2.50

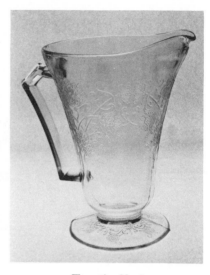

Florentine No. 2

Plate, 10 In. 8.00
Sherbet 5.25
Soup, Cream .... 4.50 to 6.00

Florentine No. 2

Soup, Cream, 4 3/4 In. 6.00
Sugar, Open 3.50
Tumbler, Flat, 3 1/2 In. 8.00
Tumbler, Flat, 4 In. ..... 6.00 to 8.00
Tumbler, Footed, 4 1/2 In. 9.00
Tumbler, 4 1/2 In. 7.95
YELLOW
Ashtray, 3 3/4 In. ..... 11.00 to 12.95
Ashtray, 5 1/2 In. ..... 18.00 to 20.00
Berry Bowl, 4 1/2 In. .... 6.00 to 8.50
Bowl, Oval, Covered, 9 In. 35.00
Bowl, 6 In. .... 15.00 to 20.00
Bowl, 8 In. .... 11.95 to 14.00
Butter, Covered .... 75.00 to 97.50
Candlestick, 2 3/4 In., Pair 30.00
Coaster .... 9.00 to 12.00
Creamer .... 5.00 to 7.00
Cup .... 3.75 to 7.00
Cup & Saucer .... 6.00 to 7.50
Gravy Boat .... 18.00 to 25.00
Gravy Boat, Underplate, 11 1/2 In. 50.00
Parfait, 6 In. .... 22.00 to 25.00
Pitcher, Cone Shape, Footed, 7 1/2 In.
.... 20.00
Pitcher, 8 In. 3.50
Plate, Grill, 10 1/4 In. 6.50
Plate, 6 In. .... 2.00 to 3.50
Plate, 8 1/2 In. .... 3.00 to 4.00
Plate, 10 In. .... 3.00 to 7.50
Platter, Oval, 11 In. ..... 5.95 to 9.50
Relish, 3 Section .... 9.00 to 15.00
Salt & Pepper .... 24.00 to 32.00
Saltshaker 14.00
Saucer .... 1.00 to 2.00
Sherbet .... 4.00 to 8.00
Soup, Cream, 4 3/4 In. .. 7.00 to 11.95
Sugar & Creamer, Lid . 16.00 to 20.00
Sugar & Creamer, Open . 4.00 to 10.00
Sugar, Covered .... 7.50 to 12.50
Sugar, Open .... 4.00 to 5.50
Tray, Condiment ...... 20.00 to 40.00

Flower & Leaf Band, see Indiana Custard
Flower Basket, see No. 615

Florentine No. 2

Tumbler, Flat, 4 In. .... 8.00 to 10.50
Tumbler, Footed, 3 1/4 In. 9.00
Tumbler, Footed, 4 In., Set Of 6 52.00
Tumbler, Footed, 4 1/2 In. 9.00
Tumbler, Footed, 5 In. . 11.00 to 16.00

Flower Garden with Butterflies

Flower Garden with Butterflies was made by the U. S. Glass Company, a firm with factories in Indiana, Ohio, Pennsylvania and West Virginia, in the late 1920s. It is found in amber, black, blue green, canary yellow, crystal, green or pink.

GREEN
  Bottle, Cologne, 7 1/2 In. 35.00
  Candy Container, Footed 49.50
  Plate, 10 1/4 In. 24.50

PINK
  Cheese & Cracker Set 32.50
  Plate, Center Handle .. 45.00 to 52.50

Flower, see Princess Feather

Fortune

Fortune was made by the Anchor Hocking Glass Company of Lancaster Ohio, from 1937 to 1938. It is found in crystal or pink.

CRYSTAL
  Berry Bowl, 4 In. .... .50 to .75
  Dish, Candy, Covered .... 5.00 to 6.00
PINK
  Berry Bowl, 4 In. .... 1.25 to 2.50
  Bowl, 4 1/2 In. 3.00

  Bowl, 5 1/4 In. 1.75
  Dish, Candy, Covered .... 4.00 to 9.00
  Plate, 6 In. 1.25
  Saucer .... 1.75 to 2.50
  Tumbler, 3 1/2 In. 3.00
  Tumbler, 4 In. 3.50

Frosted Block, see Beaded Block

Fruits

Fruits was made by the Hazel Atlas Company, a firm with factories in Ohio, Pennsylvania and West Virginia, and other companies from 1931 to 1933. It is found in crystal, green or pink.

CRYSTAL
  Tumbler 6.00
GREEN
  Cup .... 2.00 to 4.00
  Plate, 8 In. .... 1.50 to 3.75
  Saucer .... .75 to 2.00
  Sherbet 3.75

  Sherbet, Footed 9.00
  Sugar & Creamer 4.50
  Tumbler, 4 In. .... 3.50 to 5.50
PINK
  Saucer 1.50
  Tumbler, 4 In. .... 6.50 to 7.75

Garland

Garland was made by the Indiana Glass Company of Dunkirk, Indiana. It was made in crystal in 1935 and decorated milk glass in the 1950s.

CRYSTAL
  Bowl, Pink Iridescent Fruit 10.00

Georgian

Georgian was made by the Federal Glass Company of Columbus, Ohio, from 1931 to 1936. It is found in crystal, green or pink.

CRYSTAL
Berry Bowl, 4 1/2 In. 3.50
Bowl, 4 1/2 In. .... 3.00 to 3.50
Butter, Covered 42.50
Creamer, Footed, 3 In. 5.50
Cup 4.50
Cup & Saucer .... 6.00 to 7.50
Hot Plate, Center Design Only, 5 In.
.... 19.00
Plate, All Over Pattern, 9 1/4 In. 12.90
Plate, Luncheon 3.50
Plate, 6 In. .... 2.00 to 2.25
Plate, 8 In. .... 3.00 to 7.90
Plate, 9 In. 3.50
Platter, Closed Handles, 11 1/2 In. 26.50
Saucer 2.25
Sherbet .... 4.50 to 5.75
Sugar & Creamer, 3 In. 11.50
Sugar & Creamer, 4 In. 16.90
Sugar, Covered, 4 In. 19.50
Sugar, Tall 6.00
Tumbler, 4 In. 2.50
GREEN
Berry Bowl, 4 1/2 In. .... 2.25 to 5.00
Bowl, Deep, 6 1/2 In. .. 26.50 to 30.00
Bowl, Oval, 9 In. ...... 26.50 to 35.00
Bowl, 6 In. .... 5.00 to 9.00
Butter, Covered .... 35.00 to 65.00

Cake Server, Center Handle ... 18.00
Coaster 22.00
Creamer, Footed, 3 In. ... 4.00 to 6.00
Creamer, Footed, 4 In. ... 4.50 to 7.00
Cup .... 3.50 to 5.00
Cup & Saucer .... 5.50 to 8.00
Plate, 6 In. .... 1.50 to 3.50
Plate, 8 In. .... 2.50 to 5.50
Plate, 9 1/4 In. .... 6.00 to 12.00
Platter, Closed Handles, 11 1/2 In. 35.00
Saucer .... 1.50 to 2.25
Sherbet .... 2.00 to 6.25
Sugar & Creamer, Covered, Footed, 3 In.
.... 20.00
Sugar & Creamer, Footed, 3 In.   10.00
Sugar & Creamer, Open, Footed, 4 In.
.... 17.00
Sugar, Covered, Footed, 3 In. .. 24.50
Sugar, Covered, Footed, 4 In. .. 19.00
Sugar, Open, Footed, 3 In. 9.00
Sugar, Open, Footed, 4 In. 6.00
Tumbler, 4 In. .... 3.00 to 25.00
Tumbler, 5 1/4 In. 15.00
PINK
Butter 65.00
Sugar, Open 5.75
Tumbler, 3 1/4 In. 2.50

Gladioli, see Royal Lace

Gloria

Gloria was made by the Cambridge Glass Company of Cambridge, Ohio, in 1930. It is found in blue, crystal and green.

CRYSTAL
Plate, 6 In. 2.00

Tumbler, Footed, 5 Oz. 4.00
Tumbler, Footed, 10 Oz. 4.75

Gothic Arches

Gothic Arches was made by the L. E. Smith Company of Mt. Pleasant, Pennsylvania, in the 1920s. It is found in amber, green or yellow.

AMBER
Plate, 9 In. 3.00
Sherbet, Underplate 3.00
GREEN
Plate, 8 In. .... 3.50 to 4.00

YELLOW
Plate, Octagonal, 8 In. 3.50

Grape

Grape was made by the Standard Glass Manufacturing Company of Lancaster, Ohio, from 1925 to 1932. It is found in crystal, green or pink.

Grape, see also Woolworth

CRYSTAL
Tumbler, Juice 1.00
Wine, Pair 5.00
GREEN
Creamer 8.00

PINK
Pitcher, 7 3/4 In. 12.00
Sugar 8.00

Hairpin, see Newport

Hammered Band

Hammered Band was made by L. E. Smith Company of Mt. Pleasant, Pennsylvania, in the early 1930s. It is found in amethyst, black, green or pink.

AMETHYST
Plate, 9 In. 3.00
Sherbet, Cone Shape 3.00

Sherbet, Footed, Fluted, 3 1/4 In.   3.00
Sugar 3.00

Hanging Basket, see No. 615

Harp

Harp was made by the Jeannette Glass Company of Jeannette, Pennsylvania, from 1954 to 1957. It is found in crystal or crystal with a gold trim.

CRYSTAL
Cup & Saucer 2.75

Plate, 7 In. .... 2.00 to 2.50

Heritage

Heritage was made by the Federal Glass Company of Columbus, Ohio, from the late 1930s to the 1960s. It is found in blue, crystal, green or pink.

CRYSTAL
Bowl, 5 In. .... 1.50 to 4.25
Bowl, 8 1/2 In. .... 12.00 to 13.50
Bowl, 10 1/2 In. .... 4.00 to 8.00
Creamer .... 5.00 to 7.00
Cup .... 1.75 to 3.25
Cup & Saucer .... 2.00 to 5.00
Plate, 6 In. 1.00

Plate, 8 In. .... 1.50 to 3.00
Plate, 9 1/4 In. .... 3.00 to 4.00
Plate, 12 In. .... 2.00 to 8.00
Saucer .... .75 to 1.00
Sugar 6.50
Sugar & Creamer, Open 12.00 to 19.50
GREEN
Berry Bowl, 5 In. 25.00

Hexagon Optic

Hexagon Optic, sometimes called Honeycomb, was made by the Jeannette Glass Company of Jeannette, Pennsylvania, from 1928 to 1932. It is found in green or pink.

GREEN
Bowl, 4 1/2 In. 1.50
Cup 2.00
Pitcher, Footed, 9 In. .. 20.00 to 30.00
Pitcher, 5 In. 6.50
Plate, Rimmed, 10 In. 3.00
Plate, 6 In. .... .80
Plate, 8 In. .... 1.00 to 1.50
Salt & Pepper 14.00
Saltshaker 5.00
Sugar 2.00
Sugar & Creamer, Closed Handle 6.00
Tumbler, 3 In. 3.00
Tumbler, 3 3/4 In. ...... 4.00 to 5.00
Tumbler, 5 3/4 In. 5.00
Tumbler, 9 Oz. 5.00

Whiskey, 2 In. .... 1.00 to 3.00
PINK
Creamer, Closed Handles 1.75
Cup & Saucer .... 2.50 to 4.50
Cup & Saucer, Closed Handles .. 1.75
Ice Bucket 8.00
Mixing Bowl, 8 3/4 In. 6.00
Plate, 8 In. 1.50
Plate, 9 In. 1.25
Plate, 11 In. 4.00
Salt & Pepper .... 14.00 to 16.50
Saucer 1.00
Shaker 5.00
Sugar & Creamer 5.00
Tumbler, Flat, 5 3/4 In. 3.99
Tumbler, 10 Oz. 5.00

Hinge, see Patrician

Hobnail

Hobnail was made by the Hocking Glass Company of Lancaster, Ohio, from 1934 to 1936. It is found in crystal or pink.

Hobnail, see also Early American Hobnail

CRYSTAL
Creamer, Footed 4.50
Cup .... 1.50 to 2.50
Decanter, Stopper, Red Trim, 32 Oz.
.... 12.00
Goblet, Red Trim, 13 Oz. 2.25
Goblet, 8 Oz. 1.33

Pitcher, 18 Oz. .... 7.99 to 11.00
Pitcher, 67 Oz. .... 13.00 to 20.00
Plate, 6 In. .... .50
Plate, 8 1/2 In. 1.50
Sherbet, Footed, 3 1/4 In. 1.25
Tumbler, Footed, 3 1/4 In. 3.00
Tumbler, Footed, 4 1/2 In. 1.25

Tumbler, Footed, 5 In. 3.50
Tumbler, Red Trim, 4 1/2 In. ... 4.00
Tumbler, 4 In. .... .79 to 1.99
Whiskey, 2 1/4 In. ...... 2.00 to 4.00
Wine Set, Footed, 9 Piece 47.00

PINK

Bottle & Stopper, Perfume, 8 Oz. 35.00
Bowl, Ruffled, 10 In. 38.00
Cup .... 2.00 to 4.00
Cup & Saucer .... 2.25 to 4.50
Plate, 6 In. .... 1.00 to 2.00
Plate, 8 1/2 In. .... 2.75 to 7.00
Saltshaker, Flat, 3 In. 7.50
Saucer .... 1.50 to 2.50
Sherbet .... 2.00 to 2.75
Vase, Footed, Crimped, 6 1/2 In.   28.50

Hobnail

Holiday

Holiday was made by the Jeannette Glass Company of Jeannette, Pennsylvania, from 1947 to 1949. It is found in crystal, iridescent, pink or shell pink opaque.

CRYSTAL

Pitcher, 6 3/4 In. 15.00
Tumbler, Flat, 4 In. ..... 7.00 to 8.00

IRIDESCENT

Platter, Oval, 11 3/8 In. 7.50
Tumbler, Footed, 4 In. ... 5.50 to 7.00

Holiday

PINK
Berry Bowl, 5 1/8 In. .... 2.50 to 7.00
Bowl, Console, Footed, 10 3/4 In. 15.00
Bowl, Oval, 9 1/2 In. .... 6.00 to 8.00
Bowl, 7 3/4 In. .... 14.00 to 15.00
Bowl, 8 1/2 In. 11.25

Butter, Covered .... 9.00 to 30.00
Candleholder, 3 In., Pair 52.50
Creamer, Footed .... 3.00 to 6.00
Cup & Saucer, Plain ..... 3.75 to 6.00
Cup & Saucer, Rayed 5.00
Goblet, 5 3/4 In. 9.00

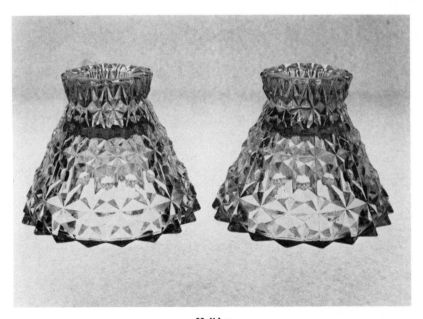

Holiday

Pitcher, 16 Oz. .... 14.00 to 45.00
Pitcher, 52 Oz. .... 19.00 to 25.00
Plate, Cake, 10 1/2 In. .. 6.00 to 45.00
Plate, 6 In. .... 1.00 to 2.50
Plate, 9 In. .... 3.00 to 7.95
Platter, 11 3/8 In. ...... 5.00 to 20.00
Saucer, Plain .... 1.00 to 2.00
Sherbet, Footed .... 2.75 to 5.00
Sugar & Creamer, Covered 15.00
Sugar, Covered .... 6.00 to 8.50
Sugar, Open 3.25
Tray, 10 1/2 In. .... 6.50 to 7.50
Tumbler, Flat, 4 In. .... 6.00 to 10.50
Tumbler, Footed, 4 In. . 11.00 to 25.00
Tumbler, Footed, 6 In. 35.00

Holiday

Homespun

Homespun was made by the Jeannette Glass Company of Jeannette, Pennsylvania, from 1939 to 1940. It is found in crystal or pink.

CRYSTAL
Butter, Covered 60.00
Creamer, Footed 3.00
Cup 2.50
Plate, 6 In. .... 1.25 to 1.50
Plate, 9 1/4 In. 5.00
Tumbler, Flat, 5 1/4 In. 6.50
Tumbler, Footed, 4 In. ... 4.00 to 5.00
Tumbler, 6 1/2 In. 9.00
PINK
Bowl, 2-Handled, 4 1/2 In. 2.50
Bowl, 4 1/2 In. 5.00
Bowl, 5 In. 7.00
Bowl, 8 1/4 In. .... 7.00 to 8.50
Butter, Covered .... 30.00 to 35.00
Coaster 5.00
Cup & Saucer .... 3.75 to 6.50
Plate, Child's .... 5.00 to 10.00
Plate, 6 In. .... 1.25 to 2.00
Plate, 9 1/4 In. .... 3.50 to 6.50
Platter, 2-Handled, 13 In. 9.00

Homespun

Saucer	1.00
Saucer, Child's	3.50 to 4.00
Sherbet, Flat, 3 1/2 In.	6.50
Sugar & Creamer, Footed	6.50
Sugar, Footed	3.00 to 4.00
Tea Set, Boxed, 14 Piece	190.00

Teapot, Child's	35.00
Tumbler, Allover Pattern	6.00
Tumbler, Flat, 4 In.	5.50 to 6.00
Tumbler, Flat, 5 1/4 In.	12.00
Tumbler, Footed, 4 In. ..	3.00 to 12.00
Tumbler, Footed, 6 1/2 In.	20.00

Honeycomb

Honeycomb was made by the Federal Glass Company of Columbus, Ohio, from 1929 to 1932. It is found in crystal, green or pink.

Honeycomb, see also Hexagon Optic

GREEN

Cup	2.00
Pitcher, 5 In.	6.50
Plate, 6 In.	.80
Sugar	2.00
Tumbler, 3 3/4 In.	4.00 to 5.00
Tumbler, 5 3/4 In.	5.00
Tumbler, 9 Oz.	5.00

PINK

Ice Bucket	8.00
Plate, 8 In.	1.50
Saucer	1.00
Sugar & Creamer	5.00
Tumbler, Flat, 5 3/4 In.	3.99
Tumbler, Footed, 5 3/4 In.	6.00
Tumbler, 3 3/4 In.	3.50

Horizontal Ribbed, see Manhattan
Horizontal Rounded Big Rib, see
Manhattan
Horizontal Sharp Big Rib, see Manhattan
Horseshoe, see No. 612

Imperial Optic Rib

Imperial Optic Rib was made by the Imperial Glass Company of Bellaire, Ohio, in 1927. It is found in amberina and blue.

BLUE

Plate, 6 1/4 In.	.75

Sherbet, Flared	1.60

Indiana Custard

Indiana Custard was made by the Indiana Glass Company of Dunkirk, Indiana, in custard or ivory in the early 1930s and in white in the 1950s.

IVORY

Bowl, Oval, 9 1/2 In. ...	7.00 to 15.50
Bowl, 8 3/4 In.	12.00 to 13.00
Butter, Covered	35.00 to 45.00

Creamer, Footed	5.00 to 9.00
Plate, 5 3/4 In.	3.00 to 6.00
Plate, 7 1/2 In.	6.00 to 7.00
Plate, 9 3/4 In.	12.00

Platter, Oval, 11 1/2 In. 20.00
Saucer 3.00
Sugar & Creamer, Footed, Covered 25.00
Sugar & Creamer, Open 15.00
Sugar, Footed, Open ..... 5.00 to 6.00

WHITE
Creamer, 3/8 In. 2.50
Saucer 1.00
Sugar 6.50

Iris

Iris was made by the Jeannette Glass Company of Jeannette, Pennsylvania, from 1928 to 1932, in 1950 and in the 1970s. The early wares are found in crystal, iridescent or pink, later wares in blue-green or red yellow.

Iris & Herringbone, see Iris

CRYSTAL
Bowl, Nutcracker 22.00
Bowl, Ruffled, 5 In. ...... 2.00 to 3.50
Bowl, Ruffled, 9 In. ...... 3.00 to 9.00
Bowl, Ruffled, 11 In. .... 5.00 to 15.00
Bowl, Straight Edge, 5 In. 2.25
Bowl, Straight Edge, 11 In. 16.95
Bowl, 7 1/2 In. .... 19.00 to 20.00
Butter, Covered .... 15.00 to 19.00
Candlestick, Double, Pair 15.00
Candy Container, Lid .. 39.50 to 47.50
Coaster 22.50
Creamer, Footed .... 1.50 to 4.50
Cup .... 4.00 to 9.00
Cup & Saucer .... 6.25 to 9.50
Goblet, 4 In. .... 5.50 to 8.00
Goblet, 5 3/4 In. .... 6.00 to 10.00
Lamp Shade .... 12.00 to 20.00
Pitcher, 7 Footed Tumblers, 6 In. 60.00
Pitcher, 9 1/2 In. ..... 12.50 to 15.00
Plate, Gold Band, 11 3/4 In. 8.00
Plate, 8 In. 18.50
Plate, 9 In. .... 9.00 to 12.50
Saucer .... 2.00 to 2.25
Sherbet, Footed, 2 1/2 In. 6.50
Sherbet, Footed, 4 In. .... 5.00 to 6.50
Sugar & Creamer, Lid .. 8.00 to 12.00
Sugar & Creamer, Open 6.25
Sugar, Covered .... 4.00 to 6.50
Sugar, Open 3.00
Tumbler, Footed, 6 In. ... 5.50 to 9.00
Tumbler, Footed, / In. ... 4.75 to 9.50
Vase, 9 In. .... 6.00 to 15.00
Wine, 4 1/4 In. .... 8.00 to 9.00
IRIDESCENT
Berry Bowl, Beaded Edge, 4 1/2 In. 4.00

Iris

Bowl, Beaded Edge, 8 1/2 In. ... 9.00
Bowl, Console, Scalloped, 12 1/2 In.
.... 12.00
Bowl, Ruffled, 9 In. 2.50
Bowl, Ruffled, 11 In. .... 4.50 to 12.00
Bowl, Straight Edge, 11 In. 6.00
Bowl, 5 In. .... 3.00 to 3.25
Bowl, 7 1/2 In. .... 10.00 to 15.00
Bowl, 8 In. 12.00
Bowl, 9 In. .... 4.00 to 6.50
Butter, Covered .... 15.00 to 30.00
Candlestick, Pair 10.00
Creamer, Footed .... 2.75 to 6.00
Cup .... 4.50 to 6.50
Cup & Saucer .... 6.50 to 8.50
Goblet, Footed, 4 In. .... 7.25 to 12.00
Pitcher .... 11.00 to 30.00
Plate, Grill 5.00
Plate, 5 1/2 In. .... 1.60 to 4.00
Plate, 8 In. 8.00
Plate, 9 In. .... 6.50 to 10.00
Plate, 11 3/4 In. .... 5.00 to 10.00
Saucer 1.50
Sherbet, 2 1/2 In. .... 3.50 to 6.00
Sugar & Creamer, Lid .. 7.50 to 12.95
Sugar, Covered .... 4.00 to 7.00
Tumbler, Footed, 6 In. ... 4.50 to 7.50
Tumbler, Footed, 7 In. .. 9.00 to 10.00
Vase, 9 In. .... 3.50 to 11.50
PINK
   Lamp Shade, Crystal Center ... 25.00

Iris

Plate, Frosted, 8 In. 20.00

Jadite

Jadite was made by the Jeannette Glass Company of Jeannette, Pennsylvania, in 1936. It is found in opaque colors.

GREEN
   Bowl, Square, 4 1/4 In. 1.25
   Bowl, 6 1/2 In. 3.00
   Bowl, 9 In. 6.00
   Canister, Coffee, Round, Tall ... 15.00
   Canister, Tea, Round, Tall 15.00

   Creamer, 5 1/4 In. .... 20.00 to 22.50
   Cup & Saucer, Square ... 1.25 to 2.00
   Salt & Pepper, 4 In. .... 6.00 to 10.00
   Sugar, Square 6.00
   Vase, Bud, 6 In. 3.50

Jane-Ray

Jane-Ray was made by the Anchor Hocking Glass Company of Lancaster, Ohio, from 1945 to 1963. It is a Fire-King Dinnerware found in jade-ite.

JADE-ITE

Bowl, 5 7/8 In. 1.25
Bowl, 8 1/4 In. 2.75
Creamer .... 1.50 to 2.00
Cup 1.25
Cup & Saucer .... 1.25 to 3.00
Jug, 16 Oz. 3.50
Mug, 3 In. 1.00
Plate, 4 7/8 In. 1.00

Plate, 7 3/4 In. .... 1.00 to 1.50
Plate, 9 1/8 In. .... 1.00 to 2.00
Platter, 12 In. 2.00
Saucer .... .50 to .75
Soup, Bowl .... 1.50 to 2.50
Sugar & Creamer, Covered 6.00
Sugar, Covered .... 2.00 to 2.75
Sugar, Open 2.00

Knife & Fork, see Colonial

Lace Edge

Lace Edge was made by the Hocking Glass Company of Lancaster, Ohio, from 1935 to 1938. It is found in crystal or pink.

CRYSTAL

Bowl, 6 3/8 In. .... 2.50 to 6.50
Bowl, 9 1/2 In. .... 6.75 to 7.00
Butter, Covered 32.00
Compote, 3-Legged, Covered ... 15.00
Cookie Jar, Covered 25.00
Flower Bowl & Frog ..... 7.00 to 9.50
Plate, Grill, 10 1/2 In. 7.00
Plate, 7 1/4 In. 2.00
Plate, 8 3/4 In. .... 1.50 to 4.00
Plate, 10 1/2 In. .... 9.00 to 10.00
Relish, 3 Part, 7 1/2 In. 10.00
Relish, 3 Part, 10 1/2 In. 6.50

Saucer 3.75
Sugar 8.75
Tumbler, Footed, 5 In. 18.00
PINK
Bowl, Console, 3-Legged, 10 1/2 In. 75.00
Bowl, 6 3/8 In. .... 4.50 to 7.50
Bowl, 7 3/4 In. .... 5.00 to 15.00
Bowl, 9 1/2 In. .... 4.00 to 12.00
Butter, Covered .... 30.00 to 45.00
Candlestick, Pair 60.00
Compote, Covered, Footed, 7 In. 11.00
Cookie Jar, Frosted ... 15.00 to 40.50
Creamer .... 7.00 to 8.50

Lace Edge

Cup .... 6.00 to 10.50	Platter, 5 Part, 13 3/4 In. 13.00
Cup & Saucer .... 12.50 to 14.95	Relish, 3 Part, 7 1/2 In. 23.00
Dish, Candy, Covered 7.00	Relish, 3 Part, 10 1/2 In. 9.50
Flower Bowl 4.50	Saucer .... 2.75 to 4.00
Flower Bowl & Frog .... 7.00 to 15.00	Server, Center Handle 55.00
Luncheon Set, 3 Piece 20.00	Sherbet, Footed 25.00
Plate, Grill, 10 1/2 In. 7.50	Sugar .... 6.75 to 7.50
Plate, 7 1/4 In. .... 3.00 to 8.50	Sugar & Creamer ..... 16.00 to 17.00
Plate, 8 In. .... 4.00 to 7.50	Tumbler, Flat, 4 1/2 In. 7.25
Plate, 10 1/2 In. .... 8.00 to 11.00	Tumbler, Footed, 5 In. .. 5.50 to 24.00

Lacy Daisy, see No. 618

Lake Como

Lake Como was made by the Hocking Glass Company of Lancaster, Ohio, from 1934 to 1937. It is white with a blue decoration.

BLUE & WHITE
Cup & Saucer .... 3.50 to 4.00

Plate, 10 In. .... 3.00 to 3.50

Laurel

Laurel was made by the McKee Glass Company of Jeannette, Pennsylvania, in the 1930s. It is found in French ivory, jade green, powder blue or white opal.

GREEN	IVORY
Berry Bowl, 5 In. .... 3.00 to 3.50	Berry Bowl, 5 In. 4.00
Bowl, Oval, 9 3/4 In. 13.50	Bowl, 9 In. 7.50
Bowl, 6 In. 6.00	Bowl, 11 In. 9.50
Bowl, 9 In. 7.50	Bowl, Green Rim, 6 In. 1.55
Butter, Covered 40.00	Candlestick, 4 In., Pair 17.50
Candlestick, 4 In., Pair 10.00	Creamer, Child's ...... 20.00 to 32.50
Cup 3.80	Creamer, Footed .... 7.50 to 8.00
Cup & Saucer .... 12.00 to 15.00	Cup .... 4.00 to 7.00
Plate, Grill, 9 1/8 In. 4.95	Cup & Saucer .... 3.00 to 9.00
Plate, Straight Edge, 6 In. 2.00	Dish, Cheese, Covered . 42.50 to 49.50
Plate, 7 1/4 In. 3.80	Dish, Oval, 9 3/4 In. 7.50
Plate, 9 1/8 In. .... 4.00 to 6.00	Plate, Grill, 9 1/8 In. 6.00
Platter, Oval, 10 3/4 In. 13.50	Plate, 6 In. 1.63
Saucer 1.95	Plate, 7 1/2 In. 6.00
Sugar, Footed .... 7.50 to 9.50	Plate, 9 1/8 In. .... 1.00 to 8.00
Tumbler, 4 1/2 In. 18.00	Platter, Oval, 10 3/4 In. 15.00

Sherbet 1.28
Sugar & Creamer 20.00

Sugar, Child's .... 20.00 to 25.00

Lily Medallion, see American Sweetheart
Lincoln Drape, see Princess

Lincoln Inn

Lincoln Inn was made by the Fenton Glass Company of Williamstown, West Virginia, in the late 1920s. It is found in amethyst, black cobalt, crystal, green, jade, pink or red.

COBALT
  Bowl, 6 In. 10.00
  Goblet, Water 17.50
CRYSTAL
  Sherbet 4.00
GREEN
  Cup 5.00
  Plate, 8 In. 6.50

Saucer 2.25
Sherbet, Footed 8.50
PINK
  Plate, 8 In. 4.25
RED
  Goblet, Water 16.00
  Tumbler, Footed, 6 In. 17.00

Line 191

Line 191 was made by the Paden City Glass Company of Paden City, West Virginia, in 1928. It is found in amber, green or pink.

GREEN
  Creamer 5.00
  Sherbet 3.00

PINK
  Creamer 4.00

Little Bo Peep

Little Bo Peep was made by the Anchor Hocking Glass Company of Lancaster, Ohio, in 1940. It is an orange and green child's line on ivory.

IVORY
  Mug 5.00

Pitcher 15.00

Little Hostess, see Moderntone Little
Hostess
Loop, see Lace Edge
Lorain, see No. 615
Louisa, see Georgian
Lydia Ray, see New Century

Madrid

Madrid was made by the Federal Glass Company of Columbus, Ohio, from 1932 to 1939. It is found in amber, crystal, green, Madonna blue or pink.

AMBER

Ashtray, Square, 6 In.	65.00 to 150.00
Berry Bowl, 5 In.	1.50 to 3.75
Bowl, Console, 11 In. ...	5.50 to 10.00
Bowl, Oval, 10 In.	6.95 to 7.50
Bowl, 4 3/4 In.	3.25 to 6.50
Bowl, 7 In.	4.00 to 7.00
Bowl, 8 In.	8.00 to 15.00
Bowl, 9 1/2 In.	10.00 to 15.00
Butter, Covered	35.00 to 60.00
Candlestick, 2 1/4 In., Pair	15.00
Cookie Jar, Covered ...	18.00 to 24.95
Creamer	2.50
Cup & Saucer	3.50 to 6.00
Hot Plate & Coaster ...	20.00 to 35.00
Jar, Jam, 7 In.	6.00 to 9.50
Jello Mold	4.00 to 6.00
Pitcher, Square, 60 Oz.	28.00
Pitcher, 5 1/2 In.	16.00 to 20.00
Pitcher, 80 Oz.	31.90
Plate, Cake, 11 1/4 In.	9.00
Plate, Grill, 10 1/2 In.	6.75
Plate, 6 In.	1.50 to 4.50
Plate, 7 1/2 In.	3.00 to 8.00
Plate, 8 7/8 In.	2.00 to 4.50
Plate, 10 1/2 In.	21.50 to 22.00
Platter, Oval, 11 1/2 In.	9.00

Relish, 10 1/4 In.	5.00 to 7.50
Salt & Pepper, Flat, 3 1/2 In. ..	30.00
Salt & Pepper, Footed, 3 1/2 In.	35.00
Saucer	1.00 to 4.50
Sherbet, Cone Shape, Footed	6.00
Sherbet, Round, Flat	2.00 to 6.00
Sugar & Creamer, Lid .	18.00 to 35.00
Sugar & Creamer, Open .	5.95 to 10.00
Sugar, Open	2.50 to 6.00
Tumbler, Flat, 3 7/8 In.	11.00
Tumbler, Flat, 4 1/4 In.	12.00
Tumbler, Flat, 5 1/2 In.	12.50
Tumbler, Footed, 4 In. ..	7.50 to 12.00
Tumbler, Footed, 5 1/2 In.	16.00

BLUE

Bowl, Oval, 10 In.	15.00 to 22.00
Bowl, 8 In.	16.00
Creamer	11.00
Cup	10.00 to 12.00
Jar, Jam, 7 In.	14.00
Plate, 6 In.	5.00
Plate, 8 7/8 In.	7.50 to 12.00
Plate, 10 1/2 In.	22.50 to 25.00
Platter, Oval, 11 1/2 In.	10.00
Sherbet, Cone Shape, Footed, 6 In.	10.00
Sugar & Creamer, Open	20.00
Sugar, Open	7.50 to 11.00

Madrid

Madrid

CRYSTAL

Bowl, Oval, 10 In.	8.00
Bowl, 7 In.	6.00
Bowl, 8 In.	8.00
Butter, Covered	95.00
Candlestick, 2 1/4 In., Pair	12.00
Cookie Jar, Covered	16.50 to 30.00
Creamer	4.00
Cup	1.75 to 4.00
Hot Plate & Coaster	20.00
Jar, Jam, 7 In.	2.00 to 4.00
Pitcher, Square, 60 Oz.	39.00
Plate, Cake, 11 1/4 In.	5.00
Plate, Grill, 10 1/2 In.	5.00
Plate, 6 In.	1.00 to 2.50
Plate, 7 1/2 In.	3.75 to 5.00
Plate, 8 7/8 In.	3.75 to 4.00
Platter, Oval, 11 1/2 In.	9.00
Relish, 4 Part, 10 1/4 In.	3.50
Salt & Pepper, Footed, 3 1/2 In.	45.00
Saucer	2.00 to 4.00
Sugar, Open	3.00 to 5.00
Tumbler, Flat, 4 1/4 In.	12.00
Tumbler, Flat, 5 1/2 In.	18.00

GREEN

Berry Bowl, 5 In.	4.00
Bowl, Oval, 10 In.	11.50
Bowl, 8 In.	12.50 to 18.00
Butter, Covered	50.00 to 75.00
Creamer	3.25 to 6.50
Cup	5.00
Cup & Saucer	5.50 to 7.00
Hot Plate & Coaster	29.50
Pitcher, Square, 60 Oz.	90.00
Plate, Grill, 10 1/2 In.	5.50
Plate, 7 1/2 In.	6.00
Plate, 8 7/8 In.	4.00 to 7.00
Plate, 10 1/2 In.	12.50
Platter, Oval, 11 1/2 In.	7.00
Salt & Pepper, Flat, 3 1/2 In.	45.00
Salt & Pepper, Footed, 3 1/2 In.	69.00
Saucer	2.50 to 3.25
Sherbet	3.75 to 5.00
Sugar & Creamer, Covered	32.50
Sugar, Open	3.00 to 6.50

PINK

Berry Bowl, 5 In.	3.00
Bowl, Console, 11 In.	5.95 to 8.00
Bowl, 8 In.	15.00
Candlestick, 2 1/4 In., Pair	15.00
Console Set, Bowl & Candlesticks	14.00
Cookie Jar, Covered	21.00 to 24.95
Cup	3.00 to 5.00

Cup & Saucer	5.50 to 6.00
Plate, Cake, 11 1/4 In.	8.00
Plate, Oval, 11 1/2 In.	7.50
Plate, 6 In.	2.00
Relish, 4 Part, 10 1/4 In.	5.00
Sherbet, Cone Shape, Footed	3.50
Tumbler, 4 1/4 In.	7.00 to 8.50

Madrid

Magnolia, see Dogwood

Manhattan

Manhattan was made by the Anchor Hocking Glass Corporation of Lancaster, Ohio, from 1938 to 1941. It is found in crystal, green or pink.

CRYSTAL

Ashtray, 4 In.	3.75 to 5.00
Berry Bowl, 2-Handled, 5 3/8 In.	3.50
Berry Bowl, 2-Handled, 7 1/2 In.	6.00
Bowl, 2-Handled, 9 In.	7.00
Bowl, 4 1/2 In.	1.00 to 3.00
Bowl, 7 1/2 In.	3.50
Bowl, 9 In.	4.00 to 11.95
Candleholder, Square, 4 1/2 In., Pair	6.50
Candy Container, Covered	10.00
Coaster	1.25 to 2.50
Compote, 5 3/4 In.	1.50 to 9.50
Creamer, Oval	2.00 to 3.00
Cup	1.00 to 5.00
Cup & Saucer	4.00
Pitcher, 42 Oz.	4.00 to 9.00
Pitcher, 80 Oz.	16.00
Plate, 6 In.	1.00 to 2.50
Plate, 8 1/2 In.	2.50 to 5.00
Plate, 10 1/4 In.	2.00 to 5.95
Relish, Metal Holder & Spoon ..	6.50
Relish, 4 Part, 14 In.	4.50 to 8.00
Relish, 5 Part, Ruby Inserts, 14 In.	8.00
Salt & Pepper, 2 In.	8.00 to 15.00
Saltshaker, 2 In.	4.00
Saucer	1.25 to 2.50
Sherbet, Flat, 2 1/4 In.	4.50

Sherbet, Footed	3.00
Sugar & Creamer, Oval ..	4.50 to 9.95
Sugar, Oval	2.00 to 3.00
Tumbler, Flat, Set Of 6	12.00
Tumbler, Footed, 4 1/2 In.	4.75
Vase, 8 In.	3.00 to 5.50
Water Set, 7 Piece	33.00
Wine, 3 1/2 In.	3.00 to 5.25

GREEN

Tumbler, Footed	5.00

PINK

Bowl, Footed, 2-Handled, 9 1/2 In.	16.00
Bowl, 2-Handled, 5 3/8 In.	3.00
Candy Container, Covered	9.50
Compote, 5 3/4 In.	2.75 to 6.50
Creamer, Oval	2.25 to 4.00
Cup & Saucer	8.00
Dish, Candy, 3-Legged ...	2.75 to 4.00
Pitcher, 42 Oz.	13.00 to 22.00
Pitcher, 80 Oz.	22.00 to 32.50
Salt & Pepper, 2 In. ...	12.00 to 20.00
Sherbet, Flat, 2 1/4 In.	3.00
Sherbet, Footed, 2 1/4 In.	3.00
Sugar & Creamer, Oval .	4.00 to 18.00
Sugar, Oval	2.25 to 3.25
Tumbler, Footed	3.75 to 6.00

Many Windows, see Roulette

Mayfair Federal

Mayfair Federal was made by the Federal Glass Company of Columbus, Ohio, in 1934. It is found in amber, crystal, green or pale blue.

AMBER
- Plate, Grill, 9 1/2 In. .... 1.25 to 6.50
- Plate, 6 3/4 In. 3.00
- Saucer .... 2.00 to 3.50
- Sugar, Footed .... 4.50 to 8.00

CRYSTAL
- Bowl, 2-Handled, 10 In. 9.00
- Cup 5.00
- Plate, Grill, 9 1/2 In. 3.50
- Plate, 6 3/4 In. 4.00
- Platter, Oval, 12 In. 5.00

GREEN
- Bowl, Scalloped, 12 In. 16.00

YELLOW
- Bowl, Scalloped, Deep, 12 In. . 100.00

Mayfair Federal

Mayfair

Mayfair, sometimes called Open Rose, was made by the Hocking Glass Company of Lancaster, Ohio, from 1931 to 1937. It is found in crystal green, ice blue, pink or yellow. Reproduction shot glasses were made in 1977 in blue, green or pink.

Mayfair, see also Rosemary

AMBER
- Platter, Oval, 12 In. 10.00

BLUE
- Bowl, Covered, 10 In. 48.00
- Bowl, Scalloped, 12 In. 45.00
- Bowl, 7 In. 20.00
- Bowl, 10 In. .... 20.00 to 21.00
- Butter, Covered, 7 In. 220.00
- Celery, Divided, 10 In. 20.00
- Cup .... 18.00 to 22.50
- Cup & Saucer .... 27.50 to 32.50
- Dish, Candy, Covered 85.00
- Goblet, 7 1/4 In. ...... 50.00 to 55.00
- Pitcher, 6 In., 37 Oz. .. 40.00 to 55.00
- Pitcher, 8 In., 60 Oz. .. 50.00 to 72.50
- Plate, Grill, 9 1/2 In. .. 17.00 to 18.00
- Plate, 6 In. 5.00
- Plate, 8 1/2 In. .... 14.00 to 14.95
- Platter, Oval, 2-Handled, 12 In. 27.50
- Relish, 4 Part, 8 3/8 In. 23.95
- Salt & Pepper, Flat .. 100.00 to 135.00
- Saucer .... 6.00 to 9.00
- Server, Center Handle 30.00
- Tumbler, 3 1/2 In., 5 Oz. 42.00
- Vase, Sweet Pea ...... 45.00 to 52.50

GREEN
- Cookie Jar, Covered 400.00
- Dish, Candy, Covered 400.00 to 500.00
- Server, Center Handle .. 9.00 to 15.00
- Sugar 150.00

PINK
- Berry Bowl, 5 In. 9.50
- Bowl, Covered, 10 In. .. 20.00 to 26.00
- Bowl, Low, 11 3/4 In. . 12.00 to 22.50
- Bowl, Open, 2-Handled, 10 In. . 10.00
- Bowl, Oval, 9 1/2 In. .... 7.95 to 9.95
- Bowl, Scalloped, Deep, 12 In. .. 20.00
- Bowl, 5 1/2 In. .... 5.00 to 8.50
- Bowl, 7 In. .... 8.00 to 14.00
- Butter, Covered .... 27.50 to 35.00
- Candy Container, Lid .. 16.50 to 22.50
- Celery, Divided, 10 In. 15.00

Mayfair

Cookie Jar, Covered ...	16.50 to 21.00	Decanter & Stopper ...	65.00 to 70.00
Creamer	7.00 to 10.95	Goblet, Thin, 7 1/4 In.	50.00
Cup	6.00 to 8.50	Goblet, Water, 5 3/4 In.	24.50
Cup & Saucer	8.00 to 15.50	Goblet, 4 In.	35.00 to 40.00

Mayfair

Jug, 8 In. 16.00
Pitcher, 6 In., 37 Oz. .. 15.00 to 18.00
Pitcher, 8 In., 60 Oz. .. 18.00 to 25.00
Pitcher, 80 Oz. .... 30.00 to 42.50
Plate, Cake, Footed, 10 In. 12.50
Plate, Grill, 9 1/2 In. 15.50
Plate, Round, 6 1/2 In. 6.00
Plate, 6 In. .... 3.50 to 4.00
Plate, 8 1/2 In. .... 6.50 to 9.50
Plate, 9 1/2 In. .... 17.00 to 24.50
Platter, Oval, Open Handles, 12 In. 12.00
Salt & Pepper, Flat .... 25.00 to 32.50
Saltshaker 15.00
Server, Center Handle, Frosted, 12 In.
.... 20.00
Sherbet, Footed, 3 1/4 In. 7.95
Sherbet, Footed, 4 3/4 In. 37.50
Soup, Cream, Frosted 17.50
Soup, Cream, 5 In. .... 11.50 to 15.00
Sugar & Creamer, Open 24.95
Sugar, Open .... 7.50 to 13.75
Tumbler, Flat, 3 1/2 In. 18.00
Tumbler, Flat, 4 1/4 In. 15.00
Tumbler, Flat, 5 1/4 In. 25.00
Tumbler, Footed, 3 1/4 In. 35.00
Tumbler, Footed, 4 3/4 In. 16.00
Tumbler, Footed, 5 1/4 In. 17.00
Tumbler, Footed, 6 1/2 In. 22.00
Vase, Sweet Pea ...... 45.00 to 65.00
Whiskey, 2 1/4 In. 49.50
YELLOW
Bowl, 5 1/2 In. 95.00
Cup 100.00
Dish, Candy, Covered 350.00
Pitcher, 6 In. 250.00
Plate, 8 1/2 In. 60.00
Plate, 9 1/2 In. 75.00

Meadow Flower, see No. 618
Meandering Vine, see Madrid

Mayfair

Platter, Closed Handles, 12 In. 150.00
Relish, Divided 175.00
Relish, Undivided 100.00
Salt & Pepper, Flat 500.00

Miss America

Miss America was made by the Hocking Glass Company of Lancaster, Ohio, from 1935 to 1937. It is found in crystal, green, ice blue, pink or red. Reproduction butter dishes and shakers were made in 1977 in crystal, green, ice blue, pink or red amberina.

CRYSTAL
Berry Bowl, 6 1/4 In. 3.00

Bowl, Oval, 10 In. ...... 5.50 to 11.50
Bowl, 6 In. .... 2.75 to 12.00

Miss America

Bowl, 6 1/4 In. .... 2.00 to 5.00	Celery, 10 1/2 In. .... 4.00 to 5.00
Bowl, 8 3/4 In. 19.50	Coaster, 5 3/4 In. .... 5.00 to 9.00
Butter, Covered 130.00	Compote, 5 In. .... 5.00 to 10.00
Candy Container, Covered, 11 1/2 In.	Creamer .... 3.50 to 6.00
.... 39.50	Cup .... 2.50 to 6.00
Candy Container, Open 15.00	Cup & Saucer .... 6.00 to 7.50

Miss America

Goblet, Juice, 4 3/4 In. 15.00
Goblet, Water, 5 1/2 In. 14.25
Goblet, Wine, 3 3/4 In. 15.00
Pitcher, Ice Lip, 8 1/2 In. 55.00
Plate, Cake, Footed, 12 In. 10.95
Plate, Grill, 10 1/4 In. 6.00
Plate, 5 3/4 In. 2.00
Plate, 8 1/2 In. .... 2.00 to 4.00
Plate, 10 1/4 In. .... 6.00 to 8.00
Platter, Oval, 12 In. ..... 5.00 to 6.95
Relish, Covered, 4 Part, 8 3/4 In. 12.00
Relish, Divided, 11 3/4 In. 10.00
Salt & Pepper .... 13.00 to 20.00
Saucer .... 1.00 to 2.00
Sherbet, Footed .... 2.50 to 6.95
Sugar 4.50
Sugar & Creamer ...... 8.00 to 10.00
Tumbler, Flat, 4 In., 5 Oz. ... 12.50
Tumbler, Flat, 4 1/2 In., 10 Oz. . 8.95
Tumbler, Footed, 4 In., 5 Oz. .. 15.00
Tumbler, 6 3/4 In., 14 Oz. 17.00
GREEN
Bowl, 4 1/2 In. 11.00
Cup .... 8.00 to 9.00
Relish, 4 Part, 8 3/4 In. 5.00
PINK
Berry Bowl, 6 1/4 In. .... 4.00 to 8.50
Bowl, Oval, 10 In. ...... 7.50 to 12.00
Bowl, 8 In. .... 20.00 to 38.00
Butter, Covered 125.00
Candy Container, Covered, 11 1/2 In.
.... 70.00
Celery, 10 1/2 In. ...... 8.00 to 10.00
Coaster, 5 3/4 In. ..... 13.50 to 17.50
Compote, 5 In. .... 6.95 to 10.50
Creamer .... 7.00 to 9.50
Cup .... 6.95 to 11.50
Cup & Saucer .... 12.00 to 15.00
Goblet, Juice, 4 3/4 In., 5 Oz. . 35.00
Goblet, Water, 10 Oz. .. 20.00 to 28.00
Goblet, Wine, 3 3/4 In. 39.50
Pitcher, Ice Lip, 8 1/2 In. 70.00
Pitcher, 8 In. .... 54.50 to 70.00
Plate, Cake, Footed, 12 In. 18.50
Plate, Grill, 10 1/4 In. 11.00
Plate, 5 3/4 In. .... 2.00 to 4.50
Plate, 6 3/4 In. 7.50
Plate, 8 1/2 In. .... 6.00 to 9.00
Plate, 10 1/4 In. ...... 10.00 to 15.00
Platter, Oval, 12 In. .... 8.50 to 12.00
Relish, 4 Part, 8 3/4 In. 8.50

Salt & Pepper	30.00	Sugar & Creamer	14.00 to 22.00
Saucer	.75 to 6.50	Tumbler, Flat, 10 Oz.	18.50 to 28.50
Sherbet	2.25 to 8.75	Tumbler, Flat, 14 Oz.	32.50
Sugar	4.50 to 9.50	Tumbler, Footed, 5 Oz.	23.00 to 37.50

Moderne Art, see Tea Room

Moderntone Little Hostess Party Set

Moderntone Little Hostess Party Set was made by the Hazel Atlas Glass Company, a firm with factories in Ohio, Pennsylvania and West Virginia, in the 1940s. It was produced on the Moderntone pattern.

BLUE
Saucer 2.00
GRAY
Plate, 5 1/4 In. 1.60
Plate, 7 In. 1.00
GREEN
Cup 2.00
Saucer 2.00
MAROON
Teapot 15.00
ORANGE
Creamer 2.00
Cup 3.50

Plate, 5 In. 1.60
Saucer .... .80
Sugar 2.00
PINK
Cup 3.50
Plate, 5 1/4 In. 1.60
Saucer 2.00
TURQUOISE
Plate, 5 1/4 In. 1.60
YELLOW
Cup .... 2.00 to 3.50
Plate, 5 1/4 In. 1.60
Saucer .... 1.00 to 2.00

Moderntone

Moderntone was made by the Hazel Atlas Glass Company, a firm with factories in Ohio, Pennsylvania and West Virginia, from 1931 to 1942. It is found in amethyst, cobalt blue, crystal, platonite fired-on colors or pink.

AMETHYST
Creamer .... 3.00 to 5.00
Cup .... 2.25 to 3.25
Cup & Saucer .... 3.50 to 4.50
Plate, 5 3/4 In. .... 1.25 to 2.00
Plate, 7 3/4 In. .... 1.75 to 2.50
Plate, 8 7/8 In. .... 3.00 to 4.50
Plate, 10 1/2 In. 7.00
Platter, Oval, 11 In. 6.00
Platter, Oval, 12 In. 8.00

Salt & Pepper 12.95
Saucer .... 1.00 to 1.25
Soup, Cream, 5 In. 4.00
Soup, Flat, 7 1/2 In. 4.50
Sugar & Creamer, Open .. 6.00 to 7.00
Sugar, Open .... 3.00 to 5.00
BLUE
Ashtray, 7 3/4 In. .... 50.00 to 100.00
Berry Bowl, 5 In. ...... 7.50 to 10.00
Bowl, 4 3/4 In. 3.00

Bowl, 8 3/4 In. .... 14.00 to 20.00
Butter, Metal Covered . 50.00 to 60.00
Creamer .... 2.50 to 5.00
Cup .... 1.50 to 4.00
Cup & Saucer .... 3.75 to 5.25
Custard .... 3.50 to 6.00
Jar, Mustard, Covered . 10.00 to 13.00
Plate, 5 3/4 In. .... 1.20 to 3.00
Plate, 6 3/4 In. .... 1.75 to 4.00
Plate, 7 3/4 In. .... 3.00 to 5.00
Plate, 8 7/8 In. .... 3.00 to 7.00
Plate, 10 1/2 In. .... 7.00 to 12.00

Platter, Oval, 12 In. .... 8.00 to 12.50
Punch Set .... 60.00 to 75.00
Relish, 3 Part, Metal Holder ... 20.00
Salt & Pepper .... 13.00 to 18.50
Saucer .... 1.50 to 2.25
Sherbet .... 2.25 to 5.50
Sherbet, Footed 4.00
Soup, Cream, 4 3/4 In. ... 4.00 to 8.00
Sugar & Creamer, Metal Cover . 35.00
Sugar & Creamer, Open . 5.95 to 10.00
Sugar, Open .... 2.75 to 5.00
Tumbler, 9 Oz. .... 6.00 to 12.00
Whiskey 8.00

Moderntone

Moderntone

CRYSTAL
Bowl, 8 3/4 In. 12.50
Creamer 1.50
Plate, 5 3/4 In. .... 1.00 to 2.25
Plate, 8 7/8 In. .... 1.50 to 1.75
Platter, Oval, 12 In. ... 10.50 to 12.50
Saucer 2.00
Soup, Cream, 4 3/4 In. 3.00
Sugar & Creamer, Open 7.00
GREEN
Platter, Oval, 12 In. 3.50
Sugar, Open .... 1.50 to 2.00
Tumbler, 4 In. 6.00
Tumbler, 5 Oz. 1.00
Tumbler, 9 Oz. 2.50
PINK
Bowl, 4 3/4 In. 2.00
Bowl, 8 3/4 In. 6.00
Plate, 8 7/8 In. 2.00

Salt & Pepper, Footed ... 8.00 to 9.50
Saucer 1.00
Sugar & Creamer 4.00
WHITE
Creamer 2.00
Plate, Red Bands, 8 7/8 In. 2.00
Salt & Pepper .... 4.50 to 12.00
Salt & Pepper, Red Bands 5.00
Sherbet 1.40
Soup, Cream, 4 3/4 In. 1.50
Sugar, Red Bands 2.00
Tumbler, Flat 3.50
Tumbler, Footed 2.50
YELLOW
Creamer .... 2.00 to 2.75
Salt & Pepper 10.00
Saucer 1.00
Sugar 2.00
Sugar & Creamer 4.25

Moondrops

Moondrops was made by the New Martinsville Glass Company of New Martins-ville, West Virginia, from 1932 to 1940. It is found in amber, amethyst, black, cobalt, crystal, dark green, ice blue, jadite, light green, pink, red or smoke.

AMBER

Bowl, Ruffled, 3 Legged 12.75
Bowl, 6 3/4 In. 3.50
Celery, 11 1/2 In. 9.95
Cup 3.50
Cup & Saucer .... 5.50 to 6.50
Goblet, 4 In. 7.50
Plate, 6 In. 1.50
Plate, 8 1/2 In. .... 2.75 to 3.50
Plate, 9 1/2 In. 4.50
Sherbet, 2 5/8 In. 5.50
Sugar & Creamer, 4 In. 12.00
Tumbler, Footed, 9 Oz. 9.50
Whiskey, Handle, 2 3/4 In. 7.50

AMETHYST

Bowl, Footed, 9 3/4 In.   19.00 to 20.00
Bowl, Ruffled, 3-Legged, 9 3/4 In. 19.00
Bowl, 2-Handled, Oval, 9 3/4 In. 17.00
Goblet, Metal Base, 3 Oz. 9.00
Platter, Oval, 12 In. 15.00
Relish, Chrome Cover, 3 Part .. 30.00

COBALT BLUE

Pitcher, 6 7/8 In. 110.00
Plate, 8 1/2 In. 4.00
Saucer 2.00
Whiskey, 2 Oz. 4.50

DARK GREEN

Ashtray, 6 In. 10.00
Saucer 2.00

ICE BLUE

Cup & Saucer 7.50

LIGHT GREEN

Butter, Covered 250.00
Sugar, 4 In. 7.50
Tumbler, Footed, 3 1/4 In. 5.50
Whiskey, 2 Oz. 4.00

PINK

Creamer, 3 3/4 In. 3.00
Whiskey, Handle, Footed, 2 3/4 In. 7.50

RED

Bowl, Ruffled, 3-Legged, 9 1/2 In. 24.00
Cocktail Shaker, Handle, Metal Top
.... 17.50
Creamer, 2 3/4 In. ...... 6.25 to 7.00
Cup .... 6.00 to 7.00
Goblet, Wine, Metal Stem, 5 1/8 In. 8.00
Goblet, Wine, 4 In., 4 Oz. 10.00 to 12.00
Plate, 6 1/8 In. 2.50
Saucer 2.00
Sugar & Creamer, 2 3/4 In. 22.50
Sugar, 2 3/4 In. 6.25
Whiskey, Handle, 2 Oz. 7.50

Moonstone

Moonstone was made by the Anchor Hocking Glass Company of Lancaster, Ohio, from 1941 to 1946. It is found in crystal with opalescent hobnails.

CRYSTAL

Basket, Fluted, 8 1/2 In. 25.00
Bottle, Cologne, Stopper 7.50
Bowl, Flat, Fluted, 7 3/4 In. 5.00
Bowl, Fluted, Handle, 6 1/2 In. . 4.50
Bowl, Fluted, 9 1/2 In. 9.50
Bowl, 5 1/2 In. .... 2.25 to 7.50
Candleholder, Pair ...... 9.00 to 10.00
Candy Container, Covered, 6 In. 12.00
Cigarette Container, Covered ... 10.00
Creamer .... 4.00 to 6.00
Cup .... 3.50 to 6.00
Cup & Saucer 5.00
Dish, Candy, Clover Shape 6.50
Dish, Candy, Heart Shape, Handle 6.00
Goblet, 10 Oz. 8.00
Plate, Fluted, 10 In. ..... 7.00 to 8.00
Plate, 6 1/4 In. .... 2.00 to 3.50

Plate, 8 In. .... 3.25 to 4.25
Puff Box, Covered, Round, 4 3/4 In.
.... 10.00
Relish, Divided, 7 3/4 In. 8.50
Salt & Pepper 30.50
Saucer .... 1.50 to 2.25
Shaker 27.50
Sherbet .... 2.50 to 5.00
Sherbet, Footed .... 3.50 to 5.00
Sugar & Creamer, Footed 7.00
Sugar, Footed .... 3.00 to 3.50
Sugar, Open 3.50
Tumbler, Footed 8.50
Vase, Bud, Fluted, 5 1/2 In. 7.00
Vase, Bud, 5 1/2 In. 5.00
Vase, Fluted, Underplate, 4 1/2 In. 16.00
Vase, Fluted, 8 In. 20.00

Mt. Pleasant

Mt. Pleasant was made by the L. E. Smith Company of Mt. Pleasant, Pennsylvania, from the 1920s to 1934. It is found in black amethyst, cobalt blue, green or pink.

Mt. Pleasant

BLACK
Bowl, 2-Handled, Square, 8 In. . 13.00
Bowl, 3-Legged, 5 1/2 In. 10.00 to 18.00
Candlestick, Double Stem, Pair . 15.00
Creamer .... 7.00 to 12.00
Cup & Saucer 12.00
Cup & Saucer, Straight Edge 8.00
Cup, Straight Edge ...... 5.50 to 7.00
Pitcher, Handle, 8 In. 10.00
Plate, Cake, 2-Handled, 10 1/2 In. 15.00
Plate, 2-Handled, 8 In. 9.00
Saltshaker 10.00
Saucer, Square .... 2.50 to 3.00
Sherbet .... 3.50 to 6.00
Sugar 6.50

BLUE
Bowl, 3-Legged .... 10.00 to 18.00
Candlestick, Double Stem, Pair . 20.00
Candlestick, Single Stem, Pair . 16.00
Creamer 7.75
Cup & Saucer 7.75
Cup, Straight Edge ...... 4.75 to 5.00
Pitcher, 8 In. 7.00
Plate, Cake, 2-Handled, 10 1/2 In. 15.00
Plate, Square, 8 In. 4.00
Plate, 2-Handled, Square, 8 In. .. 8.50
Plate, 2-Handled, 6 3/4 In. 5.00
Plate, 2-Handled, 8 In. 8.50
Plate, 8 In. 6.00
Saltshaker 10.00
Saucer .... 1.50 to 2.50
Saucer, Square .... 1.75 to 2.25
Sherbet .... 5.75 to 9.00
Sugar 8.50
Sugar & Creamer 15.00
Tray, Center Handle, 6 1/2 In. . 12.00
Tumbler, Footed, 6 In. 10.00

GREEN
Plate, 2-Handled, 7 In. 5.00

PINK
Creamer 9.00

Mt. Pleasant

Mt. Vernon

Mt. Vernon was made by the Cambridge Glass Company of Cambridge, Ohio, in 1933. It is found in amber, carmen, crystal, blue or green.

CRYSTAL
Goblet, Water 6.00

Goblet, Wine 5.00
Tray, Round, 13 In. 10.00

New Century

New Century was made by the Hazel Atlas Glass Company, a firm with factories in Ohio, Pennsylvania and West Virginia, from 1930 to 1935. It is found in amethyst, cobalt, crystal, green or pink.

AMETHYST
Tumbler, Footed, 4 In., 5 Oz. ... 9.00
Tumbler, Footed, 4 7/8 In., 9 Oz. 5.00
Tumbler, 3 1/2 In., 5 Oz. . 3.00 to 5.00
Tumbler, 5 In., 10 Oz. 4.95
Tumbler, 5 1/4 In., 12 Oz. 12.00
Tumbler, 9 Oz. .... 4.00 to 5.00
COBALT
Pitcher, Ice Lip, 8 In., 80 Oz. .. 25.00
Tumbler, Footed, 4 7/8 In., 9 Oz. 4.75 to
.... 5.00
Tumbler, 5 Oz. .... 5.00 to 6.00
Tumbler, 12 Oz. .... 8.00 to 10.00

CRYSTAL
Bowl, 4 1/2 In. 2.00
Butter, Covered ...... 27.50 to 32.00
Cup & Saucer .... 3.50 to 15.00
Pitcher, Ice Lip, 8 In., 80 Oz. .. 20.00
Plate, 6 In. 2.00
Plate, 8 1/2 In. .... 3.00 to 9.00
Plate, 10 In. 2.75
Platter, Oval, 11 In. 6.00
Salt & Pepper 12.50
Saltshaker 8.00
Saucer 1.00
Sugar, Open 2.00

Tumbler, Footed, 3 1/2 In. 3.00
Tumbler, Footed, 9 Oz. 15.00
GREEN
    Bowl, 4 1/2 In. 2.00
    Bowl, 8 In. 6.50
    Creamer .... 1.20 to 7.00
    Cup 4.00
    Cup & Saucer 5.50
    Mug, 5 1/2 In. 2.00
    Pitcher, 7 3/4 In., 60 Oz. 22.50
    Plate, 6 In. 1.00
    Plate, 8 1/2 In. .... 2.00 to 3.50
    Plate, 10 In. .... 2.50 to 8.50
    Salt & Pepper .... 17.00 to 25.00
    Saltshaker 8.00
    Sherbet, Footed, 3 In. .... 2.00 to 5.00
    Soup, Cream, 4 3/4 In. ... 5.00 to 6.00
    Sugar & Creamer, Open 9.00
    Sugar, Covered 12.50
    Sugar, Open 3.80
    Tumbler, 4 1/8 In., 9 Oz. 6.75
    Tumbler, 5 Oz. .... 4.00 to 5.00
PINK
    Pitcher, Ice Lip, 80 Oz. 25.00

New Century

Tumbler, Footed, 5 Oz. .. 3.75 to 5.00

Newport

Newport was made by the Hazel Atlas Glass Company, a firm with factories in Ohio, Pennsylvania and West Viginia, from 1936 to 1940. It is found in amethyst, cobalt, pink or platonite white and fired-on colors.

AMETHYST
    Bowl, 4 1/4 In. .... 2.25 to 5.00
    Bowl, 5 1/4 In. .... 3.25 to 5.00
    Bowl, 8 1/4 In. .... 7.50 to 10.00
    Creamer .... 2.00 to 5.00
    Cup & Saucer .... 3.25 to 4.75
    Plate, 6 In. .... 1.75 to 2.25
    Plate, 8 1/2 In. .... 3.00 to 4.50
    Plate, 11 1/2 In. .... 8.75 to 9.00
    Platter, Oval, 11 3/4 In. 10.00
    Saltshaker 10.00
    Saucer 1.00

Sherbet .... 3.50 to 5.75
Soup, Cream, 4 3/4 In. ... 4.00 to 6.50
Sugar .... 2.50 to 4.50
Sugar & Creamer .... 6.00 to 8.75
Tumbler, 4 1/2 In. ..... 6.00 to 10.00
COBALT
    Bowl, 4 1/4 In. .... 2.50 to 4.00
    Bowl, 5 1/4 In. 5.00
    Creamer .... 3.00 to 5.00
    Cup 3.50
    Cup & Saucer .... 4.00 to 5.00
    Plate, 6 In. .... 1.50 to 2.25

Plate, 8 1/2 In. .... 4.00 to 5.50
Plate, 11 1/2 In. 10.00
Platter, Oval, 11 3/4 In. 12.00
Saltshaker .... 9.50 to 11.00
Saucer .... 1.00 to 3.00
Sherbet .... 3.60 to 4.00
Soup, Cream, 4 3/4 In. ... 4.00 to 6.50
Sugar .... 3.00 to 4.50
Sugar & Creamer .... 6.00 to 9.00
Tumbler, 4 1/2 In. 18.00

PINK
Berry Bowl, 4 1/4 In. .... 2.00 to 5.00

WHITE
Creamer .... 1.75 to 3.00
Cup 1.50
Plate, 6 In. .... .85
Plate, 8 1/2 In. 1.75
Plate, 11 1/2 In. 5.00
Salt & Pepper .... 9.00 to 10.00
Saucer 1.00
Sherbet .... 1.50 to 2.15
Soup, Cream, 4 3/4 In. 3.00

Newport

Sugar .... 1.00 to 3.00
Sugar & Creamer .... 5.00 to 5.50

No. 610

No. 610, sometimes called "Pyramid," was made by the Indiana Glass Company of Dunkirk, Indiana, from 1926 to 1932. It is found in black, crystal, green, pink or yellow. It was again produced from 1974 to 1975.

GREEN
Bowl, Oval, 9 1/2 In. 17.50
Relish, Handle, 4 Section 17.50
Sugar 5.00
Tumbler, Footed, 8 Oz. . 9.00 to 12.00

PINK
Sugar & Creamer 19.50

YELLOW
Pitcher 150.00

No. 610

No. 612

No. 612, sometimes called "Horseshoe," was made by the Indiana Glass Company of Dunkirk, Indiana, from 1931 to 1933. It is found in crystal, green, pink or yellow.

GREEN

Bowl, Oval, 10 1/2 In. 14.50
Bowl, 7 1/2 In. .... 8.00 to 13.50
Bowl, 8 1/2 In. 12.50
Bowl, 9 1/2 In. .... 15.00 to 20.00
Creamer .... 5.00 to 9.50
Cup 6.00
Cup & Saucer .... 5.00 to 9.50
Dish, Candy, Covered, Metal Holder
.... 150.00
Pitcher, 8 1/2 In. 169.50
Plate, 6 In. .... 1.25 to 2.50
Plate, 8 3/8 In. .... 1.75 to 5.00
Plate, 11 In. .... 5.50 to 6.50
Platter, Oval, 10 3/4 In. 12.00
Relish, Footed, 3 Part ... 7.00 to 15.00
Saucer .... 1.00 to 3.00
Sherbet .... 7.00 to 10.00
Sugar & Creamer ..... 12.00 to 19.00
Sugar, Open .... 5.00 to 10.00

YELLOW

Bowl, Oval, 10 1/2 In. . 12.00 to 12.95
Bowl, 6 1/2 In. 10.50
Bowl, 7 1/2 In. 7.00
Bowl, 8 1/2 In. 14.50
Creamer 7.00
Cup 4.00
Cup & Saucer .... 6.50 to 7.50
Plate, 6 In. .... 1.50 to 6.00
Plate, 8 3/8 In. 6.00
Plate, 9 3/8 In. 9.50
Plate, 11 In. 12.00
Platter, Oval, 10 3/4 In. 13.00
Relish, 3 Part, Footed 16.00
Sherbet 7.95
Sugar, Open 5.50
Tumbler, Footed, 9 Oz. 10.00 to 15.00

No. 612

No. 615

No. 615 was made by the Indiana Glass Company of Dunkirk, Indiana, from 1929 to 1932. It is found in crystal, green or yellow. Reproductions were made in milk glass or olive green.

CRYSTAL
Cup .... 2.00 to 5.00
Cup & Saucer .... 5.00 to 12.00
Plate, 7 3/4 In. .... 2.00 to 3.50
Relish, Handle, 4 Part, 8 In. ... 10.00
Saucer 3.00
Tumbler, Footed, 4 3/4 In. 12.00
GREEN
Bottle & Stopper, Cologne 22.00
Bowl, 7 1/4 In. 14.95
Bowl, 8 In. 29.50
Creamer, Footed 5.00
Cup 4.50
Cup & Saucer 15.00
Plate, 7 3/4 In. .... 4.00 to 7.00
Platter, 11 1/2 In. ..... 12.50 to 22.00
Sherbet 10.00
Sugar & Creamer, Footed 14.00
Sugar, Footed .... 4.50 to 11.95
Tumbler, Set Of 6 .... 55.00
YELLOW
Bowl, Oval, 9 3/4 In. .. 16.00 to 22.50
Bowl, 8 In. 79.50
Creamer, Footed .... 9.00 to 10.00
Cup 5.00
Cup & Saucer .... 6.00 to 12.00
Plate, Cake, 11 1/2 In. 25.00
Plate, 5 1/2 In. .... 3.00 to 3.25

No. 615

Plate, 7 3/4 In. .... 5.00 to 7.00
Plate, 8 3/8 In. .... 5.00 to 6.50
Plate, 9 3/8 In. 6.50
Platter, 11 1/2 In. ..... 12.50 to 19.95
Relish, Handle, 4 Part, 8 In. 7.00 to 15.00
Saucer .... 2.00 to 2.75
Sherbet .... 7.00 to 14.00
Sugar & Creamer ..... 15.00 to 21.00
Sugar, Open .... 7.00 to 11.25
Tumbler, Footed, 4 3/4 In. 12.50

No. 616

No. 616, sometimes called "Vernon," was made by the Indiana Glass Company of Dunkirk, Indiana, from 1930 to 1932. It is found in crystal, green or yellow.

CRYSTAL
Creamer, Silver Trim 6.00
Cup 5.00
Cup & Saucer, Silver Trim 6.50
Cup, Silver Trim 5.00
Plate, Silver Trim, 8 In. 4.00
Tumbler, Footed, 5 In. 8.00
GREEN
Cup & Saucer 12.50

Plate, 8 In. .... 6.00 to 8.50
Plate, 11 In. 17.50
YELLOW
Plate, 8 In. .... 5.50 to 6.50
Saucer 3.50
Vase, 7 3/4 In. 35.00

No. 618

No. 618, sometimes called "Pineapple & Floral," was made by the Indiana Glass Company of Dunkirk, Indiana, from 1932 to 1937. It is found in amber, crystal, green or fired-on red. It was again produced in the late 1960s in avocado.

AMBER
  Cream Soup, 4 5/8 In. . 11.00 to 14.00
  Cup & Saucer 6.00
  Plate, 6 In. 2.25
  Plate, 8 3/8 In. .... 3.50 to 8.00
  Plate, 9 3/8 In. .... 4.00 to 7.00
  Plate, 11 1/2 In. .... 6.00 to 6.50
  Saucer 2.25
  Soup, Cream, 4 5/8 In. . 11.00 to 14.00
  Sugar & Creamer ...... 8.00 to 10.00
CRYSTAL
  Ashtray, 4 1/2 In. ...... 7.00 to 10.00
  Bowl, Oval, Handle, 10 In. 19.00
  Bowl, 6 In. .... 6.50 to 12.50

No. 618

Bowl, 7 In. .... 3.00 to 3.50
Bowl, 7 3/8 In. .... 2.50 to 5.00
Compote, Diamond Shape, 6 1/4 In. 3.50
Creamer, Diamond Shape 5.00
Cup .... 4.50 to 6.00
Cup & Saucer .... 4.50 to 7.25
Dish, Candy, Footed 2.00
Pitcher, 10 In. 6.25
Plate, Fired-On Red, 8 3/8 In. .. 1.30
Plate, 6 In. .... 1.50 to 3.50
Plate, 8 3/8 In. .... 2.00 to 6.00

Plate, 9 3/8 In. .... 3.50 to 5.50
Plate, 11 1/2 In. .... 6.00 to 11.00
Platter, Closed Handles, 11 In. . 10.00
Relish, 3 Section, 11 1/2 In. 8.00
Saucer 2.00
Sherbet .... 5.50 to 8.50
Soup, Cream, 4 5/8 In. 12.00
Sugar & Creamer, Diamond Shape 12.50
Sugar, Diamond Shape ... 3.00 to 5.00
Tumbler, 4 1/2 In., 12 Oz. 18.00
Vase .... 12.50 to 17.00

No. 620

No. 620 was made by the Indiana Glass Company of Dunkirk, Indiana, in amber in 1940, in crystal in 1933 and in dark green or milk glass in the 1950s.

AMBER
Berry Bowl, 4 1/2 In. 2.50
Bowl, 7 3/8 In. .... 6.50 to 7.00
Creamer, Footed .... 2.00 to 4.00
Cup .... 1.25 to 3.00
Cup & Saucer .... 3.25 to 4.50
Plate, Grill .... 2.00 to 5.00
Plate, 6 In. .... 1.25 to 2.25
Plate, 8 3/8 In. .... 1.50 to 3.95
Plate, 9 3/8 In. .... 2.50 to 4.00
Plate, 11 1/2 In. .... 5.00 to 6.90
Platter, 10 3/4 In. .... 3.75 to 6.00
Relish, 3 Section, 8 3/8 In. 5.00
Saucer .... .37 to 1.75
Sherbet, Footed .... 1.00 to 4.50
Soup, Cream, 4 1/2 In. ... 2.75 to 6.00
Sugar & Creamer, Footed 8.25
Sugar, Footed .... 3.00 to 4.45
Tumbler, Footed, 9 Oz. .. 5.00 to 8.00
CRYSTAL
Cup 2.25

Cup & Saucer .... 2.50 to 4.50
Plate, Grill .... 1.25 to 3.00
Plate, Grill, 10 3/8 In. 3.00
Plate, 6 In. 1.50
Plate, 8 3/8 In. 2.00
Plate, 9 3/8 In. 3.25
Plate, 11 1/2 In. .... 3.00 to 5.00
Sugar, Footed 3.50
GREEN
Bowl, 7 3/8 In. 3.00
Creamer 2.00
Cup 3.50
Cup & Saucer 2.75
Plate, 7 3/8 In. 1.75
Plate, 8 3/8 In. 3.00
Plate, 9 3/8 In. .... 2.75 to 3.00
Plate, 10 In. 3.00
Saucer 1.50
Soup, Cream, 4 1/2 In. ... 2.75 to 4.00
Sugar, Footed 2.00
Tumbler, Footed, 12 Oz. 5.00

Normandie

Normandie was made by the Federal Glass Company of Columbus, Ohio, from 1933 to 1940. It is found in amber, crystal, green, iridescent or pink.

AMBER
Berry Bowl, 5 In. .... 2.50 to 3.50
Berry Bowl, 8 1/2 In. ... 6.00 to 13.50
Bowl, Oval, 10 In. ...... 7.00 to 10.00
Bowl, 6 1/2 In. 6.00
Creamer, Footed .... 4.50 to 5.50
Cup .... 2.50 to 4.00
Cup & Saucer .... 3.00 to 5.75
Pitcher, 8 In. .... 25.00 to 45.00
Plate, Grill, 11 In. .... 3.50 to 7.50
Plate, 6 In. .... 1.00 to 2.00
Plate, 8 In. .... 3.50 to 8.00
Plate, 9 1/4 In. .... 2.50 to 5.00
Platter, 11 3/4 In. 7.00
Salt & Pepper .... 25.00 to 33.00
Saltshaker 11.00
Saucer .... 1.00 to 1.50

Normandie

Sherbet, Footed	2.00 to 6.50
Sugar & Creamer, Open	9.75
Sugar, Covered	59.50 to 62.50
Sugar, Open	3.25 to 5.50
Tumbler, 4 In.	7.95 to 8.50
Tumbler, 5 In.	11.50 to 12.50

CRYSTAL

Bowl, 6 1/2 In.	3.00
Cup & Saucer	4.50
Sherbet	3.00

GREEN

Plate, 9 1/4 In.	6.00
Saucer	1.50

IRIDESCENT

Berry Bowl, 5 In.	1.50 to 5.00
Berry Bowl, 8 1/2 In.	5.00 to 8.00
Bowl, Oval, 10 In.	9.00
Bowl, 6 1/2 In.	3.00 to 6.00
Creamer, Footed	2.50 to 4.00
Cup	2.25 to 5.00
Cup & Saucer	4.00 to 6.50

Oatmeal Lace, see Princess Feather

Plate, Grill, 11 In.	2.50 to 5.00
Plate, 6 In.	1.50 to 2.00
Plate, 9 1/4 In.	7.00 to 8.00
Platter, 11 3/4 In.	5.00 to 7.00
Saucer	.95 to 3.00
Sherbet, Footed	3.00 to 5.75
Sugar & Creamer, Open .	8.00 to 10.00
Sugar, Open	3.00 to 3.25

PINK

Berry Bowl, 5 In.	3.00 to 5.00
Berry Bowl, 8 1/2 In.	15.50
Cup	1.75 to 4.00
Cup & Saucer	4.00 to 6.50
Plate, Grill, 11 In.	4.00
Plate, 6 In.	1.50 to 3.00
Plate, 8 In.	3.00 to 6.50
Plate, 9 1/4 In.	3.50
Platter, 11 3/4 In.	6.00
Salt & Pepper	24.00 to 35.00
Saucer	1.00 to 2.25
Sherbet, Footed	2.00 to 5.00

Old Cafe

Old Cafe was made by the Anchor Hocking Glass Company of Lancaster, Ohio, from 1936 to 1938 and again in 1940. It is found in crystal, pink or ruby red.

CRYSTAL

Bowl, Closed Handle, 9 In.	3.50
Dish, Candy, Closed Handles, 8 In.	5.00
Dish, Candy, Red Cover ..	6.50 to 9.50
Plate, 6 In.	1.25
Saucer	1.00
Sherbet, Footed	2.50
Vase, 7 1/4 In.	6.00

PINK

Bowl, Closed Handles, 9 In.	3.25
Bowl, Handle, 5 In.	2.50
Bowl, 2-Handled, 5 In.	3.00
Bowl, 5 1/2 In.	1.50 to 6.50
Cup	1.50 to 2.50
Cup & Saucer	4.00 to 6.50
Dish, Candy, Closed Handles, 8 In.	4.00

Dish, Olive, 6 In.	1.50 to 2.25
Plate, 6 In.	2.00
Plate, 10 In.	4.50 to 9.50
Saucer	1.50 to 2.50
Sherbet	2.50
Tumbler, 3 In.	2.25
Tumbler, 4 In.	2.50

RUBY RED

Bowl, Closed Handle, 9 In.	9.00
Bowl, 5 1/2 In.	9.00
Cup	2.75 to 5.00
Cup & Saucer	5.00
Dish, Candy, Low, Closed Handles, 8 In.	7.50
Saucer	2.00

Old English

Old English was made by the Indiana Glass Company of Dunkirk, Indiana. It is found in amber, crystal, green or pink.

CRYSTAL
   Eggcup 12.00
GREEN
   Berry Bowl, 4 In. 8.50

Pitcher, Open 45.00
Tumbler, Footed, 4 1/2 In. 8.50
PINK
Fruit Stand, Footed, 11 In. 12.00

Old Florentine, see Florentine No. 1
Open Lace, see Lace Edge
Open Rose, see Mayfair
Open Scallop, see Lace Edge
Optic Design, see Raindrops
Optic Rib, see Imperial Optic Rib
Oregon Grape, see Woolworth
Oriental Poppy, see Florentine No. 2

Ovide

Ovide was made by the Hazel Atlas Glass Company, a firm with factories in Ohio, Pennsylvania and West Virginia, from 1930 to 1935. It is found in black, green, white with an Art Deco design and fired-on colors.

BLACK
   Luncheon Set, 14 Piece 45.00
   Plate, 8 In. 3.00
   Sugar & Creamer 12.00
GREEN
   Bowl, Console, 11 In. 6.00
   Bowl, 5 1/2 In. 3.50
   Cup .... 1.00 to 2.50
   Cup & Saucer .... 2.25 to 3.50

Saucer .... .75
Sherbet 1.25
Sugar & Creamer 6.00
RED
   Creamer 4.00
YELLOW
   Bowl, Console, 11 In. 6.00
   Creamer 4.00

Oyster & Pearl

Oyster & Pearl was made by the Anchor Hocking Glass Company of Lancaster, Ohio, from 1938 to 1940. It is found in crystal, pink, ruby red, or white with fired-on green or pink.

CRYSTAL
   Bowl, Heart Shape, Handle, 5 1/4 In.
   .... 7.00
   Candlholder, 3 1/2 In., Pair 15.00
   Relish, Divided, Oval, 10 1/4 In. 2.25
PINK
   Bowl & Underplate, 6 1/2 In. .. 12.00
   Bowl, Closed Handles, 6 1/2 In. . 6.50
   Bowl, Heart Shape, Handle, 5 1/4 In.
   .... 4.00

Bowl, 10 1/2 In. .... 7.25 to 10.00
Candleholder, Pair, 3 1/2 In. 9.00
Plate, 13 1/4 In. .... 4.50 to 5.00
Relish, Divided, Oval, 10 1/4 In. 6.50
RUBY RED
   Bowl, Console 14.00
   Bowl, Heart Shape, Handle, 5 1/4 In.
   .... 6.00
   Candleholder, 3 1/2 In., Pair ... 25.00
   Plate, 13 1/2 In. ...... 14.00 to 18.00

Paneled Aster, see Madrid
Paneled Cherry Blossom, see Cherry
Blossom
Pansy & Doric, see Doric & Pansy
Parrot, see Sylvan
Party Line, see Line 191

Patrician

Patrician was made by the Federal Glass Company of Columbus, Ohio, from 1933 to 1937. It is found in amber, crystal, green, pink or yellow.

AMBER
Berry Bowl, 5 In.	2.50 to 5.50
Berry Bowl, 8 1/2 In.	5.50 to 11.50
Bowl, Oval, 12 In.	9.00 to 14.50
Bowl, 6 In.	7.50 to 10.00
Butter, Covered	30.00 to 50.00
Cookie Jar, Covered	25.00 to 37.50
Creamer	2.75 to 7.00
Cup	2.75 to 6.50
Cup & Saucer	6.95 to 9.50
Dish, Jam, 6 1/2 In.	12.00
Pitcher, 8 In.	40.00 to 49.50
Plate, Grill, 10 1/2 In.	6.00
Plate, 6 In.	2.25 to 3.75
Plate, 7 1/2 In.	4.00 to 8.75
Plate, 9 In.	3.00 to 5.00
Plate, 10 1/2 In.	2.00 to 5.00
Platter, Oval, 11 1/2 In.	14.00
Salt & Pepper	18.00 to 27.50
Saltshaker	12.00
Saucer	1.50 to 3.95
Sherbet	3.50 to 6.00
Soup, Cream, 4 3/4 In.	5.00 to 6.50
Sugar & Creamer, Covered	24.95
Sugar & Creamer, Open	7.00 to 12.50
Sugar Shaker	12.50
Sugar, Covered	18.50
Sugar, Open	3.00 to 10.00
Tumbler, Flat, 5 Oz.	10.95
Tumbler, Flat, 9 Oz.	19.50
Tumbler, Flat, 14 Oz.	24.50
Tumbler, Footed, 8 Oz.	30.00

CRYSTAL
Berry Bowl, 8 1/2 In.	8.00
Bowl, 6 In.	4.50 to 6.00
Butter, Covered	57.50 to 60.00
Cookie Jar, Covered	35.00
Cup	1.80 to 4.00
Plate, Grill, 10 1/2 In.	5.00
Plate, 9 In.	3.00
Platter, Oval, 11 1/2 In.	5.00
Salt & Pepper	25.00
Soup, Cream, 4 3/4 In.	2.50
Sugar, Open	5.00

GREEN
Berry Bowl, 5 In.	2.50 to 5.75
Berry Bowl, 8 1/2 In.	8.00 to 9.50
Bowl, Oval, 12 In.	11.00
Bowl, 6 In.	7.50 to 9.50
Butter, Covered	70.00 to 75.00
Cookie Jar, Covered	15.50 to 175.00
Creamer	5.00

Patrician

Cup .... 3.50 to 4.50
Cup & Saucer .... 5.75 to 9.00
Plate, Grill, 10 1/2 In. 7.00
Plate, 7 1/2 In. .... 2.75 to 6.00
Plate, 9 In. .... 3.75 to 6.00
Plate, 10 1/2 In. 17.50
Salt & Pepper .... 28.00 to 40.00
Saltshaker 18.00
Saucer 2.00
Sherbet .... 3.00 to 6.50
Soup, Cream, 4 3/4 In. .. 6.00 to 15.00
Sugar & Creamer, Covered 45.00
Sugar & Creamer, Open . 8.00 to 12.00
Sugar, Open .... 3.50 to 5.00
Tumbler, Flat, 4 1/2 In., 9 Oz. . 12.50
Tumbler, Footed, 5 1/4 In. 16.50
Tumbler, 4 In., 5 Oz. 16.50

PINK
Berry Bowl, 5 In. .... 4.00 to 5.00
Berry Bowl, 8 1/2 In. ... 8.00 to 12.50
Bowl, Oval, 12 In, ... 7.50
Bowl, 6 In. 8.00
Butter, Covered ..... 175.00 to 180.00
Creamer .... 3.50 to 6.00
Cup .... 3.75 to 5.00
Cup & Saucer .... 8.50 to 9.00
Jar, Jam, 6 1/2 In. 6.00
Pitcher, 8 In. 85.00
Plate, Grill, 10 1/2 In. 7.50
Plate, 9 In. .... 3.00 to 4.50
Plate, 10 1/2 In. .... 9.00 to 16.00

Patrician

Platter, Oval, 11 1/2 In. 9.00
Salt & Pepper .... 55.00 to 85.00
Saucer 4.00
Sherbet 4.75
Soup, Cream 10.00
Sugar & Creamer, Open . 8.00 to 10.00
Tumbler, 4 1/2 In., 9 Oz. 12.50

Peacock & Wild Rose

Peacock & Wild Rose was made by the Paden City Glass Company of Paden City, West Virginia, in the 1930s. It is found in green or pink.

GREEN
Bowl, Center Handle, 10 1/2 In.   14.00
Bowl, Footed, 9 1/4 In. 13.50
Cake Plate 12.50
Compote, 6 1/4 In. 11.00
Vase, 10 In. 32.50

PINK
Bowl, Flat, 8 1/2 In. 11.00
Candlestick, 5 In. Across, Pair . 14.00
Plate, 10 1/2 In. 12.00
Sugar, Footed, 4 1/4 In. 8.50

Peacock Reverse

Peacock Reverse was made by the Paden City Glass Company of Paden City, West Virginia. It is found in cobalt blue or red.

BLUE
   Plate 15.00
   Tumbler .... 22.00 to 25.00
RED
   Bowl, Square, 8 In. 30.00

Candlestick, Pair ...... 50.00 to 55.00
Plate 15.00

Pear Optic

Pear Optic was made by the Federal Glass Company of Columbus, Ohio, from 1929 to 1930. It is found in green.

GREEN
   Cup 1.00
   Cup & Saucer 2.50

Plate, 8 1/2 In. 1.50
Sherbet 1.00

Pebbled Band, see Hammered Band

Penny Line

Penny Line was made by the Paden City Glass Company of Paden City, West Virginia, in 1932. It is found in amber, blue, green, pink or ruby.

AMBER
   Jar, Powder, Celluloid Lid 7.00

GREEN
   Goblet, 4 3/4 In. 3.50

Petal Swirl, see Swirl

Petalware

Petalware was made by the MacBeth Evans Glass Company, a firm with factories in Indiana, Ohio and Pennsylvania, from 1930 to 1940. It is found in blue, cobalt, cremax, crystal, green, monax, pink or fired- on blue, green, red or yellow. Some pieces have painted decorations.

BLUE
   Ashtray 2.75
   Bowl, 5 3/4 In. .... 3.00 to 5.00
   Creamer 2.50
   Cup .... 2.50 to 3.50
   Cup & Saucer 4.50
   Mustard & Metal Cover 5.00
   Pitcher, 80 Oz. 6.00
   Plate, 6 In. .... 1.75 to 3.00
CREMAX
   Bowl, 8 3/4 In. 8.50

Cup 3.00
Cup & Saucer .... 3.75 to 4.75
Cup, Gold Rim 2.50
Luncheon Set, Gold Rim, 17 Piece 55.00
Plate, Gold Leaf & Lattice, 8 In. 2.60
Plate, Gold Line & Flower, 8 In. 2.50
Plate, Gold Rim, 11 In. 3.00
Plate, Pastel Band, 8 In. 3.00
Plate, 6 In. .... 1.30 to 2.00
Plate, 8 In. .... 1.50 to 2.75

Plate, 9 In. .... 3.00 to 3.25
Plate, 11 In. 3.00
Salver, 12 In. 4.75
Saucer 1.00
Saucer, Gold Line & Flower 1.00
Saucer, Pastel Band 1.50
Soup, Cream, 4 1/2 In. 3.50
Sugar & Creamer 7.50
Sugar, Open .... 3.25 to 3.50

CRYSTAL
Cup 4.00
Plate, 8 In. .... 2.50 to 4.00
Platter, Oval, 13 In. 2.75
Saucer .... 1.50 to 1.75
Sugar & Creamer 6.00

MONAX
Bowl, 5 3/4 In. .... 2.75 to 4.00
Bowl, 8 3/4 In. 4.50
Cake Set, 7 Piece 25.00
Creamer 6.00
Creamer, Gold Rim 6.50
Cup .... 2.50 to 5.00
Cup & Saucer .... 3.00 to 5.00
Cup, Gold Rim 2.50
Lampshade, 7 In. 6.00
Plate, Gold Design, 8 In. 5.00
Plate, Gold Rim, 8 In. ... 2.50 to 5.00
Plate, Red Flower, 6 In. 1.50
Plate, Red Flower, 8 In. 2.50
Plate, Red Flower, 9 In. 3.50
Plate, Red Flower, 11 In. 5.00
Platter, Oval, 13 In. ... 10.00 to 15.00
Platter, Round, 11 In. 7.00
Saucer .... 1.00 to 3.50
Saucer, Gold Rim .... 1.00 to 3.50

Petalware

Saucer, Red Flower 1.00
Server 13.00
Sherbet, Low, Footed 3.50

Petalware

Soup, Cream, 4 1/2 In. ... 3.50 to 7.00
Sugar .... 1.95 to 5.00
Sugar & Creamer ...... 6.00 to 12.00
Sugar & Creamer, Red Flower .. 6.00
Sugar, Gold Rim .... 3.25 to 6.50
PINK
Bowl, 5 3/4 In. .... 3.00 to 5.00
Creamer 3.00
Cup .... 2.25 to 4.00
Cup & Saucer .... 3.95 to 5.00
Lampshade, Monax Inside 20.00
Plate, 6 In. .... 1.25 to 1.75

Plate, 8 In. .... 1.50 to 3.00
Plate, 9 In. .... 3.50 to 3.75
Plate, 11 In. 5.00
Platter, Oval, 13 In. ..... 4.50 to 6.50
Relish, 5 Part 6.00
Saucer .... 1.00 to 1.50
Sherbet, Low, Footed .... 2.00 to 3.50
Soup, Cream, 4 1/2 In. ... 3.50 to 5.00
Sugar .... 2.95 to 3.50
Sugar & Creamer 8.00
RED
Cup 2.25

Philbe

Philbe was made by the Anchor Hocking Glass Company of Lancaster, Ohio, in 1940. It is found in blue, blue with platinum or pink.

BLUE
Trivet, 8 In. .... 7.00 to 10.00

PINK
Trivet, 8 In. .... 7.00 to 10.00

Pillar Flute

Pillar Flute was made by the Imperial Glass Company of Bellaire, Ohio. It is found in green, light blue and Rose Marie (pink).

LIGHT BLUE
Creamer 7.00
Cup 5.00

Saucer 3.50
Vase, Tulip, 6 In. 8.00

Pillar Optic

Pillar Optic was made by the Hocking Glass Company of Lancaster, Ohio, in 1935.

GREEN
Sugar & Creamer 5.00

Pineapple & Floral, see No. 618
Pinwheel, see Sierra

Pioneer

Pioneer was made by the Federal Glass Company of Columbus, Ohio. It was made in pink in the 1930s, crystal in the 1940s and some pieces were still being made in crystal in 1973.

CRYSTAL
  Bowl, Frosted, 10 1/2 In. 5.00
  Plate, 11 1/2 In. 5.00
PINK
  Compote, Footed, 6 In. 8.75

Cup & Saucer 6.00
Plate, 7 1/2 In. .... 1.95 to 2.00
Plate, 10 In. 3.95

Poinsettia, see Floral
Poppy No. 1, see Florentine No. 1
Poppy No. 2, see Florentine No. 2

Pretzel

Pretzel was made by the Indiana Glass Company of Dunkirk, Indiana, in the 1930s in crystal. Some pieces were again produced in the 1970s.

CRYSTAL
  Creamer .... 2.00 to 4.00
  Cup .... 1.50 to 4.00
  Cup & Saucer .... 2.50 to 4.50
  Plate, Cake, 11 1/2 In. 4.00
  Plate, Closed Handles, 6 In. 2.00
  Plate, Fruit Center, 6 In. 1.00
  Plate, Fruit Center, 9 3/8 In. ... 3.00

Plate, 6 In. .... 1.50 to 2.00
Plate, 8 3/8 In. .... 1.50 to 3.50
Plate, 9 3/8 In. 2.50
Relish, Oblong, 10 1/4 In. 4.00
Saucer .... .50 to 1.75
Soup, Flat, 7 1/2 In. ..... 1.50 to 4.00
Sugar .... 2.50 to 4.00
Sugar & Creamer .... 2.75 to 7.95

Primo

Primo was made by the U. S. Glass Company, a firm with factories in Indiana, Ohio, Pennsylvania and West Virginia, in 1932. It is found in green and yellow.

GREEN
  Cup 3.50
  Cup & Saucer 7.50
  Plate, 7 1/2 In. 4.50
YELLOW
  Cup 4.00
  Plate, Cake, 3-Legged 15.00
  Plate, Grill 3.50
  Plate, 7 1/2 In. 4.00
  Saucer 2.00
  Sugar 5.00
  Sugar, Open 4.00
  Tray, 10 1/2 In. 4.50

Primus, see Madrid

Primo

Princess Feather

Princess Feather was made by the Westmoreland Glass Company of Grapeville, Pennsylvania, in the 1920s and the 1930s. It is found in aqua, crystal, green or pink. It was again produced in amber in the 1960s.

CRYSTAL
Candy Container, Covered, Footed 14.00
Goblet, Footed, 8 Oz. 5.00
Sherbet 3.00
GREEN
Custard 1.10
Plate, 4 1/2 In. .... .90

Sherbet, Footed, 3 1/2 In. 4.80
Tumbler, 5 Oz. 1.10
Tumbler, 9 Oz. 1.25
PINK
Sherbet 4.00
Sherbet, Long Stem, 4 1/2 In. ... 4.80

Princess

Princess was made by the Hocking Glass Company of Lancaster, Ohio, from 1931 to 1935. It is found in amber, blue, green, pink or yellow.

AMBER
Cup 3.00
Cup & Saucer .... 5.00 to 5.50
Plate, Grill, 9 1/2 In. 4.00
Plate, 5 1/2 In. 2.00
Plate, 8 In. .... 2.50 to 4.50
Plate, 9 1/2 In. .... 4.50 to 5.00
Tumbler, Flat, 5 1/4 In., 12 Oz.   15.00
GREEN
Berry Bowl, 4 1/2 In. .. 13.00 to 13.50
Bowl, Hat Shape, 9 1/2 In. 16.00
Bowl, Octagon, 9 In. ... 12.00 to 12.95
Bowl, Oval, 10 In. .... 6.95 to 9.50

Bowl, 5 In. .... 8.00 to 15.00
Butter, Covered .... 37.50 to 50.00
Candy Container, Covered 27.50
Cookie Jar, Covered ... 20.00 to 25.00
Creamer .... 5.95 to 7.75
Cup .... 3.50 to 6.00
Cup & Saucer .... 6.00 to 8.50
Dish, Candy, Covered .. 20.00 to 25.00
Pitcher, 6 In. 20.00
Pitcher, 8 In. .... 20.00 to 27.50
Plate, Grill, 2-Handled, 9 In. 6.50
Plate, Grill, 2-Handled, 12 1/2 In.   7.00
Plate, Grill, Handled, 10 1/2 In. .   5.50

Princess

Princess

Plate, Grill, 9 1/2 In. 6.50	Bowl, Oval, 10 In. 8.50
Plate, 6 In. .... 1.75 to 3.00	Bowl, 5 1/2 In. .... 7.00 to 9.00
Plate, 8 In. .... 4.00 to 7.50	Butter, Covered .... 45.00 to 55.00
Plate, 9 In. .... 10.00 to 10.50	Candy Container, Covered 27.00
Plate, 9 1/2 In. .... 7.00 to 18.00	Candy Container, Open 17.50
Platter, Closed Handled, 12 In. .. 9.50	Cookie Jar, Covered ... 17.50 to 18.00
Relish, 4 Section, 7 1/2 In. 13.00	Creamer .... 5.00 to 7.50
Salt & Pepper .... 22.50 to 30.00	Cup .... 3.00 to 5.00
Saltshaker, 5 1/2 In. .... 9.75 to 10.00	Cup & Saucer .... 4.50 to 6.50
Saucer .... 2.00 to 2.75	Dish, Candy, Covered .. 19.95 to 22.50
Sherbet, 5 1/2 In. .... 2.00 to 3.50	Pitcher, 6 In. .... 16.00 to 16.50
Soup, Flat, 7 3/4 In. 55.00	Pitcher, 8 In. .... 22.50 to 25.00
Spice Shaker .... 12.95 to 34.75	Plate, Cake, Footed, 10 In. 10.00
Sugar & Creamer 7.00	Plate, Grill, 9 1/2 In. 5.00
Sugar & Creamer, Covered 12.00	Plate, Grill, 10 1/2 .... 7.50
Sugar, Covered .... 8.00 to 9.00	Plate, 5 1/2 In. .... 1.75 to 2.50
Sugar, Open 6.00	Plate, 8 In. .... 3.50 to 4.00
Tumbler, Flat, 9 Oz. 14.00	Plate, 9 In. .... 6.00 to 7.50
Tumbler, Flat, 12 Oz 15.00	Relish, 4 Section .... 7.00 to 10.00
Tumbler, Footed, 10 Oz. 18.00	Salt & Pepper .... 23.00 to 28.50
Tumbler, Footed, 12 1/2 Oz. ... 22.00	Saltshaker .... 12.00 to 12.95
Tumbler, 3 In. 12.50	Sherbet .... 3.50 to 8.00
Vase, 8 In. .... 8.50 to 16.00	Sugar & Creamer, Open 10.00
PINK	Sugar, Open 5.00
Berry Bowl, 4 1/2 In. .... 4.00 to 5.00	Tumbler, Flat, 5 Oz. 14.75
Bowl, Hat Shape, 9 1/2 In. 12.50	Tumbler, Flat, 9 Oz. 10.50
Bowl, Octagon, 9 In. 12.00	Tumbler, Flat, 12 Oz 12.00

Tumbler, Footed, 10 Oz. 11.00
Tumbler, Footed, 12 1/2 Oz. ... 17.50
Vase, 8 In. .... 10.00 to 12.00
Water Set, 8 In., 9 Piece 160.00
YELLOW
Bowl, Oval, 10 In. ..... 17.00 to 25.00
Creamer .... 5.00 to 7.50
Cup .... 3.00 to 5.50
Cup & Saucer .... 4.95 to 7.50
Pitcher, 8 In. .... 35.00 to 42.00
Plate, 2-Handled, 9 1/2 In. 4.50
Plate, Grill, 2-Handled, 11 1/2 In. 5.50
Plate, 5 1/2 In. .... 2.00 to 2.50

Plate, 8 In. .... 3.00 to 5.00
Plate, 9 1/2 In. .... 4.50 to 7.00
Plate, 10 In. 10.00
Salt & Pepper .... 45.00 to 65.00
Saltshaker 18.00
Sherbet 15.00
Sugar & Creamer, Covered 25.00
Sugar, Covered 10.00
Tumbler, Flat, 5 Oz 14.00
Tumbler, Flat, 12 Oz. 14.00
Tumbler, Flat, 4 In., 9 Oz. 12.50 to 16.00
Tumbler, Footed, 10 Oz. 15.00

Pyramid, see No. 610

Queen Anne

Queen Anne was made by the Anchor Hocking Glass Company of Lancaster, Ohio, in 1940. It was also made in beverage sets only in 1940 by the Hazel Atlas Glass Company. It is found in crystal and pink.

CRYSTAL
Butter .... 13.00 to 15.00
Tumbler, 4 In., 9 Oz. 4.00
PINK
Bowl, Footed, Handle, 5 1/4 In. 15.00

Bowl, Footed, Handle, 8 1/2 In. 30.00
Platter, 13 1/2 In. 40.00
Server, Center Handle, 12 1/2 In. 40.00

Queen Mary

Queen Mary was made by the Hocking Glass Company of Lancaster, Ohio, from 1936 to 1940. It is found in crystal, pink or ruby red.

CRYSTAL
Ashtray 2.50
Bowl, One Handle, 4 In. 2.00
Bowl, 4 In. 2.00
Bowl, 5 In. .... 1.00 to 2.50
Bowl, 6 In. .... 1.00 to 2.25
Bowl, 7 In. 5.00
Bowl, 8 3/4 In. .... 4.00 to 6.00
Butter, Covered .... 15.00 to 18.00
Candlestick, Double, 4 1/2 In., Pair 15.00
Candy Container, Covered 15.00
Cigarette Jar, Covered 10.00
Coaster .... 1.50 to 2.00
Creamer .... 2.75 to 3.00
Cup .... 2.00 to 4.00

Cup & Saucer 4.75
Dish, Candy, Covered .. 13.00 to 18.50
Plate, Cake, Footed, 12 1/2 In. .. 3.50
Plate, 6 In. .... .95 to 1.50
Plate, 8 1/2 In. .... 2.00 to 3.00
Plate, 9 3/4 In. .... 3.00 to 8.50
Plate, 12 In. .... 3.00 to 4.50
Relish, 3 Section, 12 In. 5.00
Salt & Pepper .... 8.00 to 10.00
Salt & Pepper, Red Top 12.00
Saltshaker 8.00
Saucer .... 1.00 to 1.50
Sherbet, Footed .... 1.75 to 4.00
Sugar & Creamer .... 4.00 to 7.00
Sugar, Open .... 2.50 to 3.50

Tumbler, Footed, 10 Oz. 11.00
PINK
　Berry Bowl, 5 In. .... 2.00 to 3.00
　Berry Bowl, 8 3/4 In. 2.50
　Berry Set, 7 Piece 22.50
　Bowl, Handle, 4 In. ...... 1.25 to 2.00
　Bowl, 2-Handled, 5 1/2 In. 2.00
　Bowl, 4 In. .... 1.25 to 3.00
　Bowl, 5 In. 2.50
　Bowl, 6 In. .... 1.00 to 5.00
　Bowl, 7 In. 7.50
　Butter, Covered .... 30.00 to 69.00
　Coaster 2.00
　Creamer .... 2.50 to 3.00
　Cup .... 1.75 to 4.00

Cup & Saucer .... 3.00 to 5.00
Dish, Candy, Covered .. 10.00 to 13.00
Plate, 6 In. .... 1.00 to 1.50
Plate, 9 3/4 In. .... 6.00 to 13.50
Relish, 4 Section, 14 In. 6.50
Saucer 1.50
Sherbet .... 1.50 to 4.00
Sugar .... 2.75 to 3.50
Sugar & Creamer .... 4.00 to 8.00
Tumbler, Flat, 3 1/2 In. 4.50
Tumbler, Footed, 5 In. 8.00
Tumbler, 4 In. .... 2.25 to 6.00
RUBY RED
Ashtray .... 2.50 to 3.50

Radiance

Radiance was made by the New Martinsville Glass Company of New Martinsville, West Virginia, from 1936 to 1939. It is found in amber, cobalt, crystal, ice blue or red.

RED
　Cup 8.00

Sugar 10.00
Tumbler, 4 3/4 In. 12.50

Raindrops

Raindrops was made by the Federal Glass Company of Columbus, Ohio, from 1929 to 1933. It is found in crystal or green.

Raindrops, see also Colony

CRYSTAL
　Whiskey, 1 7/8 In. ...... 1.00 to 1.50
GREEN
　Cup 2.00

Cup & Saucer .... 2.00 to 3.00
Tumbler, 3 In. .... 2.50 to 3.50
Tumbler, 5 In. 3.50
Whiskey, 1 7/8 In. ...... 2.25 to 2.50

Raspberry, see Laurel
Ribbed, see Manhattan

Ribbon

Ribbon was made by the Hazel Atlas Glass Company, a firm with factories in Ohio, Pennsylvania and West Virginia, in the early 1930s It is found in black, crystal or green.

Ribbon Candy, see Pretzel

CRYSTAL

Bowl, 8 In.	7.00
Creamer	4.00
Cup & Saucer	4.00
Plate, 6 1/4 In.	1.00
Plate, 8 In.	3.00
Salt & Pepper	16.00
Saucer	1.00
Sherbet	3.25
Sugar	3.50

GREEN

Berry Bowl, 4 In.	4.50
Berry Bowl, 8 In.	8.00
Bowl, 9 In.	12.50
Creamer	2.50 to 3.00
Cup	2.00 to 4.00
Cup & Saucer	6.50
Dish, Candy, Covered	20.00 to 25.00
Plate, 6 1/4 In.	1.00 to 2.00
Plate, 8 In.	1.50 to 3.00
Salt & Pepper	9.00 to 13.00
Saltshaker	3.00 to 5.00
Saucer	1.00 to 2.00
Sherbet	2.50 to 3.00
Sugar & Creamer	6.50
Sugar, Open	2.50 to 4.00
Tumbler, Footed, 6 1/2 In., 13 Oz.	6.75

Ring

Ring was made by the Hocking Glass Company of Lancaster, Ohio, from 1927 to 1932. It is found in blue, crystal, green, pink, red and crystal with rings of black, pink, orange, platinum, red or yellow.

BLUE

Decanter Set	20.00

CRYSTAL

Bowl, 7 1/4 In.	4.00
Cocktail Shaker, Aluminum Top	9.00
Cup, Platinum Rings	1.75
Decanter & Stopper, Multicolor Rings	17.00
Decanter & Stopper, Red Rings	12.00
Decanter & Stopper, 6 Jiggers	25.00
Goblet, 7 1/2 In.	4.50 to 6.00
Pitcher, 8 1/2 In.	8.00 to 15.00
Plate, Off Center Ring, 6 In.	4.50
Plate, Platinum Rings, 6 1/2 In.	1.00
Plate, Platinum Rings, 8 In.	1.25
Plate, 6 1/4 In.	1.25
Plate, 8 In.	1.50 to 5.00
Salt & Pepper	8.00
Server, Center Handle	4.00 to 8.00
Sherbet, 4 3/4 In.	2.25 to 2.50
Sugar & Creamer, Platinum Rings	4.00
Sugar, Platinum Rings	2.50
Tumbler, Flat, 3 1/2 In.	3.25
Tumbler, Flat, 5 1/2 In.	2.50
Tumbler, Flat, 9 Oz.	4.00
Tumbler, Footed, 3 1/2 In.	3.25
Tumbler, Footed, 5 1/2 In.	3.00
Tumbler, Footed, 6 1/2 In.	4.00
Tumbler, Multicolor Rings, 3 3/4 In.	2.75
Tumbler, Multicolor Rings, 5 1/4 In.	3.25
Tumbler, Platinum Rings, 3 1/2 In.	2.50
Whiskey Set, 6 Piece	22.00
Whiskey, Multicolor Rings, 2 In.	2.50
Wine Set, 7 Piece	28.00

GREEN

Bowl, 8 In.	3.50
Creamer	2.50
Cup	1.75 to 2.50
Cup & Saucer	4.50
Cup, Platinum Rings	1.75
Decanter & Stopper	15.00
Dessert Set, Platinum Ring, 24 Piece	52.50
Goblet, 7 1/2 In.	5.00
Ice Bucket	4.00
Ivy Ball, Stemmed	25.00
Plate, Multicolor Rings, 11 In.	3.50
Plate, Off-Center Ring, 6 In.	1.75
Plate, Platinum Rings, 6 1/4 In.	1.00
Plate, 6 In.	.75 to 1.50
Plate, 8 In.	1.25 to 4.50
Server, Center Handle	15.00 to 16.50
Sherbet, Footed, 4 3/4 In.	4.00
Sherbet, Multicolor Ring, 4 3/4 In.	4.00

Tumbler, Flat, 3 1/2 In.	3.00	Tumbler, 5 1/8 In.	2.50
Tumbler, Footed, 6 1/2 In.	4.00	Tumbler, 9 Oz.	4.00
Tumbler, Orange & Black Rings, 9 Oz.		Whiskey, 2 In.	2.00
....	3.00		
Tumbler, Platinum Rings, 5 1/8 In.			
....	3.00		

Rock Crystal

Rock Crystal was made by the McKee Glass Company of Jeannette, Pennsylvania, from the 1920s to the 1930s. It is found in amber, blue- green, cobalt, crystal, green, pink, red or yellow.

AMBER
Bowl, Footed, 7 In.	10.00
Candlestick, Pair, 8 1/2 In.	25.00
Compote, Footed, 7 In.	27.50
Goblet, Footed	13.00
Plate, Cake, Pedestal, 11 In. ...	24.75

BLUE GREEN
Pitcher, Covered, 9 1/8 In. ...	125.00

CRYSTAL
Bowl, 4 1/2 In.	3.75
Candlestick, Double, 5 1/2 In., Pair	15.00
Cruet & Stopper, 6 Oz.	35.00
Eggcup	6.75
Goblet, Footed, 3 1/2 Oz.	6.00
Goblet, Footed, 6 Oz.	6.00
Goblet, Footed, 8 Oz.	8.00
Pitcher, 6 1/2 In.	75.00
Plate, 7 In.	2.25
Plate, 7 1/4 In.	3.00
Relish, 5 Part, 11 1/2 In.	9.00

Sundae, Low, Footed, 6 Oz.	5.00
Tumbler, Concave, 12 Oz.	10.00
Tumbler, 5 Oz.	7.00

GREEN
Plate, Cheese, 10 1/2 In.	18.50

PINK
Goblet, 3 Oz.	15.50
Goblet, 6 Oz.	14.00
Goblet, 8 Oz.	15.00
Server, Center Handle	17.50
Sherbet, Low, Stemmed, 3 1/2 In.	6.00

RED
Compote	12.00
Compote & Underplate	20.00
Goblet, Low, Stemmed, 8 Oz. ..	26.00
Plate, 7 1/2 In.	12.00
Plate, 10 In. .... 12.50 to 18.00
Tray, Oval, 13 1/4 In.	28.00
Tumbler, Flat, 5 Oz.	22.00
Tumbler, Flat, 9 Oz.	24.00

Romanesque, see Gothic Arches
Rope, see Colonial Fluted

Rose Cameo

Rose Cameo was made by the Belmont Tumbler Company of Bellaire, Ohio, in 1933. It is found in green.

GREEN
Bowl, 4 1/2 In. .... 1.25 to 3.00	

Bowl, 5 In. .... 1.50 to 3.25	
Goblet, 5 In.	8.00

| Plate, 7 In. .... | 1.50 to 3.00 |
| Sherbet .... | 1.50 to 4.00 |

Tumbler, Cone Shape, Footed, 5 In. 4.50
Tumbler, Footed, 5 In. ... 4.50 to 6.50

Rose Lace, see Royal Lace

Rosemary

Rosemary was made by the Federal Glass Company of Columbus, Ohio, from 1935 to 1937. It is found in amber, crystal, green or pink.

Rosemary, see also Mayfair Federal

AMBER

Berry Bowl, 5 In.	1.75 to 3.00
Bowl, Oval, 10 In.	6.00 to 10.00
Creamer	5.50 to 7.50
Cup	3.00
Cup & Saucer	4.50 to 5.00
Plate, 6 3/4 In.	1.50 to 4.25
Plate, 9 1/2 In.	2.75 to 6.00

Platter, Oval, 12 In.	5.00 to 7.00
Saucer	1.00 to 2.00
Soup, Cream, 5 In.	5.00 to 6.00
Sugar	3.95 to 7.00
Sugar & Creamer ...,..	5.50 to 10.00
Tumbler, 4 1/4 In.	4.50 to 8.00

GREEN

| Plate, Grill .... | 6.00 |

Rosemary

Rosemary

Plate, 6 3/4 In. 2.25
Plate, 9 1/2 In. .... 4.75 to 5.50
Saucer 1.50
PINK
Bowl, 5 In. .... 3.50 to 4.25
Bowl, 6 In. 4.50
Cup & Saucer 6.50
Plate, Grill 5.00
Plate, 9 1/2 In. .... 3.50 to 6.00
Sugar 5.00

Rosemary

Roulette

Roulette was made by the Hocking Glass Company of Lancaster, Ohio, from 1935 to 1939. It is found in green or pink.

CRYSTAL
Bowl, 9 In. 5.00
Cup 2.50
Plate, 6 In. 1.00
Plate, 8 1/2 In. 2.25
GREEN
Bowl, 9 In. .... 5.00 to 9.50
Cup .... 2.00 to 5.00
Cup & Saucer .... 2.25 to 5.50
Measuring Cup, Marked Kellogg . 7.50
Plate, 6 In. .... 1.00 to 1.50
Plate, 8 1/2 In. .... 1.25 to 3.50
Plate, 12 In. .... 2.50 to 5.00

Saucer .... .50 to 3.50
Sherbet .... 2.00 to 4.50
Tumbler, Flat, 12 Oz. 9.95
Tumbler, Footed, 10 Oz. 8.00
Tumbler, 9 Oz. 5.00
Whiskey, 2 1/2 In. 5.50
PINK
Cup & Saucer 4.00
Pitcher, 8 In. 16.00
Tumbler, 9 Oz. 5.00
Tumbler, 12 Oz. 8.50
Tumbler, 3 1/2 In., 8 Oz. 5.00

Round Robin

Round Robin, manufacturer unknown, was made in the early 1930s. It is found in green or iridescent.

GREEN
Cup 4.00
Plate, 6 In. .... 1.00 to 1.25

Sherbet .... 2.25 to 2.50

Roxana

Roxana was made by the Hazel Atlas Glass Company, a firm with factories in Ohio, Pennsylvania and West Virginia, in 1932. It is found in crystal, white or yellow.

YELLOW
Bowl, 5 In. .... 2.00 to 3.00
Bowl, 6 In. .... 3.00 to 4.50

Saucer .... 1.00 to 1.75
Sherbet .... 2.00 to 3.50

Royal Lace

Royal Lace was made by the Hazel Atlas Company, a firm with factories in Ohio, Pennsylvania and West Virginia, from 1934 to 1941. It is found in amethyst, blue, crystal, green or pink.

AMETHYST
Sherbet, Metal Holder 25.00
BLUE
Berry Bowl, 10 In. 22.50
Bowl, Console, 3-Legged, Straight Edge
.... 37.50
Bowl, Console, 3-Legged, 10 In. 32.00
Bowl, Oval, 11 In. ..... 20.00 to 25.00
Bowl, 5 In. 18.00
Candleholder, Rolled Edge, Pair 55.00
Candleholder, Ruffled Edge, Pair 45.00
Candleholder, Straight Edge, Pair 45.00
Cookie Jar, Covered .. 65.00 to 100.00
Creamer .... 13.00 to 18.00
Creamer & Plate, 8 1/2 In. 32.50
Cup .... 12.00 to 17.00
Cup & Saucer .... 14.50 to 19.00
Hot Toddy Set 80.00
Pitcher & 8 Glasses 195.00
Pitcher, 7 In., 54 Oz. .. 59.50 to 70.00
Pitcher, 8 In., 68 Oz. 65.00
Pitcher, 8 1/2 In. 105.00
Plate, Grill, 9 7/8 In. 17.50
Plate, 6 In. .... 3.50 to 6.00
Plate, 8 1/2 In. .... 8.50 to 16.00
Plate, 10 In. .... 15.00 to 17.50
Platter, Oval, 13 In. ... 22.50 to 27.00
Salt & Pepper ...... 120.00 to 150.00
Saucer .... 3.00 to 5.00
Sherbet 10.00
Sherbet, Metal Holder . 10.00 to 14.50
Soup, Cream, 4 3/4 In. . 12.50 to 18.00
Sugar & Creamer, Covered 40.00

Sugar, Covered .... 50.00 to 55.00
Sugar, Open .... 14.00 to 14.50
Tumbler, 3 1/2 In. .... 16.00 to 18.00
Tumbler, 4 1/8 In. .... 16.00 to 16.95
Tumbler, 4 7/8 In. .... 15.00 to 27.00
Tumbler, 5 3/8 In. 28.50
CRYSTAL
Bowl, 3-Legged, Rolled Edge, 10 In. 15.00
Bowl, 3-Legged, Ruffled Edge, 10 In.
.... 15.00
Bowl, 3-Legged, 10 In. 15.00
Butter, Covered 90.00
Candleholder, Rolled Edge, Pair 16.00
Candleholder, Ruffled, Pair 20.00
Cookie Jar, Covered ... 16.00 to 35.00

Royal Lace

Creamer .... 6.00 to 9.00
Cup .... 4.50 to 5.50
Cup & Saucer 7.50
Pitcher, 68 Oz. 25.00
Pitcher, 96 Oz. 40.00
Plate, Grill 3.50
Plate, 6 In. 3.75
Plate, 8 1/2 In. 6.50
Plate, 10 In. 5.00
Platter, Oval, 13 In. 12.00
Salt & Pepper .... 30.00 to 33.00
Salt Dip 7.50
Saucer 1.50
Sherbet, Insert 3.00
Soup, Cream, 4 3/4 In. .... 3.50 to 6.00
Sugar & Creamer 10.50
Sugar, Covered 15.00
Sugar, Open .... 3.00 to 5.50
Tumbler, 12 Oz. 8.00
Tumbler, 3 1/2 In. ...... 5.00 to 8.00
Tumbler, 4 1/8 In., 9 Oz. 5.00
GREEN
Berry Bowl, 5 In. 15.00
Berry Bowl, 10 In. 20.00
Bowl, Oval, 11 In. 10.00
Bowl, 3-Legged, Rolled Edge, 10 In. 18.50
Bowl, 3-Legged, Ruffled Edge, 10 In.
.... 30.00
Bowl, 3-Legged, Straight Edge, 10 In.
.... 25.00
Butter, Covered 195.00
Candleholder, Rolled, Pair 40.00
Cookie Jar, Covered ... 32.50 to 37.00
Creamer 8.50

Cup .... 6.50 to 7.00
Cup & Saucer .... 9.50 to 12.00
Pitcher, Straight Edge, 54 Oz. 50.00 to
.... 64.50
Pitcher, 8 In., 68 Oz. 75.00
Pitcher, 86 Oz. 75.00
Pitcher, 96 Oz. 100.00
Plate, Grill, 9 7/8 In. 10.00
Plate, 6 In. 3.50
Plate, 8 1/2 In. .... 6.00 to 8.00
Plate, 10 In. .... 8.00 to 10.00
Platter, Oval, 13 In. ... 15.00 to 23.00
Salt & Pepper .... 65.00 to 85.00
Sherbet .... 8.50 to 12.00
Soup, Cream, 4 3/4 In. ... 6.00 to 8.00
Sugar, Covered 25.00
Sugar, Open .... 6.00 to 7.50
Tumbler, Flat, 3 1/2 In. 18.00
Tumbler, 9 Oz 15.00
Tumbler, 12 Oz. 18.00
PINK
Berry Bowl, 5 In. 15.00
Berry Bowl, 10 In. ...... 7.50 to 9.00
Bowl, Oval, 11 In. 12.00

Royal Lace

Bowl, 3-Legged, 10 In.	17.00
Butter, Covered	70.00 to 75.00
Candleholder, Straight Edge, Pair	13.00
Candlestick, Rolled Edge, Pair .	20.00
Cookie Jar, Covered	25.00
Creamer	5.00 to 8.50
Cup & Saucer	7.50 to 8.00
Dish, Nut	95.00
Pitcher, 68 Oz.	32.50 to 40.00
Pitcher, 7 In., 44 Oz.	50.00
Pitcher, 8 In.	44.00
Pitcher, 8 1/2 In.	85.00
Plate, Grill	7.50 to 8.00
Plate, 6 In.	3.00 to 3.95
Plate, 8 1/2 In.	6.50 to 8.00
Plate, 10 In.	8.95
Platter, Oval, 13 In.	10.00
Salt & Pepper	29.00 to 60.00
Saucer	2.50 to 3.50
Sherbet	6.50 to 7.50
Soup, Bowl	7.50
Soup, Cream	6.50
Sugar	5.75 to 6.50
Sugar & Creamer, Covered	20.00
Sugar, Covered	14.50 to 22.00
Sugar, Open	4.00
Tumbler, Flat, 4 In.	8.50
Tumbler, 9 Oz.	10.50
Tumbler, 10 Oz.	12.50
Tumbler, 3 1/2 In.	8.50 to 10.00
Tumbler, 5 3/8 In.	14.00 to 19.50

Royal Ruby

Royal Ruby was made by the Anchor Hocking Glass Company of Lancaster, Ohio, from 1939 to the 1960s and again in 1977. It is found in red.

RED

Ashtray, Square, 4 1/2 In.	2.75
Berry Bowl, Square, 4 1/2 In.	3.00 to 4.00
Berry Bowl, 4 1/2 In.	2.00
Berry Bowl, 8 1/2 In.	6.50
Berry Set, 7 Piece	20.00
Bowl, Console, 11 1/2 In.	15.00
Bowl, Oval, 8 In.	8.50
Candleholder	1.50
Cigarette Box, Covered	12.00
Creamer, Flat	2.50 to 4.00
Creamer, Footed	5.00
Cup & Saucer	4.00
Cup & Saucer, Square ...	3.00 to 5.00
Cup, Round	4.00
Cup, Square	4.00
Custard	3.00
Goblet, Ball Stem	7.00 to 9.00
Ivy Ball, Square, 4 In.	4.00
Mustard Pot, Ruby Top, Crystal Base	
....	3.50

Royal Ruby

Cameo, water bottle

Block, sherbet

Cameo, creamer & sugar

Cherry Blossom, tumbler

Circle, goblet

Colonial, wine goblet

Colonial, pitcher

Colonial "X", candy jar

Riviera, by Homer Laughlin, assorted colors

Florentine No. 2, candy dish

Fiesta, by Homer Laughlin, assorted colors

Iris, candy dish

Florentine No. 2, tumbler

Dutch Petitpoint, Salem

Mayfair, cookie jar

Harlequin, by Homer Laughlin, assorted colors

New Century, bowl

Moondrops, winged candleholder

Moonstone, vase

No. 612, creamer & sugar

Primo, tumbler

Normandie, oval vegetable bowl

Petalware, mustard pot

Ribbon, candy dish

Royal, pitcher

Royal Lace, ruffled candleholders

Swirl, double candleholder

Royal Ruby, pitcher

Sharon, candy dish

Sylvan, sherbet

Tea Room, creamer & sugar

Waterford, sandwich plate

Twisted Optic, candy dish

White Ship, pitcher

Windsor, fruit bowl

Calico Fruit, covered bowl

Crocus, by Hall, plate

Rosebud, by Coors, plate

Caliente, by Paden City, plate

Bittersweet, by Hall, plate

Pitcher, Tilted, Swirl, 3 Oz. 25.00
Pitcher, Tilted, 42 Oz. 12.00
Plate, Square, 7 3/4 In. 2.50
Plate, 6 1/2 In. 3.00
Plate, 7 In. 2.50
Plate, 7 3/4 In. .... 2.00 to 3.00
Plate, 9 In. .... 3.50 to 5.00
Plate, 9 1/4 In. 3.50
Punch Set, Pedestal, 13 Piece .. 40.00
Saucer, Round .... 1.50 to 2.00
Saucer, Square .... 1.50 to 2.00
Sherbet, Collared Bottom 2.50
Sherbet, Flat 3.00
Sherbet, Footed .... 2.00 to 5.00
Soup, Flat .... 5.50 to 6.00
Sugar & Creamer, Covered 11.00
Sugar & Creamer, Flat .. 7.50 to 10.00

Sugar & Creamer, Footed 8.50
Sugar, Flat .... 4.00 to 5.00
Sugar, Footed .... 3.00 to 6.50
Sugar, Footed, Covered 9.00
Tumbler, Cocktail, 3 1/2 Oz. 3.00 to 3.25
Tumbler, Ice Tea, 13 Oz. 2.00
Tumbler, Juice, 5 Oz. .... 1.50 to 3.00
Tumbler, Water, Flat, 10 Oz. ... 2.00
Tumbler, Water, Footed, 10 Oz. . 6.00
Tumbler, Water, 9 Oz. ... 2.50 to 4.00
Vase, Ivy Ball, 3 1/4 In. 3.00
Vase, 6 3/8 In. 3.25
Vase, 9 In. 6.00
Water Set, 9 Piece .... 47.50 to 50.00
Whiskey .... 1.50 to 3.00
Wine, Collared Base, 2 1/2 Oz. . 6.00

Russian, see Holiday

S Pattern

S Pattern was made by the MacBeth Evans Glass Company, a firm with factories in Indiana, Ohio and Pennsylvania, from 1930 to 1933. It is found in amber, crystal, pink, monax and crystal with amber, blue, green or platinum trim.

AMBER

Bowl, 5 1/2 In. .... 2.00 to 3.50
Creamer 3.00
Cup .... 2.00 to 2.25
Cup & Saucer .... 2.50 to 5.50
Plate, Grill 4.00
Plate, 6 In. 1.75

Plate, 8 In. .... 1.50 to 2.75
Plate, 9 1/4 In. .... 2.50 to 6.00
Saucer .... 1.00 to 1.25

S Pattern

Sherbet, Low, Footed .... 2.50 to 4.50
Sugar 3.00
Tumbler, Flat, 3 1/2 In. 3.75
CRYSTAL
Creamer .... 2.50 to 3.00
Creamer, Platinum Rim 3.00
Cup & Saucer .... 2.00 to 3.75
Cup & Saucer, Platinum Rim ... 3.50
Cup, Amber Handle 2.00
Cup, Thick .... 2.25 to 2.50
Plate, Amber Band, 8 In. 1.50
Plate, Cake, 11 In. .... 19.00 to 20.00
Plate, Gold Rim, 6 In. ... 1.00 to 1.25
Plate, Gold Rim, 8 In. 1.75
Plate, Platinum Rim, 8 In. 1.75
Plate, 6 In. 1.25
Plate, 8 In. .... 2.00 to 3.00
Plate, 9 1/4 In. 2.50
Saucer .... .75 to 1.25
Saucer, Platinum Rim 1.75
Sherbet, Gold Rim 3.00
Sherbet, Low, Footed, Amber Rim 4.00
Sugar 2.50
Sugar & Creamer 6.50
Sugar & Creamer, Amber Handle 10.00
Sugar, Amber Rim 2.50
Sugar, Platinum Rim 2.20
Tumbler, Flat, 12 Oz. 6.00
Tumbler, Platinum Rim, 4 3/4 In. 6.00
Tumbler, 10 Oz. 5.00
Tumbler, 3 1/2 In. ...... 3.00 to 3.50
Tumbler, 4 In., 9 Oz. .... 3.00 to 4.00
GREEN
Pitcher, Dogwood Style, 80 Oz.   30.00

S Pattern

Sail Boat, see White Ship
Sailing Ship, see White Ship

Sandwich Anchor Hocking

Sandwich was made by the Anchor Hocking Glass Company of Lancaster, Ohio, from 1939 to 1964. It is found in amber, crystal, forest green, pink, red or white. In 1977 they produced a line of cookie jars.

AMBER
Bowl, 6 1/2 In. 3.00
Cookie Jar, Covered 22.50
Cup 2.50
Cup & Saucer .... 4.50 to 5.00
Plate, 9 In. 3.00

CRYSTAL
Bowl 3.25
Bowl, Oval, 8 1/4 In. .... 3.00 to 6.50
Bowl, Scalloped, 6 1/2 In. 6.50
Bowl, 4 7/8 In. .... 1.25 to 4.00
Bowl, 6 In. 2.75

Sandwich Anchor Hocking

Bowl, 6 1/2 In. .... 2.50 to 6.50
Butter, Covered .... 20.00 to 23.00
Cookie Jar, Covered 15.00
Creamer .... 3.00 to 3.75
Cup .... 2.00 to 3.00
Cup & Saucer .... 2.50 to 4.50
Custard .... 1.00 to 3.00
Custard Liner 6.00
Pitcher, Ice Lip, 2 Qt. 40.00
Plate, 7 In. 2.95
Plate, 8 In. 3.75
Plate, 9 In. .... 2.75 to 5.00
Plate, 10 1/2 In. .... 3.75 to 4.00
Plate, 12 In. 6.00
Punch Bowl & Base 12.50
Punch Cup 1.50
Saucer 1.25
Sherbet, Footed .... 2.00 to 3.50
Sugar & Creamer, Covered 12.50
Sugar & Creamer, Open .. 4.00 to 7.75
Tumbler, Footed, 9 Oz. .. 6.00 to 8.50
Tumbler, 5 Oz. .... 1.00 to 3.00
Tumbler, 9 Oz. 5.00
FOREST GREEN
Bowl, Oval, 8 1/4 In. 27.50

Bowl, 4 7/8 In. .... 3.00 to 4.00
Bowl, 6 1/2 In. .... 14.50 to 18.50
Bowl, 7 In. 22.50
Cookie Jar, Open ..... 15.00 to 16.00
Creamer .... 9.00 to 10.00
Cup & Saucer .... 14.50 to 16.00
Custard .... 1.50 to 2.50
Pitcher, 2 Qt. .... 135.00 to 150.00
Pitcher, 6 In. 65.00
Plate, 9 In. 19.00
Sherbet 2.00
Sugar, Open 8.50
Tumbler, 5 Oz. .... 1.50 to 2.50
Tumbler, 9 Oz. .... 2.25 to 4.00
PINK
Bowl, Scalloped, 8 In. 12.00
Bowl, Smooth, 8 In. 10.00
RED
Bowl, Scalloped, 8 In. 22.50
Bowl, 4 7/8 In. 8.00
Bowl, 5 1/4 In. 7.00
Sugar & Creamer 22.00
WHITE
Punch Cup .... .75 to 1.25
Punch Set .... 25.00 to 28.00

Sandwich Indiana

Sandwich was made by the Indiana Glass Company of Dunkirk, Indiana, from the 1920s to the 1970s. It is found in amber, crystal, green, pink, red or teal blue. Reproductions were made in 1969 in amber, blue, crystal or red.

BLUE
Sherbet, Footed 6.00
CRYSTAL
Ashtray 1.00
Ashtray Set, Card Suits 9.00
Bowl, Hexagonal, 6 In. 3.00
Candleholder, 3 1/2 In. 5.50
Cookie Jar, Covered 22.00
Creamer .... 1.50 to 2.50
Cup .... 1.25 to 3.00
Cup & Saucer 4.00
Goblet, 9 Oz. 10.50
Plate, 6 In. 1.00

Plate, 8 In. .... 2.50 to 3.00
Plate, 8 3/8 In. .... 2.00 to 4.95
Plate, 10 1/2 In. .... 4.00 to 6.95
Saucer 1.50
Sherbet, Footed, 3 1/4 In. 3.50
Sugar & Creamer, Tray .. 8.00 to 9.00
GREEN
Ashtray, Diamond 2.00
Plate, Oval, 8 In. 4.50
RED
Bowl, 8 1/4 In. 12.50
Sugar & Creamer 30.00

Sawtooth, see English Hobnail
Saxon, see Coronation
Scroll & Star, see Princess Feather
Shamrock, see Cloverleaf

Sharon

Sharon was made by the Federal Glass Company of Columbus, Ohio, from 1935 to 1939. It was made in amber, crystal, green or pink. Reproductions were made in amber, blue, green or pink in 1976.

AMBER
Berry Bowl, 5 In. .... 3.50 to 4.00
Berry Bowl, 8 1/2 In. .... 2.50 to 6.00
Bowl, Oval, 9 1/2 In. .... 6.50 to 7.00
Bowl, 6 In. .... 3.00 to 9.00
Bowl, 10 1/2 In. .... 8.50 to 15.00
Butter, Covered .... 28.00 to 40.00
Creamer, Footed .... 4.00 to 5.00
Cup .... 4.00 to 4.50
Cup & Saucer .... 1.95 to 5.50
Dish, Candy, Covered .. 19.00 to 23.00
Dish, Cheese, Covered   90.00 to 150.00
Jar, Jam, 7 1/2 In. .... 12.00 to 20.00
Pitcher, Ice Lip, 80 Oz. 55.00
Plate, Cake, Footed, 12 In. 15.00
Plate, 6 In. .... 2.00 to 3.25
Plate, 7 1/2 In. .... 4.95 to 8.00
Plate, 9 1/2 In. .... 4.00 to 5.50

Platter, Oval, 12 1/2 In. 9.00
Salt & Pepper .... 19.00 to 25.00
Saltshaker 10.00
Saucer .... 1.25 to 4.50
Sherbet .... 3.00 to 8.00
Soup, Cream, 5 In. ..... 9.00 to 15.00
Soup, Flat, 7 1/2 In. .... 9.00 to 12.00
Sugar & Creamer, Covered 20.00
Sugar, Covered ...... 12.00 to 20.00
Sugar, Open .... 3.00 to 7.00
Tumbler, Flat, 4 1/8 In.   12.50 to 13.00
Tumbler, Footed, 6 1/2 In. 25.00 to 35.00
Tumbler, 5 1/4 In., 12 Oz. 17.50
CRYSTAL
Plate, Cake, Metal Lid, Wooden Knob
.... 15.00
GREEN
Berry Bowl, 5 In. .... 5.00 to 6.00

Berry Bowl, 8 1/2 In. 12.50
Bowl, Oval, 9 1/2 In. .. 10.00 to 10.80
Bowl, 6 In. 12.50
Bowl, 10 1/2 In. ...... 16.50 to 25.00
Butter, Covered .... 50.00 to 59.50
Creamer, Footed .... 6.00 to 12.50
Cup 6.00
Cup & Saucer .... 8.50 to 10.75
Dish, Candy, Covered 95.00
Jar, Jam, 7 1/2 In. .... 17.50 to 25.00
Plate, Cake, Footed, 11 1/2 In. . 29.50
Plate, 6 In. 3.00
Plate, 7 1/2 In. .... 5.50 to 12.50
Plate, 9 1/2 In. .... 7.00 to 8.00
Platter, Oval, 12 1/2 In. 10.80
Punch Set, Base, 12 Cups 45.00
Salt & Pepper .... 40.00 to 60.00
Saucer .... 2.00 to 3.00
Soup, Cream, 5 In. 15.00
Sugar, Covered ...... 24.00 to 25.00
Sugar, Open .... 6.00 to 10.50
Tumbler, 9 Oz. 28.00
Tumbler, 12 Oz. 35.00

Sharon

Sharon

PINK

Berry Bowl, 5 In.	3.50 to 4.50
Berry Bowl, 8 1/2 In.	6.00 to 9.50
Bowl, Oval, 9 1/2 In. ...	7.50 to 13.50
Bowl, 6 In.	6.50 to 8.00
Bowl, 10 1/2 In.	10.00 to 14.75
Butter, Covered	25.00 to 35.00
Creamer	3.50 to 7.00
Cup	4.50 to 5.50
Cup & Saucer	6.00 to 7.00
Dinner Set, With Butter, 53 Piece	250.00
Dish, Candy, Covered ..	20.00 to 30.00
Jar, Jam, 7 1/2 In.	40.00
Pitcher, Ice Lip, 80 Oz.	60.00
Pitcher, 5 Tumblers, 80 Oz. ...	100.00
Plate, Cake, Footed, 11 1/2 In. .	15.00

Plate, 6 In.	1.75 to 6.00
Plate, 7 1/2 In.	9.00
Plate, 9 1/2 In.	5.75 to 11.00
Platter, Oval, 12 1/2 In.	14.00
Salt & Pepper	29.00
Saucer	3.50 to 5.50
Sherbet, Footed	4.50 to 9.50
Soup, Cream, 5 In.	12.50 to 16.95
Soup, Flat, 7 1/2 In. ...	10.00 to 17.50
Sugar & Creamer, Covered	17.00 to 22.50
Sugar & Creamer, Open .	7.95 to 12.00
Sugar, Covered	15.00
Sugar, Open	3.50 to 7.50
Tumbler, Flat, 9 Oz.	14.50
Tumbler, Flat, 12 Oz.	18.00

Shell, see Petalware

Shirley Temple

Shirley Temple was a cobalt blue and white decorated ware that was given away as premiums. Companys such as U. S. Glass, Hazel Atlas Glass Company (1934-1942) and others produced wares. Creamers and sugars, bowls, plates and mugs were made.

COBALT BLUE

Bowl	25.00 to 55.00

Creamer	15.00 to 20.00
Mug	30.00 to 40.00

Sierra

Sierra was made by the Jeannette Glass Company of Jeannette, Pennsylvania, from 1931 to 1933. It is found in green or pink.

GREEN

Berry Bowl, 8 1/2 In.	7.25 to 9.95
Berry Set, 7 Piece	27.50
Bowl, Oval, 9 1/4 In.	22.00
Bowl, 5 1/2 In.	3.00 to 6.00
Butter, Covered	32.00 to 45.00
Creamer	7.00 to 8.50
Cup	4.00 to 6.00
Cup & Saucer	7.50 to 9.00
Pitcher, 6 1/2 In.	40.00 to 40.50
Plate, 6 In.	2.95 to 4.00
Plate, 9 In.	6.00 to 7.95

Salt & Pepper	20.00 to 25.00
Saucer	1.00 to 2.00
Sugar, Covered	10.00 to 15.00
Sugar, Open	7.50
Tray, 2-Handled	5.50
Tumbler, Footed, 4 1/2 In.	18.50

PINK

Berry Bowl, 8 1/2 In.	7.25 to 8.50
Bowl, Oval, 9 1/4 In. ...	9.95 to 14.00
Bowl, 5 1/2 In.	3.50 to 6.00
Butter, Covered	30.00 to 37.50
Creamer	5.50 to 8.50

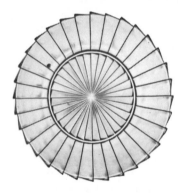

Sierra

Cup .... 3.00 to 4.50
Cup & Saucer .... 4.00 to 8.50
Pitcher, 6 1/2 In. ..... 25.00 to 35.00
Plate, 9 In. .... 3.50 to 7.00

Platter, Oval, 11 In. .... 8.50 to 10.00
Salt & Pepper .... 16.00 to 27.50
Saucer .... 1.50 to 2.50
Sugar & Creamer, Covered 20.00
Sugar, Covered .... 7.00 to 12.50
Sugar, Open 5.00
Tray, 2-Handled .... 5.00 to 8.00
Tumbler, Footed, 4 1/2 In. 15.00

Smocking, see Windsor
Snowflake, see Doric

Spiral Flutes

Spiral Flutes was made by the Duncan Miller Glass Company of Washington, Pennsylvania. Amber, crystal or green were made in 1924, pink in 1926.

AMBER
Sugar 4.50
GREEN
Bowl, Console 14.00

Sherbet, 5 In. 5.00
Soup, Bowl, Rimmed, 7 In. 4.00
PINK
Plate, 7 3/8 In. .... 3.00 to 3.50

Spiral Optic, see Spiral

Spiral

Spiral was made by the Hocking Glass Company of Lancaster, Ohio, from 1928 to 1930. It is found in green.

GREEN
Bowl, 5 3/8 In. .... 2.00 to 3.00
Bowl, 8 In. 5.00
Butter, Covered 10.00
Candy Container, Covered 12.00
Champagne 4.00
Creamer, Flat .... 4.00 to 5.00
Creamer, Footed .... 4.00 to 5.00
Cup .... 1.50 to 4.00
Cup & Saucer .... 2.90 to 3.00
Ice Bucket .... 9.00 to 12.00
Pitcher, Rope Rim, 7 5/8 In. ... 18.00

Pitcher, 7 5/8 In. ..... 11.00 to 16.25
Plate, 6 In. .... .75 to 1.00
Plate, 8 In. .... 1.00 to 3.00
Plate, 8 1/4 In. 1.50
Plate, 9 In. 3.00
Preserve, Covered ...... 8.50 to 18.00
Salt & Pepper .... 15.00 to 25.00
Saucer .... 1.00 to 2.00
Server, Center Handle 18.00
Sherbet .... 1.50 to 3.00
Sugar & Creamer, Flat 5.00
Sugar, Footed 4.00

Spun

Spun was made by the Imperial Glass Company of Bellaire, Ohio, in 1935. It is found in crystal, aqua, fired-on orange, red and all pastel colors.

BLUE
Tumbler, Flat, 10 Oz. 6.00

Starlight

Starlight was made by the Hazel Atlas Glass Company, a firm with factories in Ohio, Pennsylvania and West Virginia, from 1938 to 1940. It is found in cobalt, crystal, pink or white.

CRYSTAL
  Bowl, 11 1/2 In. 9.00
  Bowl, 2-Handled, 5 1/2 In. 4.00
  Creamer, Oval 3.00
  Cup & Saucer 2.50
  Plate, 8 1/2 In. .... 2.00 to 3.50

Salt & Pepper .... 10.00 to 12.50
Sugar & Creamer, Oval 8.00
Sugar, Oval 3.00
WHITE
  Plate, 9 In. 3.50

Stippled Rose, see S Pattern

Strawberry

Strawberry was made by the U. S. Glass Company, a firm with factories in Indiana, Ohio, Pennsylvania and West Virginia, in the early 1930s. It is found in crystal, green, iridescent or pink.

GREEN
  Berry Bowl, Deep, 7 1/2 In. ... 11.00
  Berry Bowl, 4 In. .... 3.50 to 5.50
  Bowl, 6 1/2 In. 10.00
  Butter, Open 50.00
  Pitcher, 7 3/4 In. 92.00
  Sherbet .... 2.00 to 5.50
  Tumbler, 3 5/8 In. .... 15.00 to 20.00
PINK
  Berry Bowl, Deep, 7 1/2 In. ... 10.00
  Berry Bowl, 4 In. 6.00

Butter, Covered ...... 98.00 to 115.00
Creamer .... 8.50 to 12.50
Plate, 6 In. 3.50
Plate, 7 1/2 In. 5.50
Sherbet .... 5.00 to 5.50
Sugar, Covered, 4 5/8 In. 22.50
Tumbler, 3 5/8 In. .... 15.00 to 20.00

Sunburst

Sunburst was made by the Jeannette Glass Company of Jeannette, Pennsylvania, from 1938 to 1940.

CRYSTAL
  Bowl, Console 6.00
  Bowl, 4 3/4 In. 2.00

Candleholder, Double, Pair 8.00
Cup & Saucer 2.00
Plate, 10 In. .... 2.00 to 6.50

Sunflower

Sunflower was made by the Jeannette Glass Company of Jeannette, Pennsylvania. It is found in delphite, pink or green.

GREEN
  Ashtray, 5 In. .... 3.00 to 4.50
  Creamer .... 5.00 to 6.00
  Cup .... 4.00 to 4.50

Cup & Saucer 6.00
Plate, Cake, 3-Legged, 10 In. 8.00
Plate, 9 In. .... 4.00 to 6.50
Sugar & Creamer 15.00

Sugar, Open .... 5.00 to 6.50	
Tumbler, Footed, 4 3/4 In. 10.00	

PINK

Ashtray, 5 In. .... 2.50 to 6.00
Cup .... 4.50 to 6.50
Cup & Saucer .... 5.50 to 6.95

Plate, Cake, 3-Legged, 10 In. 5.00
Plate, 9 In. .... 4.00 to 6.45
Saucer .... 1.25 to 2.00
Sugar & Creamer, Open 10.00
Tumbler, Footed, 4 3/4 In. 10.00

Sweet Pear, see Avocado

Swirl

Swirl was made by the Jeannette Glass Company of Jeannette, Pennsylvania, from 1937 to 1938. It is found in amber, delphite, ice blue, pink or ultramarine.

DELPHITE

Bowl, 5 1/4 In. 6.00
Bowl, 9 In. 15.00
Plate, 6 1/2 In. 1.75

PINK

Bowl, 5 1/4 In. .... 1.40 to 4.00
Bowl, 9 In. .... 5.00 to 6.00

Butter, Covered ..... 110.00 to 120.00
Candlestick, Double, Pair 24.50
Coaster, 1 X 3 1/4 In. 4.00
Creamer, Footed .... 3.25 to 4.00
Cup .... 2.25 to 4.00
Cup & Saucer 5.00
Dish, Candy, Covered 57.50

Swirl

Dish, Candy, 3-Legged, Open ...   2.00
Plate, 6 1/2 In. 1.50
Plate, 7 1/2 In. 6.00
Plate, 9 1/4 In. ....   4.00 to 5.50
Plate, 12 1/2 In. ....   3.75 to 6.00
Saucer ....   1.25 to 1.50
Sherbet, Low, Footed ....   2.50 to 5.00
Tumbler, Flat, 9 Oz. 5.00
Tumbler, Footed, 9 Oz. 6.00
Vase, Footed, 6 In. 6.00

ULTRAMARINE

Bowl, 5 1/4 In. ....   4.95 to 8.00
Bowl, 9 In. ....   9.00 to 14.00
Bowl, Closed Handles, 10 In. ...   14.00
Bowl, Console, Footed, 10 1/2 In.   17.50
Butter, Covered .....   185.00 to 280.00
Candleholder, Double, Pair 18.00
Coaster, 3 1/4 In. 7.50
Creamer, Footed ....   4.00 to 6.00
Cup ....   3.25 to 5.00
Cup & Saucer ....   5.50 to 7.50
Dish, Candy, Covered ..   50.00 to 69.50
Dish, Candy, 3-Legged, Open ...   5.00
Plate, Ruffled Edge, 6 1/2 In. ...   2.25
Plate, Ruffled Edge, 9 1/4 In. ...   5.00
Plate, Ruffled Edge, 12 1/2 In. ..   7.50
Plate, 6 1/2 In. 4.50
Plate, 7 1/4 In. ....   4.50 to 7.50
Plate, 8 In. ....   4.00 to 5.75
Plate, 9 1/4 In. 7.00
Plate, 10 1/2 In. 14.00
Plate, 12 1/2 In. 15.00
Salt & Pepper ....   18.50 to 25.00
Saltshaker ....   8.00 to 9.25
Saucer ....   2.00 to 2.50
Sherbet, Low, Footed ....   5.00 to 5.95
Sugar & Creamer, Footed 15.00
Sugar, Footed ....   5.00 to 6.00
Tumbler, Flat, 9 Oz. 11.00
Tumbler, Flat, 12 Oz, ...   19.95
Tumbler, Footed, 9 Oz. 12.50
Vase, 8 1/2 In. 15.00

Swirl

Swirled Big Rib, see Spiral
Swirled Sharp Rib, see Diana

Sylvan

Sylvan was made by the Federal Glass Company of Columbus, Ohio, from 1931 to 1932. It is found in amber, crystal or green.

AMBER
Plate, 5 3/4 In. 4.00
Platter, Oval, 11 1/4 In. 35.00
Sherbet, Cone Shape, Footed 9.00
CRYSTAL
Berry Bowl, 5 In. . . . . . . 7.50 to 10.00
Cup 10.00
Plate, Grill, 10 1/2 In. 7.50
GREEN
Bowl, Oval, 10 In. . . . . . 15.00 to 20.00
Bowl, 7 In. . . . . 15.00 to 16.00
Bowl, 8 In. 45.00
Butter, Covered . . . . . 195.00 to 225.00
Creamer . . . . 15.00 to 18.50
Cup & Saucer . . . . 14.50 to 20.00
Pitcher, 8 1/2 In. . . . 450.00 to 500.00
Plate, Grill, 10 1/2 In. 12.00
Plate, 5 3/4 In. . . . . 5.00 to 10.00
Plate, 7 1/2 In. . . . . 4.00 to 9.50
Plate, 9 In. . . . . 12.00 to 18.00
Platter, Oval, 11 1/4 In. 20.00
Salt & Pepper 150.00
Sherbet, Cone Shape, Footed . . . 10.00
Sugar & Creamer, Covered 75.00
Sugar, Open . . . . 10.00 to 15.00
Tumbler, Flat, 5 1/2 In. 75.00
Tumbler, Footed, 5 3/4 In. 75.00

Tassel, see Princess

Sylvan

Tea Room

Tea Room was made by the Indiana Glass Company of Dunkirk, Indiana, from 1926 to 1931. It is found in amber, crystal, green or pink.

GREEN
Candleholder, Pair . . . . . 19.00 to 29.50
Creamer, Footed, 4 In. 8.00
Creamer, Rectangular . . . 9.50 to 10.00
Ice Bucket . . . . 22.00 to 25.00
Lamp, 9 In. 30.00
Sugar & Creamer, Rectangular . 18.00
Sugar & Creamer, Tray, 4 In. . . 27.00
Sugar & Creamer, 4 In. 18.00
Sugar, Rectangular . . . . . . 7.00 to 9.50
Sugar, 4 In. . . . . 6.00 to 8.00
Toothpick 15.00
Tumbler, Footed, 5 In. 9.00
Tumbler, Footed, 6 Oz. . 9.00 to 14.00

Tumbler, Footed, 8 1/2 Oz. 25.00
Tumbler, Footed, 9 Oz. 10.00
Tumbler, 11 Oz. . . . . . . 17.00 to 25.00
Tumbler, 12 Oz. . . . . . . 17.00 to 25.00
Vase, Ruffled Top, 9 In. 15.00
PINK
Bowl, Oval, 9 1/2 In. 25.00
Creamer, Rectangular . . . . 7.00 to 9.00
Creamer, 4 In. . . . . 7.00 to 7.75
Pitcher & Tumblers, Set 240.00
Pitcher, 64 Oz. 65.00
Relish, Divided . . . . 7.00 to 9.00
Salt & Pepper 20.00
Sherbet . . . . 3.50 to 7.50

Sugar & Creamer, Rectangular .   16.95
Sugar & Creamer, Tray, 4 In. ..   20.00
Sugar, Rectangular ...... 5.00 to 7.00
Sugar, 4 In. .... 5.00 to 8.50
Tumbler, 9 Oz. 9.00

Teardrop

Teardrop was made by the Duncan Miller Glass Company of Washington, Pennsylvania, in 1934.

CRYSTAL
Bonbon, Handle, 6 In. 4.00
Bowl, Flared, 5 In. 12.00
Cup 3.00
Cup & Saucer 5.00
Goblet 8.00

Mayonnaise Set, 3 Piece 15.00
Nappy, 2-Handled, 5 In. 4.00
Plate, 2-Handled, 6 In. 4.00
Plate, 8 In. 3.50
Salt & Pepper 5.00

Thistle

Thistle was made by the MacBeth Evans Glass Company, a firm with factories in Indiana, Ohio and Pennsylvania, from 1929 to 1930. It is found in crystal, green, pink or yellow.

GREEN
Berry Bowl, 5 1/2 In. .. 10.00 to 10.75
Luncheon Set, 3 Piece 20.00
Saucer .... 3.00 to 3.50
PINK
Bowl, 5 1/2 In. .... 8.50 to 10.00
Cup 8.00

Cup & Saucer .... 11.00 to 12.00
Plate, 8 In. 7.50
Saucer 3.00

Threading, see Old English
Three Parrot, see Sylvan
Thumbprint, see Pear Optic
Tiered Block, see Line 191
Tiered Semi-Optic, see Line 191

Twisted Optic

Twisted Optic was made by the Imperial Glass Company of Bellaire, Ohio, from 1927 to 1930. It is found in amber, green or pink.

AMBER
Candlestick, 3 In., Pair 10.00
Cup & Saucer 3.50
Pitcher, 64 Oz. .... 7.00 to 15.00
Plate, 8 In. .... 1.50 to 1.75

Sherbet .... 1.50 to 2.00
GREEN
Candy Container, Covered 12.00
Goblet, Footed, 7 1/2 In. 3.50
Goblet, Set Of 5 .... 15.00

Plate, 6 In. 1.00
Plate, 8 In. .... 1.25 to 2.00
Sherbet .... 1.50 to 2.00
Sugar & Creamer 8.00
PINK
  Candlestick, 3 In., Pair 12.50
  Candy Container, Covered 12.00

Creamer 2.50
Cup & Saucer 2.00
Pitcher, 64 Oz. 15.00
Plate, 6 In. .... .80 to .90
Plate, 8 In. .... 2.00 to 2.50
Sherbet 1.50

Vernon, see No. 616
Verticle Rib, see Queen Mary

Victory

Victory was made by the Diamond Glass-Ware Company of Indiana, Pennsylvania, from 1929 to 1932. It is found in amber, black, cobalt blue, green or pink.

AMBER
  Plate, 6 In. 1.00
  Plate, 9 In. .... 2.50 to 6.50
GREEN
  Bowl, Oval, 9 In. 6.00
  Bowl, 6 1/2 In. 4.00
  Creamer 3.50
  Cup .... 3.00 to 5.00
  Cup & Saucer 4.00
  Plate, 6 In. 1.50

  Plate, 8 In. 4.00
  Plate, 9 In. 3.50
  Saucer .... 1.25 to 2.00
  Server, Center Handle 12.00
PINK
  Cup .... 3.00 to 5.00
  Plate, 8 In. 4.00
  Saucer 1.25
  Server, Center Handle 10.00
  Sugar 7.50

Vitrock

Vitrock was made by the Hocking Glass Company of Lancaster, Ohio, from 1934 to 1937. It is found in white and fired-on colors.

WHITE
  Bowl, Cereal, 7 1/2 In. 1.50
  Creamer, Oval 2.50

Sugar, Oval 2.50

Vivid Bands, see Petalware
Waffle, see Waterford

Waterford

Waterford was made by the Hocking Glass Company of Lancaster, Ohio, from 1938 to 1944. It is found in crystal, pink, white or yellow. It was later produced in the 1950s in green.

CRYSTAL

Ashtray, 4 In. 1.75
Berry Bowl, 4 3/4 In. .... 1.50 to 2.50
Berry Bowl, 8 1/4 In. .... 4.50 to 9.00
Bowl, 4 1/2 In. .... 2.00 to 4.00
Bowl, 5 1/2 In. .... 4.50 to 6.00
Bowl, 8 1/4 In. .... 3.50 to 6.50
Butter, Covered .... 12.00 to 14.00
Coaster, 4 In. .... .90 to 2.50
Creamer, Oval .... 1.50 to 3.00
Cup .... 1.75 to 3.75
Cup & Saucer .... 2.50 to 4.50
Goblet, 5 1/4 In. .... 5.00 to 8.50
Goblet, 5 5/8 In. .... 5.00 to 8.50
Lamp, Ball Shape, 4 In. 20.00
Lazy Susan, Metal Swival Cup . 20.00
Pitcher, Juice 15.00
Pitcher, Tilted, Ice Lip, 80 Oz. . 15.00
Pitcher, Tilted, 42 Oz. 11.00
Plate, Cake, Handle, 10 1/4 In. . 5.00
Plate, 6 In. .... 1.00 to 2.00
Plate, 7 1/8 In. .... 1.25 to 3.25
Plate, 9 5/8 In. .... 2.50 to 4.00
Plate, 13 3/4 In. .... 2.50 to 5.00
Relish, 6 Section, 14 In. 9.00
Salt & Pepper, 4 In. ..... 8.00 to 9.00
Salt & Pepper, 6 In. ..... 6.75 to 9.00
Saltshaker, Red Lid 1.00

Waterford

Waterford

Saltshaker, 4 In. .... 2.50 to 3.00
Saltshaker, 6 In. 3.00
Saucer .... .50 to 2.50
Sherbet, Footed, 5 1/4 In. 3.50
Sugar & Creamer, Covered, Oval 10.00
Sugar, Oval, Covered .... 3.00 to 7.00
Sugar, Oval, Open .... 1.50 to 3.00
Tumbler, Footed, 4 7/8 In. 8.00
Tumbler, Footed, 6 In. 5.00
GREEN
Berry Set, 9 Piece 25.00
Plate, 13 3/4 In. 5.00
PINK
Berry Bowl, 4 3/4 In. .... 3.00 to 5.00

Bowl, 5 1/2 In. 4.00
Butter, Covered 135.00
Cup .... 4.75 to 5.00
Cup & Saucer .... 10.00 to 12.50
Plate, Cake, Handle, 10 1/4 In. . 5.00
Plate, 9 5/8 In. .... 4.00 to 8.50
Plate, 13 3/4 In. .... 6.00 to 8.00
Saucer .... 2.00 to 3.50
Sherbet, Footed 4.00
Sugar & Creamer, Oval, Covered 14.50
Sugar, Oval, Open 4.95
Tumbler, Footed, 4 7/8 In. 8.00

Wedding Band, see Moderntone
Westmoreland, see Princess Feather
White Sail, see White Ship

White Ship

White Ship was made by the Hazel Atlas Glass Company, a firm with factories in Ohio, Pennsylvania and West Virginia, in 1938. It is found in a blue and white decorated beverage set.

BLUE
Pitcher, 80 Oz. 25.00
Tumbler 5.00
Tumbler, 5 Oz. .... 4.00 to 5.00

Tumbler, 9 Oz. .... 5.00 to 7.00
Tumbler, 10 Oz. .... 3.00 to 5.00
Tumbler, 12 Oz. 4.50

Wild Flower, see No. 618
Wildrose with Apple Blossom, see Flower
Garden with Butterflies
Wildrose, see Dogwood

Windmill

Windmill was made by the Hazel Atlas Glass Company, a firm with factories in Ohio, Pennsylvania and West Virgina. It is found in blue.

BLUE
Cocktail Mixer 8.00
Ice Bucket 8.00

Tumbler, Flat, 4 1/2 In. 4.00

Windsor

Windsor was made by the Jeannette Glass Company of Jeannette, Pennsylvania, from 1936 to 1946. It is found in amberina, crystal, delphite, green or pink.

AMBERINA
Pitcher, 52 Oz. 12.50
CRYSTAL
Berry Bowl, 4 3/4 In. 2.75
Butter, Covered ...... 15.00 to 25.00
Candlestick, Pair .... 7.95 to 11.50
Creamer .... 3.00 to 3.50
Cup .... 1.25 to 2.50
Cup & Saucer 3.50
Dish, Candy, Covered 12.50
Jar, Powder, Covered 8.00
Pitcher, 16 Oz. 8.00
Pitcher, 20 Oz. 3.50
Pitcher, 52 Oz. 10.75
Plate, 2-Handled, 10 1/2 In. 4.00
Plate, 9 In. .... 2.75 to 2.95
Plate, 13 5/8 In. .... 4.25 to 5.00
Punch Bowl, Stand, 8 Cups 35.00
Saltshaker 2.50
Sugar & Creamer, Covered 9.75
Sugar, Covered .... 3.50 to 4.00
Tumbler, Footed, 3 In. 5.25
Tumbler, Footed, 4 In. ... 2.50 to 3.50
Tumbler, 5 Oz. 3.00
Tumbler, 9 Oz. 6.00
DELPHITE
Ashtray .... 30.00 to 39.50
GREEN
Ashtray .... 25.00 to 35.00

Berry Bowl, 4 5/8 In. 2.25
Bowl, Boat Shape, 7 X 11 3/4 In. 18.00
Bowl, Oval, 9 1/2 In. ... 7.50 to 12.00
Butter, Covered .... 50.00 to 75.00
Candlestick, 9 1/2 In. 10.00
Coaster, 3 1/4 In. ...... 5.00 to 10.50
Creamer .... 5.00 to 6.95
Cup .... 3.00 to 4.75

Windsor

Windsor

Cup & Saucer .... 6.00 to 7.50
Jar, Powder, Covered 7.00
Pitcher, 48 Oz. .... 15.00 to 22.00
Pitcher, 6 3/4 In., 52 Oz. 30.00 to 35.00
Plate, 2-Handled, 10 1/4 In. ... 10.00
Plate, 6 In. .... 2.50 to 6.00
Plate, 7 In. .... 3.50 to 6.50
Plate, 13 1/2 In. .... 8.00 to 11.00
Platter, Oval, 11 1/2 In. 8.25
Salt & Pepper .... 19.50 to 25.00
Saltshaker 11.00
Saucer 2.00
Sherbet .... 3.50 to 4.50
Soup, Cream, 5 In. 10.00
Sugar 5.00
Tray, 4 1/8 X 9 In. 15.00
Tray, 8 1/2 X 9 3/4 In. 12.50
Tumbler, 4 In., 9 Oz. .... 7.00 to 9.00
PINK
Ashtray .... 16.00 to 25.00
Berry Bowl, 4 3/4 In. .... 3.00 to 3.50
Berry Bowl, 8 1/2 In. .... 4.00 to 5.00
Bowl, Boat Shape, 7 X 11 3/4 In. 15.00
Bowl, Oval, 9 1/2 In. 5.00
Bowl, Round, Handle, 9 In. 4.95 to 6.00
Bowl, 3-Legged, 7 1/8 In. 5.50
Bowl, 5 1/2 In. .... 4.75 to 8.50
Butter, Covered .... 23.00 to 30.00
Coaster, 3 1/4 In. .... 4.50 to 6.50
Creamer .... 3.00 to 5.00

Cup .... 4.00 to 4.50
Cup & Saucer 4.95
Glass, Ice Tea, 12 In. 9.50
Pitcher, 4 1/2 In., 16 Oz. 25.00
Pitcher, 52 Oz. 22.00
Pitcher, 6 Tumblers 47.50
Plate, 2-Handled, 10 1/4 In. 6.00
Plate, 6 In. .... 1.00 to 3.50
Plate, 7 In. .... 1.75 to 6.50
Plate, 9 In. .... 3.00 to 6.00
Plate, 13 1/2 In. .... 6.00 to 8.00
Plate, 15 1/2 In. ...... 10.00 to 12.00
Platter, Oval, 11 1/2 In. 7.50
Salt & Pepper .... 15.00 to 30.00
Saucer 1.50
Sherbet .... 2.00 to 5.50
Soup, Cream, 5 In. 7.95
Sugar & Creamer, Covered 14.95
Sugar, Covered .... 6.00 to 7.50
Sugar, Open .... 2.50 to 5.00
Tray, Square, 4 In. 4.00
Tumbler, 3 1/4 In. ...... 3.50 to 8.00
Tumbler, 5 In. 9.50
Water Set, 7 Piece 45.00

Winged Medallion see Madrid

Woolworth

Woolworth was made by the Westmoreland Glass Company of Grapeville, Pennsylvania, in the early 1930s. It is found in blue, crystal, green and pink.

CRYSTAL
Plate .... 3.00 to 4.00

GREEN
Plate 3.00
Sugar & Creamer ...... 8.00 to 10.00

X Design

X Design was made by the Hazel Atlas Glass Company, a firm with factories in Ohio, Pennsylvania and West Virginia, from the 1920s to the 1930s. It is found in blue, crystal, green or pink.

BLUE
Bowl, 10 1/2 In. 20.00
Butter, Covered 19.50
CRYSTAL
Bowl, 8 In. 4.00
Bowl, 9 1/2 In. .... 3.75 to 6.00
Butter, Covered .... 3.00 to 7.25
Cocktail Shaker, Face On Side . 18.00
Mixing Bowl Set, 4 Piece 15.00
Pitcher, 60 Oz. 10.00
Reamer .... 6.00 to 10.00
Refrigerator Jar, Covered, Square 12.00

Tumbler, 5 Oz. 2.50
Tumbler, 9 Oz. 4.50
GREEN
Jar, Refrigerator, Oblong 6.50
Mixing Bowl, 7 1/2 In. 6.50
Mixing Bowl, 8 1/2 In. 5.00
Reamer .... 12.00 to 18.00
Reamer, Insert 7.25
PINK
Butter, Covered 10.00
RITZ BLUE
Reamer 85.00

Refrigerator Ware

Refrigerator sets were made by the Hall China Company, East Liverpool, Ohio, from the late 1930s. For Westinghouse the company made Patrician in 1938, Emperor in 1939, Aristocrat in 1940-1941 and Prince in 1952. They also made King and Queen ovenware to match the Refrigerator Ware. Sears Roebuck, Montgomery Ward, Hotpoint and General Electric also used Hall Refrigerator Ware. The company also made some pieces sold with the Hall name. They were Bingo in the late 1930s, Plaza in the 1930s to the 1960s and Norris.

Hotpoint, Blue, Water Server 8.00
Hotpoint, Dresden Blue, Water Server 20.00
Hotpoint, Gray, Leftover, Addison 9.00
Hotpoint, Maroon, Leftover 15.00
Hotpoint, Red, Leftover, 4 In. .... 6.00 to 15.00

Hotpoint, Yellow, Leftover, 8 1/2 In. 10.00
Montgomery Ward, Delphinium Blue, Water Jug 18.00
Montgomery Ward, Delphinium Blue, Water Server, Covered 18.00
Sears Roebuck, Cadet Blue, Leftover, 3-End-Section 8.50
Westinghouse, Canary, Butter, Covered, Emperor 9.00
Westinghouse, Canary, Leftover, Prince 4.50
Westinghouse, Canary, Roaster, Covered, King 9.00
Westinghouse, Daffodil & Blue, Water Server, Prince 8.00
Westinghouse, Delphinium Blue, Roaster, Covered 9.00
Westinghouse, Delphinium Blue, Water Server, Patrician 15.00
Westinghouse, Garden Green, Leftover, Aristocrat 8.00
Westinghouse, Green, Butter 5.00
Westinghouse, Green, Refrigerator Set, Server, Butter 5.00

Reproductions of Depression Glass
(List based on information from Depression Glass Glaze and other sources)

Pattern	Object	Year reproduction first reported	How to tell the original from the reproduction
Avocado	Pitcher, blue	1974	Not an original color
Avocado	Pitcher, frosted pink	1974	Not an original color
Avocado	Pitcher, green	1979	Darker than original
Avocado	Pitcher, pink	1974	More orange than original
Avocado	Pitcher, red amethyst	1974	Not an original color
Avocado	Pitcher, yellow	1974	Not an original color
Avocado	Tumbler, blue	1974	Not an original color
Avocado	Tumbler, green	1979	Darker than original
Avocado	Tumbler, frosted pink	1974	Not an original color
Avocado	Tumbler, pink	1974	More orange than original
Avocado	Tumbler, red amethyst	1974	Not an original color
Avocado	Tumbler, yellow	1974	Not an original color
Bottom's-Up	Tumbler, black	1979	No patent date on reproduction, lacks detail
Bottom's-Up	Tumbler, custard	1979	No patent date on reproduction, lacks detail
Bottom's-Up	Tumbler, jade	1979	No patent date on reproduction, lacks detail
Bubble	Ashtray, square, 3 sizes, red	1977–1978	

Pattern	Object	Year reproduction first reported	How to tell the original from the reproduction
Bubble	Bowl, 4½ in., red	1977–1978	
Bubble	Bowl, 8 in., red	1977–1978	
Bubble	Ivy ball, red	1977–1978	
Bubble	Punch cup, red	1977–1978	
Bubble	Vase, 3¾ in., red	1977–1978	Ruffled top
Cape Cod	Dinner set	1978	
Cherry Blossom	Butter dish, dark green	1976	Not an original color
Cherry Blossom	Butter dish, light blue	1976	Not an original color
Cherry Blossom	Butter dish, light green	1976	
Cherry Blossom	Butter dish, pink	1976	
Cherry Blossom	Butter dish, child's size, cobalt blue	1973	Never an original, crude decorations
Cherry Blossom	Butter dish, child's size, iridescent	1973	Never an original, crude decorations
Cherry Blossom	Butter dish, child's size, light green	1973	Never an original, crude decorations
Cherry Blossom	Butter dish, child's size, pink	1973	Never an original, crude decorations

Pattern	Object	Year reproduction first reported	How to tell the original from the reproduction
Cherry Blossom	Cup, blue delphite	1977	
Cherry Blossom	Cup, child's size, pink, possibly other colors	1973	Pronounced collar base, crude decorations
Cherry Blossom	Pitcher, blue	1979	Pattern almost obscure, sharply defined panel ridges, bottom scallops thicker and flatter than original
Cherry Blossom	Pitcher, pink	1979	Pattern almost obscure, sharply defined panel ridges, bottom scallops thicker and flatter than original
Cherry Blossom	Plate, child's size, blue	1973	Off color
Cherry Blossom	Plate, child's size delphite	1973	Off color
Cherry Blossom	Plate, child's size, green	1973	Off color
Cherry Blossom	Plate, child's size, pink	1973	Off color
Cherry Blossom	Salt & pepper shaker, blue delphite	1977	Scalloped glass ledge below top is rounded on original, more squared off on reproduction

Pattern	Object	Year reproduction first reported	How to tell the original from the reproduction
Cherry Blossom	Salt & pepper shaker, green	1977	Scalloped glass ledge below top is rounded on original, more squared off on reproduction
Cherry Blossom	Salt & pepper shaker, pink	1977	Scalloped glass ledge below top is rounded on original, more squared off on reproduction
Cherry Blossom	Saucer, blue	1973	Off color
Cherry Blossom	Saucer, green	1973	Off color
Cherry Blossom	Saucer, pink	1973	Off color
Cherry Blossom	Tumbler, footed, pink	1979	Pattern almost obscure, sharply defined panel ridges, bottom scallops thicker and flatter than original
Indiana Sandwich	Dinner set, amber	1969	Not an original color
Indiana Sandwich	Dinner set, dark blue	1969	Not an original color
Indiana Sandwich	Dinner set, crystal	1978	
Indiana Sandwich	Dinner set, red	1969	

Pattern	Object	Year reproduction first reported	How to tell the original from the reproduction
Iris	Candy dish (bottom only), multicolored	1976	Does not have rayed bottom
Iris	Vase, multicolored	1976	Does not have rayed bottom
Madrid	Dinner set, amber	1976–1979	Marked '76, new mold
Mayfair	Shot glass, blue	1977	Not an original color
Mayfair	Shot glass, green	1977	Not an original color
Mayfair	Shot glass, pink	1977	Lighter than original color
Miss America	Butter dish, amberina	1977	Knob is larger on reproduction
Miss America	Butter dish, crystal	1977	Knob is larger on reproduction
Miss America	Butter dish, green	1977	Knob is larger on reproduction
Miss America	Butter dish, ice blue	1977	Knob is larger on reproduction
Miss America	Butter dish, pink	1977	Knob is larger on reproduction
Miss America	Salt & pepper, crystal	1977	
Miss America	Salt & pepper, green	1977	
Miss America	Salt & pepper, pink	1977	

Pattern	Object	Year production first reported	How to tell the original from the reproduction
Royal Ruby	Tumbler, 7 oz.	1977–1978	Anchor Hocking catalog lists as "Newport," sides taper to base unlike original
Royal Ruby	Tumbler, 9 oz.	1977–1978	Anchor Hocking catalog lists as "Newport," sides taper to base unlike original
Royal Ruby	Tumbler, 12 oz.	1977–1978	Anchor Hocking catalog lists as "Newport," sides taper to base unlike original
Royal Ruby	Tumbler, 16 oz.	1977–1978	Anchor Hocking catalog lists as "Newport," sides taper to base unlike original
Sandwich	Cookie jar, covered, clear	1977	One inch higher than original
Sharon	Butter dish, amber	1976	Off color
Sharon	Butter dish, blue	1976	Not an original color
Sharon	Butter dish, dark green	1976	Not an original color
Sharon	Butter dish, light green	1976	Knob higher than original, other noticeable variations
Sharon	Butter dish, pink	1976	Knob higher than original, other noticeable variations
Sharon	Cheese dish, green	1977	

American Dinnerware

Introduction

The ceramic dinnerware that was made in America from the 1930s through the 1950s is just attracting the 1980 collectors. Some refer to it as "Depression dinnerware," but the name used by the manufacturers was "American dinnerware" and that is the name that most researchers hope will be the term used by collectors and dealers.

Pottery, porcelain, semiporcelain, ironstone, and other ceramic ware are included in the category of dinnerware. Most of them were made in potteries located in Southern Ohio, and in West Virginia near the Ohio River. Each factory made many patterns for sale to gift shops and department stores. They also made special patterns that stores could use either as premiums and give away free or sell for low prices or for any other types of store promotions.

American dinnerware patterns fall into six categories. The first to be rediscovered by collectors and the first to be reproduced have been the solid-colored pottery lines such as "Fiesta" or "Harlequin." Some of this type of dinnerware originally was also made in California potteries.

Many manufacturers preferred hand-painted decorations on their dinnerware. Included in this group are the pieces made by Southern Potteries under the name "Blue Ridge" and the pottery by Stangl picturing fruit, flowers, or birds.

An unusual type of dinnerware made by Harker, and others, was "Cameo Ware": A solid-color plate embellished with a white decoration that appears to be cut into the colored glaze.

Realistically shaped pieces resembling corn were produced by several makers; the most important was "Corn King" by the Shawnee Pottery Company. Green and yellow dishes were made in full sets. Other sets of dishes in three-dimensional shapes include the "Little Red Riding Hood" line, and many cookie jars and salt and pepper shakers.

Some of the dishes were made in very modern shapes with solid-color decorations. The innovative shapes and subtle earth-tone colorings made them a favorite in the 1940s and 1950s—e.g., wares designed by Russel Wright and made by several firms, and the "Tricorne" line by Salem.

Most of the dinnerware was decorated with decal designs: colored, printed patterns applied to the dishes. The most famous of these designs, "Autumn Leaf," was made for and sold by the Jewel Tea Company. Mexican-inspired designs such as "Mexicana" by Homer Laughlin were popular during the late 1930s. The Hall China Company made a lot of decal-decorated ware, including "Poppy," "Red Poppy," and "Crocus." Black silhouette designs against light-colored dishes were popular in the 1930s—e.g., "Silhouette" by the Crooksville China Company and "Taverne" by the Hall China Company.

Thousands of American dinnerware designs have been made since 1930 and the research has just begun. A partial list of patterns, makers, shapes, and dates is included in the back of this book.

It is important to remember that the descriptions of dinnerware may include many strange names. Some are the factory names, some names refer to the pattern (decorations applied to the piece), and many of the names were used by the factory to describe the shape: e.g., "Taverne" is a pattern," "Laurel" is the shape of the dish used to make that pattern, and "Taylor-Smith-Taylor" is the name of the company that made the dinnerware.

Pieces of American dinnerware are being discovered in attics, basements, garage sales, flea markets, and antique shops. The publications that offer them through the mail use descriptions that often include both the pattern and the shape name. It is important to learn to recognize the shapes that were used by each maker.

This book has been written as a guide to the marketplace. For more in-depth study read the specialized books about each factory listed in the Bibliography.

Bibliography

Bougie, Stanley J. and David A. Newkirk. *Red Wine Dinnerware.* Monticello, MN, 1980.

Cunningham, Jo. *The Autumn Leaf Story.* Springfield, MO: Haf-a-Productions, 1976.

Duke, Harvey. "Superior Quality Hall China." Otisville, MI: *Depression Glass Daze,* 1977.

Eaklor, Thomas W. *A Collector's Guide to Russel Wright.* Privately Printed: 1912 S. Street, N.W., #1, Washington, DC: 1978.

Fridley, A. W. *Catalina Pottery: The Early Years 1927–1937.* Costa Mesa, CA: Rainbow Publications, 1977.

Hayes, Barbara, and Jean Bauer. *The California Pottery Rainbow.* Privately Printed: 1629 W. Washington Blvd., Venice, CA , 1975.

Huxford, Bob and Sharon. *The Collectors Encyclopedia of Fiesta.* Paducah, KY: Collector Books, 1976.

Kerr, Ann. *The Steubenville Saga.* Privately Printed: P.O. Box 437, Sidney, OH, 1979.

Lehner, Lois. *Ohio Pottery And Glass Marks and Manufacturers.* Des Moines, IA: Wallace-Homestead, 1978.

Nelson, Maxine Feek. *Versatile Vernon Kilns.* Costa Mesa, CA: Rainbow Publications, 1978.

Newbound, Betty and Bill. *Southern Potteries Inc. Blue Ridge Dinnerware.* Privately Printed: 4567 Chadsworth, Union Lake, MI, 1979

Rehl, Norma. *The Collectors Handbook of Stangl Pottery.* Flemington, NJ: Democrat Press, 1979.

Riederer, LaHoma and Charles Bettinger. *Fiesta II: A Collector's Guide to Fiesta, Harlequin, and Riviera Dinnerware.* Privately Printed: P.O. Box 2733, Monroe, LA, 1976.

Simon, Dolores. *Shawnee Potter.* Paducah, KY: Collector Books, 1977.

Hall Teapots

The Hall China Company of East Liverpool, Ohio, started working in 1903. In 1920 they started making a line of teapots. Each pot has a special design name but may be made in a variety of colors.

Accordian Pleats, see Round Robin

Airflow, Cadet, Gold Flowers	25.00
Airflow, Cobalt & Gold	20.00
Airflow, Lettuce & Gold	20.00
Airflow, Poppy Red	28.00
Airflow, Turquoise & Gold	20.00
Airflow, Yellow & Gold	17.50
Aladdin, Black	12.00
Aladdin, Black, Gold Trim, Round Lid	18.00
Aladdin, Black, Infuser	20.00 to 25.00
Aladdin, Black, Oval Lid	15.00
Aladdin, Cadet	10.00 to 18.50
Aladdin, Cobalt, Gold Trim, Round Lid	18.00
Aladdin, Daffodil, Infuser	12.00
Aladdin, Delphinium, Gold Trim	17.00
Aladdin, Emerald	12.00 to 15.00
Aladdin, Forest Green, Gold Trim, Round Lid	18.00
Aladdin, Marine	12.00
Aladdin, Matte Black, Infuser	25.00
Aladdin, Red, Marine, Gold Trim	18.00
Aladdin, Red, Pink, Gold Trim	10.00
Aladdin, Yellow, Gold Trim, Round Lid	18.00
Albany, Cobalt, Gold Decoration	35.00
Albany, Mahogany & Gold	20.00
Albany, Turquoise	15.00
Albany, Turquoise, Gold Decoration	20.00
Automobile, Canary	30.00
Baltimore, Cadet & Gold	22.50
Baltimore, Maroon	22.50
Baltimore, Pink	7.50
Basket, Delphinium, Silver Decoration	45.00
Basketball, Chinese Red	20.00
Boston, Camellia, Gold Trim, 6 Cup	20.00
Boston, Canary, Gold Trim, 6 Cup	20.00
Boston, Cobalt, Gold Trim, 6 Cup	20.00
Boston, Delphinium, Gold Trim, 6 Cup	20.00
Boston, Golden Glo, 8 Cup	30.00
Boston, Green, Gold Trim, 6 Cup	20.00
Boston, Monterrey, Gold Trim, 6 Cup	20.00
Boston, Yellow, Gold Trim, 6 Cup	18.00 to 20.00
Cleveland, Cobalt, Gold Butterflies	15.00
Cleveland, Green, Gold Butterflies	20.00
Cleveland, Yellow, Gold Design	35.00
Disraeli, Pink	18.00

Doughnut, Forest Green 14.50
French, Cadet 18.50
French, Celadon & Gold, 4 Cup 14.00
French, Cobalt & Gold, 6 Cup 10.00
French, Daffodil, Gold Daisies, 12 Cup 45.00
French, Turquoise, Gold Daisy 18.00
French, Turquoise, 6 Cup 16.00
French, Yellow, Gold Daisies 16.00
Hollywood, Camellia & Gold 12.00
Hollywood, Maroon 17.50
Hollywood, Maroon & Gold, 6 Cup 18.00
Hollywood, Yellow & Gold .... 15.00 to 17.00
Hook Cover, Cadet .... 7.50 to 13.00
Hook Cover, Cadet, Gold Decoration .... 15.00 to 18.00
Hook Cover, Delphinium, Gold Trim 15.00
Hook Cover, Ivory, Gold Trim 20.00
Lipton, Camellia 7.50
Lipton, Cobalt, Gold Trim 10.00
Lipton, Delphinium 18.00
Los Angeles, Cobalt, 8 Cup 25.00
Los Angeles, Matte Black, Gold Handle & Trim 16.00
Manhattan, Blue & Gold, 4 Cup 16.00
Manhattan, Celadon & Gold 14.00
Manhattan, Green & Gold, 4 Cup .... 10.00 to 14.00
Manhattan, Ivory, Roses, 4 Cup 10.00
Manhattan, Yellow, Gold Trim, 4 Cup 10.00
McCormick, Maroon 13.00
Melody, Chinese Red 20.00
Moderne, Canary, Gold Trim 10.00
Moderne, Daffodil 20.00
New York, Camellia & Gold, Cup 17.50
New York, Cobalt, Gold Trim, 2 Cup 7.00
New York, Emerald & Gold, 4 Cup 7.00
New York, Green Lustre, 2 Cup 10.00
New York, Ivory, Gold Flowers, 2 Cup 12.00
New York, Pink, 6 Cup 15.00
New York, Rose 8.75
Parade, Camellia 10.00
Parade, Canary 12.00
Parade, Canary & Gold 18.00
Parade, Daffodil .... 9.00 to 12.00
Parade, Rose 10.00
Parade, Yellow 12.00
Philadelphia, Brown, Gold Trim, 8 Cup 17.50
Philadelphia, Cobalt, Gold Circles, 8 Cup 15.00
Philadelphia, Cobalt, 7 Cup 15.00
Philadelphia, Daffodil, Gold Decoration, 6 Cup 18.00
Philadelphia, Pink, 6 Cup 20.00
Saf-Handle, Cobalt, 4 Cup 15.00
Sani-Grid, Cadet 12.00
Sani-Grid, Chinese Red, 6 Cup .... 12.00 to 18.50
Sani-Grid, Cobalt, Gold Handle 15.00

Star, Camellia 12.00
Star, Turquoise .... 12.00 to 19.00
Streamline, Black, Gold Trim 20.00
Streamline, Canary 20.00
Streamline, Cobalt, Gold Trim 15.00
Streamline, Delphinium, Gold Trim 15.00
Streamline, Emerald 20.00
Streamline, Ivory, Silhouette 18.00
Surfside, Emerald 50.00
Tea for Two, Stock Green 4.00
Victoria, Celadon .... 12.00 to 22.50
Windshield, Camellia 15.00
Windshield, Camellia & Gold 12.00
Windshield, Cobalt, Gold Roses 15.00
Windshield, Delphinium & Gold 15.00
Windshield, Ivory, Gold Dot .... 10.00 to 20.00
Windshield, Maroon, Gold Roses .... 12.00 to 15.00

Amberstone

Amberstone was made by the Homer Laughlin China Company, Newell, West Virginia, about 1967. It is a brown decorated ware on a Fiesta body shape. It was made exclusively for supermarket promotions.

Berry Bowl	1.50	Pie Baker	17.00
Bowl, Fruit, 5 1/2 In.	3.00	Plate, Salad, 7 1/4 In.	2.50
Bowl, Vegetable, 9 In.	8.00	Plate, 10 1/4 In.	4.00
Bread & Butter, 6 1/4 In.	1.50	Saltshaker	4.00
Cup & Saucer Set	5.00	Saucer	1.00

Autumn Leaf

Autumn Leaf china was made for the Jewel Tea Company from 1936. Hall China Company, East Liverpool, Ohio, Crooksville China Company, Crooksville, Ohio, Harker Potteries, Chester, West Virginia, and Paden City Pottery, Paden City, West Virginia, made dishes with this design.

Bean Pot, Handle	135.00	Cookie Jar, Big Ear	65.00
Berry Bowl, 5 1/2 In.	4.50	Cookie Jar, Tootsie	45.00 to 50.00
Bowl, Cereal	5.00 to 6.00	Cookware Set, 7 Pieces	65.00
Bowl, Fruit	2.00 to 2.50	Creamer	5.00 to 15.00
Bowl, Fruit, 5 1/2 In.	2.00	Creamer, Sunshine	5.00 to 6.00
Bowl, Mixing	7.00 to 20.00	Creamer, 4 1/2 In.	9.00
Bowl, Salad, 9 In.	6.00 to 15.00	Cup	1.75 to 5.00
Bowl, Stacking, Covered Set	32.00	Cup & Saucer	3.25 to 6.50
Bowl, Sunshine, 6 1/4 In.	10.00	Custard	2.50 to 4.00
Bowl, Sunshine, 7 1/2 In.	6.00	Dish, Pickle	8.00
Bowl, Sunshine, 9 In.	8.00	Drippings Jar, Covered	7.00 to 15.00
Bowl, Utility, 7 1/2 In.	8.00	Fluted Baker, 4 In.	3.50 to 6.00
Bowl, Utility, 9 In.	10.00	Gravy Boat	7.00 to 12.50
Bowl, Vegetable, Oval	6.00 to 7.50	Jar, Grease	9.00
Bowl, Vegetable, Oval, 10 1/2 In.	18.00	Jar, Marmalade	10.00
Bowl, Vegetable, 9 In.	12.00	Jar, Marmalade, 3 Piece	30.00 to 35.00
Bowl, 5 In.	3.00	Mug	17.00
Bowl, 5 1/2 In.	2.50 to 4.00	Mustard Pot, 3 Piece	22.00 to 35.00
Bowl, 5 5/8 In.	2.25	Pepper, Shaker, Range	5.00
Bowl, 6 In.	3.00	Percolator, Electric	150.00
Bowl, 6 1/4 In.	2.00 to 8.00	Pie Baker	8.00
Casserole Set	35.00	Pie Baker, 4 Small Fluted Bakers	22.00
Casserole, Covered	18.00 to 25.00	Pitcher, Utility, 6 In.	7.50 to 12.00
Clock	300.00	Plate, Cake, 9 1/2 In.	6.00 to 15.00
Coaster	4.00 to 5.00	Plate, 6 In.	2.50 to 2.75
Coffee Server, 8 1/2 In.	16.00 to 28.00	Plate, 7 In.	2.25 to 3.75
Coffee, Irish	4.00	Plate, 7 1/2 In.	5.00
Coffeepot	25.00 to 30.00	Plate, 8 In.	3.50
Coffeepot, Sunshine	22.00 to 25.00	Plate, 9 In.	3.00 to 5.00

Plate, 10 In. .... 4.25 to 10.00
Platter, 11 In. 8.00
Platter, 13 In. 12.00
Platter, 14 In. 10.00
Sauce 2.50
Saucer .... 1.00 to 1.75
Shaker, Handle, Large 15.00
Shaker, Range, Pair ... 10.00 to 15.00
Shaker, 2 1/2 In., Pair 6.50
Sifter 17.50
Soup, Cream .... 4.50 to 17.50
Soup, Flat .... 5.50 to 60.00
Sugar & Creamer, Open 12.00
Sugar & Creamer, Ruffled, Covered 14.50
Sugar, Covered .... 3.50 to 6.00
Sugar, Sunshine 6.00
Teapot, Aladdin .... 16.00 to 25.00
Teapot, Long Spout 38.00
Thermos 200.00
Tray, Glass, Wooden Handle ... 55.00
Tray, Oval, 18 3/4 In. 15.00
Tumbler, Frosted, 7 Oz. 10.00
Tumbler, Frosted, 14 Oz. 14.00
Underplate 9.50
Vase 100.00

Autumn Leaf

Warmer, Oval 85.00
Water Jug .... 12.00 to 15.00
Water Jug .... 12.00 to 15.00
Water Jug, Ice Lip, 5 1/2 Pt. 10.00 to
.... 18.00

Ballerina

Ballerina was made by Universal Potteries, Cambridge, Ohio, from 1952 to 1956. It was made in Forest Green, Burgundy, Chartreuse, Dove Gray, Sierra Rust, Moss Rose and Pine Cone.

CLEAR
  Bowl, 7 3/4 In. 2.50
BURGUNDY
  Bowl, 9 1/4 In. 3.00
  Plate, 6 1/8 In. 1.00
  Plate, 9 1/4 In. 2.25

GRAY
  Plate, 6 1/8 In. 1.00
  Plate, 9 1/4 In. 2.25
GREEN
  Plate, 6 1/8 In. 1.00
  Plate, 9 1/4 In. 2.25

Banded

Banded was first made by the Hall China Company, East Liverpool, Ohio, in 1937. It is the name of both a solid color line and of the shape for some decal-decorated pieces.

RED
  Pitcher 8.00

Syrup, Covered 20.00

Bauer, see Ring

Blue Bouquet

Blue Bouquet was made by the Hall China Company, East Liverpool, Ohio, in the early 1950s through the early 1960s as a premium for Standard Coffee, New Orleans, Louisiana.

Bowl, Salad	12.00	Pitcher, 6 In.	5.00
Bowl, Vegetable, 9 3/8 In.	11.00	Plate, 6 3/8 In.	2.00
Bowl, 6 In.	4.00	Plate, 11 In.	4.50
Bowl, 6 1/2 In.	4.75	Spoon	12.50
Bowl, 11 3/4 In.	12.00	Sugar, Boston	5.00
Casserole, Big Lip	12.00	Water Jug, Colonial	8.00
Cup & Saucer	6.00		

Blue Parade, see Rose Parade

Blueberry

Blueberry (pattern No. 3770) was first made by Stangl Pottery, Trenton, New Jersey, in 1950.

Cup, Stangl	2.00
Nappy, 5 1/2 In., Stangl	3.00

Blueberry

Brown-Eyed Susan

Brown-Eyed Susan was first made by the Vernon Kilns, Vernon, California, in the 1940s.

Bowl, 9 In.	4.00	Plate, Chop, 12 In.	5.00
Eggcup	12.50		

Calico Fruit

Calico Fruit was made by Universal Potteries, Cambridge, Ohio, a firm that started in 1934.

Casserole, Covered 15.00
Leftover, Covered 5.00
Pie Server 10.00

Calico Fruit

Caliente

Caliente was made by the Paden City Glass Company of Paden City, West Virginia.

Bowl, 5 In. .... .75 to 1.00   Plate, 10 In. 1.00
Plate, Handles, 7 In. .... .50

Cameo Rose, see White Rose

Cameo Ware

Cameo Ware was made by Harker China Company, Chester, West Virginia. The design is white and appears to be cut into the blue or pink background. Several patterns of Cameo Ware are known, including floral and animal designs.

BLUE
Bowl, Harker 5.50
Saucer, Square, Harker 1.50
Sugar & Creamer, Harker 8.50

PINK
Creamer, Harker 4.00
Plate, Square, 7 In., Harker 1.50
Plate, 9 In., Harker 3.00

Casualstone

Casualstone was made by Coventry in the 1970s.

Cup & Saucer .... 5.00   Plate, 10 1/4 In. 4.00

Cat Tail

Cat Tail was made by Universal Potteries, Cambridge, Ohio, for Sears, Roebuck and Company from 1934 to 1956.

Bowl, Oval, 9 In. 8.50
Bowl, Salad 5.00
Bowl, 6 In. 3.50
Casserole, 8 1/4 In. 10.00
Creamer .... 2.00 to 3.00
Pitcher, Milk, 6 1/4 In. 10.00
Pitcher, Water 4.00
Plate, 10 In. 4.00
Platter, Oval, 11 3/4 In. . 3.50 to 7.00
Platter, Oval, 13 In. 4.00
Platter, Oval, 13 1/2 In. . 4.50 to 8.00
Spoon, Serving 5.00
Water Jug 7.50
Water Jug, Covered, 1 Qt. 12.00

Cat Tail

Colonial Dogwood

Colonial Dogwood was made by Stangl Pottery, Trenton, New Jersey.

Cup & Saucer, Stangl 7.00

Colorado

Colorado, maker unknown.

BROWN

Bean Pot, Covered, Molded Handles
.... 10.00
Bowl, Cereal, 5 1/2 In. 3.00
Cup & Saucer 5.00

Dutch Oven, 9 1/2 In. 12.00
Mug, Handle 5.00
Plate, 9 1/2 In. 3.00
Sugar, Covered 6.00

Coors, see Rosebud

Corn King

Corn King was made by Shawnee Pottery Company, Zanesville, Ohio, before 1954. The color was changed slightly in 1954 and the pattern was renamed Corn Queen.

Bowl, Cereal	5.00	Salt & Pepper	16.00
Bowl, Fruit, Covered	12.00	Shaker, Corn	3.50
Butter, Covered	25.00	Shaker, Milk	7.50
Casserole, Covered	18.00	Shaker, 3 1/2 In.	4.00
Cookie Jar	20.00	Shaker, 5 In.	8.00
Creamer .... 7.00 to	13.00	Sugar, Covered .... 10.00 to	22.00
Dish, Relish	7.00	Teapot .... 20.00 to	35.00
Mug	20.00	Teapot, Individual	42.00
Plate, 7 In.	4.00		

Corn Queen

Corn Queen was made by Shawnee Pottery Company, Zanesville, Ohio, from 1954 to 1961.

Butter, Covered	32.00	Shaker, 5 1/2 In., Pair	15.00
Mug	18.00	Sugar, Open	10.00
Pitcher, Cream	12.00		
Pitcher, Milk, 8 1/2 In.	28.00		
Shaker, 3 1/2 In., Pair	9.50		

Crab Apple

Crab Apple was made by Southern Potteries Inc., Ervin, Tennessee, under the trade name Blue Ridge after 1930, before 1957.

Plate, 5 1/2 In., Blue Ridge	2.00	Saucer, Blue Ridge	1.25

Crocus

Crocus was made by Hall China Company, East Liverpool, Ohio, in the 1930s. It is sometimes called Holland. Another pattern called Crocus was made by Stangl Pottery, Trenton, New Jersey.

Bowl, Fruit	4.50	Bowl, Sunshine, No.4	12.00
Bowl, Salad	15.00	Bowl, Vegetable, Round	15.00
Bowl, Sunshine, No.3	10.00	Bowl, Vegetable, 10 1/4 In. 10.00 to	15.00

Casserole, Covered, Sunshine	5.00
Coffeepot With Grinder	25.00
Cup	8.00
Cup & Saucer .... 7.00 to	7.50
Drippings Jar	15.00
Gravy Boat .... 10.00 to	12.50
Jar, Pretzel, Open	10.00
Pie Server, 8 1/4 In.	5.50
Plate .... 6.50 to	7.50
Plate, 6 1/4 In.	3.00
Plate, 7 In.	4.00

Plate, 7 In., Stangl	2.00
Plate, 8 1/4 In.	6.00
Platter, 11 1/2 X 8 3/4 In.	15.00
Platter, 13 3/4 In. X 10 1/4 In.	9.00 to
....	18.00
Saltshaker	8.00
Saucer	2.50
Shaker, Pair	16.00
Soup, Flat, 8 1/4 In.	6.00
Sugar & Creamer, Covered 15.00 to 25.00	

Cumberland

Cumberland was made by Southern Potteries Inc., Ervin, Tennessee, under the trade name Blue Ridge after 1930, before 1957.

Saucer, Blue Ridge 1.25

Dogwood

Dogwood was made by Homer Laughlin China Company, Newell, West Virginia. Another pattern with the same name was introduced by Stangl Pottery Company, Zanesville, Ohio, in 1965.

Cup, Stangl .... 3.00 to 5.00   Saucer, 6 In., Homer Laughlin .. 1.00

Eggshell Theme

Eggshell Theme was made by Homer Laughlin China Company, Newell, West Virginia, in the 1940s.

Bowl, Vegetable, Oval, 9 In.	9.00	Plate, 8 In.	1.50
Creamer, Footed	3.00	Plate, 10 In.	2.25
Plate, 6 In.	1.25	Platter, 15 1/2 In.	9.50

Eureka Serenade

Eureka Serenade was made by Hall China Company, East Liverpool, Ohio.

Coffeepot, Stepdown	25.00	Plate, 7 In.	3.00
Creamer, O Line	5.00	Plate, 9 In.	3.50
Cup	3.50	Saucer	1.50

Fiesta

Fiesta was introduced in 1936 by Homer Laughlin China Company, Newell, West Virginia. It was made until 1972.

ANTIQUE GOLD
Plate, 6 In. 75
BLUE
Ashtray .... 9.00 to 16.00
Base, Syrup 28.00
Bowl, Fruit, 4 3/4 In. 4.50 5.50
Bowl, Fruit, 5 1/2 In. 5.00
Bowl, Nested, No.1, 6 In. 10.00
Bowl, 5 1/2 In. .... 4.00 to 5.00
Bowl, 9 In. 5.50
Bowl, 9 1/2 In. 20.00
Casserole, Covered 22.00
Coffeepot, Embossed Mark 10.00 to 35.00
Creamer, Stick .... 6.50 to 12.50
Cup & Saucer .... 6.50 to 12.50
Cup & Saucer, After Dinner ... 22.50
Eggcup, Embossed Mark 12.00 to 18.00
Gravy Boat .... 6.00 to 12.50
Jar, Marmalade, Covered 60.00
Mug 7.50
Mug, Tom & Jerry 11.00
Mustard Pot 35.00
Mustard Pot, Covered .. 35.00 to 50.00
Nappy, Embossed Mark, 8 1/2 In. 6.00
Pitcher, Disk, Water, 2 Qt. 16.00 to 22.00
Pitcher, Tilt 10.00
Pitcher, 8 Tumblers 32.00
Plate, Chop, 13 In. ..... 4.50 to 12.00
Plate, Ink Mark, 8 In. ... 6.00 to 7.00
Plate, 6 In. .... .75 to 2.00
Plate, 7 In. .... 1.50 to 3.00
Plate, 9 In. .... 1.00 to 4.00
Plate, 10 In. .... 1.00 to 5.00
Plate, 12 In. 8.00
Plate, 15 In. 9.00
Platter, Oval, 12 In. .... 7.00 to 10.00
Salt & Pepper 5.00
Saucer .... .75 to 2.00
Shaker .... 2.00 to 3.50
Soup, Cream .... 6.00 to 12.50
Soup, Flat 12.00
Spoon 30.00
Sugar 3.50
Sugar & Creamer 12.50
Sugar, Covered .... 8.00 to 9.00
Teapot 20.00

Tray, Utility 7.00
Tumbler, Juice, 5 Oz. ... 6.50 to 10.00
Tumbler, Water 18.00
Tumbler, 10 Oz. ...... 12.95 to 14.00
Vase, 6 In. 12.00
Vase, 8 In. 65.00
CHARTREUSE
Ashtray 18.00
Bowl, Embossed, 6 In. 9.00
Bowl, Fruit, 4 3/4 In. 5.00
Bowl, Fruit, 5 1/2 In. 6.50
Bowl, 4 1/2 In. .... 5.50 to 12.00
Creamer .... 4.00 to 6.00
Cup & Saucer, Ink Mark 14.00

Fiesta

Eggcup .... 13.50 to 22.00
Nappy, 8 1/2 In. 12.50
Pitcher, Water .... 10.75 to 18.50
Plate, Ink Mark, 6 In. ... 3.00 to 7.00
Plate, Ink Mark, 7 In. 3.50

Plate, Ink Mark, 9 In. ... 3.25 to 5.00
Plate, 8 In. .... 9.00 to 12.00
Plate, 10 In. 18.00
Plate, 12 1/2 In. 6.00
Plate, 15 In. 25.00
Platter, Oval, 12 In. ... 12.00 to 14.00
Salt & Pepper 7.00
Saltshaker 4.00
Saucer .... 2.00 to 10.00
Soup, Flat, 8 In. ...... 10.00 to 20.00
Water Jug, 1/2 Gal. 15.00
Water Jug, 2 Pt. ...... 18.50 to 22.50

DARK BLUE
Pie Server 30.00

DARK GREEN
Bowl, Embossed Mark, 6 In. ... 11.00
Bowl, Fruit, 4 3/4 In. 5.50
Bowl, Fruit, 5 1/2 In. 6.50
Mug 18.00
Plate, Ink Mark, 6 In. 3.00
Plate, Ink Mark, 7 In. 3.50
Plate, Ink Mark, 8 In. 9.00
Plate, Ink Mark, 9 In. 4.50

FOREST GREEN
Ashtray 18.00
Creamer 5.00
Salt & Pepper 10.00
Water Jug, 2 Pt. 18.00

GRAY
Ashtray .... 18.00 to 19.50
Bowl, Fruit, 4 3/4 In. 5.00
Bowl, Fruit, 5 1/2 In. .... 6.00 to 7.00
Bowl, Vegetable 10.00
Bowl, 4 1/2 In. 12.00
Bowl, 5 1/2 In. 14.00
Bowl, 6 In. 18.00
Creamer 5.00
Cup 7.00
Cup & Saucer .... 9.50 to 14.00
Eggcup 13.50
Mug .... 20.00 to 29.00
Mug, Tom & Jerry 16.00
Nappy, 8 1/2 In. .... 8.00 to 12.50
Plate, Grill 18.00
Plate, Ink Mark, 7 In. ... 3.50 to 8.00
Plate, Ink Mark, 8 In. 9.00
Plate, Ink Mark, 9 In. 4.50
Plate, Ink Mark, 10 In. . 5.00 to 15.00
Plate, 6 In. .... 1.50 to 3.00
Plate, 15 In. 30.00
Platter, 15 In. .... 3.00 to 14.00
Salt & Pepper 7.00

Shaker 3.50
Soup, Cream .... 10.00 to 15.00
Soup, Flat 10.00
Sugar 7.50
Water Jug, 2 Pt. 20.00

GREEN
Ashtray 16.50
Base, Syrup 28.00
Bowl, Fruit, 4 3/4 In. 5.00
Bowl, Fruit, 5 1/2 In. ... 3.00 to 10.00
Bowl, Nested 15.00
Bowl, Salad 35.00
Bowl, Stack Set 65.00
Bowl, Vegetable 10.00
Bowl, 4 1/2 In. .... 3.50 to 12.00
Bowl, 5 1/2 In. .... 4.00 to 15.00
Bowl, 6 In. .... 4.50 to 18.00
Bowl, 8 1/2 In. 6.00
Bowl, 9 1/2 In. 20.00
Candleholder, Bulb 10.00
Carafe 30.00
Casserole 24.00
Casserole, Covered, 8 1/2 In. ... 50.00
Creamer .... 5.00 to 20.00
Creamer, Stick 5.00
Cup .... 4.00 to 9.00
Cup & Saucer .... 7.00 to 12.00
Eggcup .... 13.50 to 16.00
Fork .... 17.00 to 27.50
Gravy Boat .... 10.00 to 20.00
Mug .... 20.00 to 29.00
Mug, Tom & Jerry .... 12.00 to 16.00
Mustard Pot, Covered 20.00
Nappy, 5 1/2 In. 5.00
Nappy, 8 1/2 In. .... 7.50 to 15.00
Nappy, 9 1/2 In. 12.00
Pitcher, Water .... 16.00 to 18.50
Plate, Calendar, Good Luck 27.50
Plate, Chop, 13 In. 10.00
Plate, Deep, 8 1/2 In. ... 6.00 to 12.50
Plate, Grill, 10 1/2 In. .. 8.00 to 15.00
Plate, 6 In. .... .75 to 9.00
Plate, 7 In. .... 2.00 to 8.00
Plate, 9 In. .... 1.50 to 12.00
Plate, 10 In. .... 4.50 to 10.00
Platter, Holder, 13 In. 55.00
Platter, 12 In. .... 3.00 to 14.00
Relish Side Insert 5.00
Salt & Pepper 7.00
Saucer .... .75 to 3.00
Shaker .... 2.00 to 18.00
Soup, Cream .... 6.00 to 20.00

Soup, Flat 7.75
Sugar .... 1.50 to 3.50
Sweetmeat 12.00
Tray, Utility 7.00
Tumbler, Juice, 5 Oz. ... 9.00 to 10.00
Tumbler, 10 Oz. 12.00
Vase, Bud .... 15.00 to 18.00
Vase, 8 In. 65.00
Water Jug, 2 Pt. ...... 10.00 to 22.50

LIGHT GREEN

Ashtray 15.00
Bowl, Embossed Mark, 6 In. 9.00
Bowl, Fruit, 4 3/4 In. 4.50
Bowl, Fruit, 5 1/2 In. 5.00
Bowl, 5 1/2 In. .... 4.50 to 8.00
Candleholder, Bulb 15.00
Casserole .... 15.00 to 24.00
Cup & Saucer, After Dinner ... 22.50
Cup & Saucer, Ink Mark 12.50
Eggcup, Embossed 18.00
Fork 30.00
Nappy, Embossed Mark, 8 1/2 In. 9.00
Plate, Compartment, 11 1/2 In. . 15.00
Plate, Ink Mark, 6 In. 2.00
Plate, Ink Mark, 7 In. 2.00
Plate, Ink Mark, 8 In. 7.50
Plate, 7 In. 2.50
Plate, 9 In. .... 1.50 to 3.00
Plate, 10 In. 7.50
Saucer, Ink Mark .... .75 to 1.50
Soup, Cream, Embossed Mark .. 10.00
Teapot, Covered, Embossed Mark 18.00
Tumbler, Embossed Mark, 10 Oz. 14.00
Tumbler, Juice, 5 Oz. 10.00

MEDIUM GREEN

Cup 6.00
Cup & Saucer, Ink Mark 20.00
Gravy Boat 10.00
Mug .... 25.00 to 29.50
Mug, Tom & Jerry, Ink Mark . 45.00
Plate, Ink Mark, 7 In. 10.00
Plate, Ink Mark, 8 In. 15.00
Plate, Ink Mark, 9 In. 12.50
Plate, 6 In. 7.50

OLD IVORY

Ashtray .... 8.00 to 8.50
Bowl, Fruit, 4 3/4 In. .... 4.50 to 5.00
Bowl, Fruit, 5 1/2 In. .... 4.50 to 5.00
Bowl, Vegetable 10.00
Bowl, 5 In. 5.50
Bowl, 8 1/2 In. .... 6.00 to 20.00
Coffeepot 28.50

Creamer 4.00
Creamer, Stick 5.00
Cup 7.00
Cup & Saucer .... 6.50 to 13.75
Eggcup, Embossed Mark 18.00
Gravy Boat 14.00
Jar, Marmalade, Covered 37.50 to 40.00
Mug 29.00
Mug, Tom & Jerry 20.00
Nappy 9.50
Pitcher, Disk .... 16.00 to 22.00
Plate, American Potter Mark, 10 In.
.... 14.75
Plate, Chop, 13 In. ...... 5.00 to 6.00
Plate, Chop, 15 In. 7.50
Plate, Compartment, 10 1/2 In . 12.50
Plate, Deep, 8 In. 6.00
Plate, Grill, 10 1/2 In. 15.00
Plate, Ink Mark, 6 In. ... 1.00 to 2.00
Plate, Ink Mark, 7 In. ... 2.00 to 2.50
Plate, Ink Mark, 8 In. 7.50
Plate, Ink Mark, 9 In. ... 3.00 to 4.00
Plate, 10 In. .... 4.50 to 6.00
Platter, Oval .... 6.00 to 14.00
Platter, 11 1/2 In. 7.00
Relish Side Insert 5.00
Salt & Pepper 7.00
Saucer .... .50 to 2.00
Shaker 9.00
Soup, Cream .... 8.00 to 9.00
Soup, Flat 8.00
Sugar 5.00
Sugar, Covered .... 7.50 to 10.00
Teapot, Covered 28.00
Tray, Utility .... 7.50 to 9.00
Tumbler, Juice, 5 Oz. 10.00

RED

Ashtray 18.00
Bowl, Embossed Mark, 5 1/2 In. 13.50
Bowl, Fruit, 4 3/4 In. .... 5.00 to 9.00
Bowl, Fruit, 5 1/2 In. ... 6.00 to 14.00
Bowl, Nested, Embossed Mark, 8 In.
.... 30.00
Bowl, Salad 35.00
Bowl, Salad, Footed 135.00
Bowl, 4 1/2 In. 5.25
Bowl, 8 1/2 In. 20.00
Bowl, 9 1/2 In. 15.00
Candleholder, Bulb, Pair 15.00
Candlestick, Tripod 75.00
Carafe 40.00
Coffeepot, Embossed Mark 15.00

Compote, 12 In. 45.00
Creamer, Embossed Mark   5.50 to 8.00
Cup 7.00
Cup & Saucer .... 7.50 to 12.00
Cup & Saucer, After Dinner ... 27.00
Eggcup, Embossed Mark 18.00 to 28.00
Gravy Boat .... 10.50 to 20.00
Jar, Marmalade, Covered 65.00
Mug 15.00
Mug, Tom & Jerry, Ink Mark . 45.00
Mustard Pot, Covered 75.00
Nappy, 8 1/2 In. ...... 10.00 to 12.50
Pepper Shaker 5.00
Pitcher, Disk 35.00
Pitcher, Ice Lip 20.00
Plate, Chop, 15 In. 15.00
Plate, Deep, 8 In. 8.00
Plate, Ink Mark, 6 In. ... 1.50 to 7.00
Plate, Ink Mark, 7 In. ... 3.00 to 8.00
Plate, Ink Mark, 9 In. ... 2.00 to 6.00
Plate, 13 In. 25.00
Plate, 14 1/2 In. 7.00
Platter, Oval, Ink Mark, 12 In.   12.00
Saucer, Ink Mark .... 1.50 to 3.00
Soup, Cream .... 12.00 to 20.00
Soup, Flat, 8 In. ...... 14.00 to 20.00
Soup, Onion 35.00
Spoon 32.50
Sugar .... 1.50 to 8.50
Sugar & Creamer, Stick 16.00
Sugar, Covered 15.00
Sweetmeat 22.50
Tumbler, Water 25.00
Vase, Bud, Embossed Mark 9.75 to 25.00
Vase, 10 In. 108.00
Water Jug, 2 Pt. 16.50
ROSE
Bowl, Fruit, 4 3/4 In. 5.50
Bowl, Fruit, 5 1/2 In. .... 3.00 to 6.50
Bowl, Vegetable 10.00
Bowl, 4 1/2 In. 6.00
Bowl, 6 In. .... 11.00 to 18.00
Casserole, Covered 45.00
Coffee Server 42.50
Cup 12.00
Cup & Saucer 3.50
Eggcup .... 13.50 to 22.00
Gravy Boat 20.00
Mug .... 22.00 to 29.00
Plate, Ink Mark, 6 In. ... 2.00 to 3.00
Plate, Ink Mark, 7 In. .... .75 to 8.00
Plate, Ink Mark, 8 In. ... 4.50 to 9.00

Plate, Ink Mark, 9 In. .. 1.50 to 12.00
Plate, 10 In. 5.00
Plate, 13 In. 25.00
Platter, 12 In. .... 3.00 to 14.00
Saucer .... 1.50 to 2.00
Shaker 5.00
Sugar, Embossed Mark 5.00
Tumbler, Juice, 5 Oz. ... 9.00 to 11.00
Water Jug, 2 Pt. ...... 10.00 to 22.50
TURF GREEN
Bowl, Soup 9.00
Bowl, 4 3/4 In. 5.00
Casserole, Covered 25.00
Gravy Boat 8.00
Pitcher, Water 22.00
Platter, 13 In. 9.50
Saucer 2.00
Shaker 3.50
Tumbler 10.00
TURQUOISE
Ashtray, Ink Mark .... 13.50 to 18.00
Base, Relish 8.00
Base, Syrup .... 11.00 to 28.00
Bowl, Fruit, 4 3/4 In. .... 3.50 to 5.00
Bowl, Fruit, 5 1/2 In. 5.00
Bowl, Salad .... 16.00 to 32.00
Bowl, Vegetable 10.00
Bowl, 6 In. .... 4.50 to 8.00
Candleholder, Bulb 10.00
Candleholder, Bulb, Pair 22.00
Candlestick, Tripod 35.00
Casserole, Handle, Covered 22.00
Coffeepot 28.50
Compote, 12 In. 14.50
Creamer 5.00
Cup .... 6.50 to 8.00
Cup & Saucer, After Dinner ... 22.50
Cup & Saucer, Ink Mark   6.50 to 18.50
Jar, Marmalade .... 45.00 to 47.50
Mug 16.00
Mug, Tom & Jerry 14.00
Nappy, 8 1/2 In. 8.00
Pitcher, Water, 2 Qt. .. 12.50 to 18.50
Plate, American Mark, 10 In. .. 16.00
Plate, Chop, Ink Mark, 13 In. ... 9.00
Plate, Deep, 8 In. 6.00
Plate, Grill, 10 1/2 In. 15.00
Plate, Ink Mark, 6 In. .... .75 to 3.00
Plate, Ink Mark, 7 In. ... 2.00 to 8.00
Plate, Ink Mark, 8 In. 7.50
Plate, Ink Mark, 9 In. ... 1.50 to 4.00
Plate, Ink Mark, 10 In. 7.50

Plate, 12 In. 9.50
Plate, 15 In. 8.00
Platter, Oval, 13 In. .... 5.00 to 10.00
Relish Side Insert ...... 5.00 to 12.00
Saucer .... .75 to 5.00
Shaker 2.00
Soup, Cream .... 6.00 to 10.00
Soup, Flat 6.25
Sugar 1.50
Sweetmeat .... 12.00 to 15.00
Syrup .... 55.00 to 65.00
Syrup, Covered 75.00
Tumbler, Juice, 5 Oz. .. 10.00 to 14.00
Vase, Bud 18.00
YELLOW
Bowl, Fruit, 4 3/4 In. .... 3.50 to 4.50
Bowl, Fruit, 5 1/2 In. .... 4.00 to 8.00
Casserole, Handle 15.00
Coffeepot 20.00
Compote, 12 In. 32.50
Creamer .... 3.00 to 5.00
Cup .... 6.00 to 7.50
Cup & Saucer .... 6.00 to 16.00
Eggcup, Embossed Mark 15.00 to 18.00
Gravy Boat .... 7.50 to 12.00
Jar, Marmalade 40.00
Mug .... 9.00 to 17.00
Mug, Tom & Jerry .... 14.00 to 16.00
Mustard Pot, Covered 45.00
Nappy, Embossed Mark, 8 1/2 In. 12.00
Nappy, 4 1/2 In. 5.00
Nappy, 5 1/2 In. 5.00
Nappy, 9 1/2 In. 12.00

Pitcher, Juice .... 5.00 to 50.00
Pitcher, Water .... 13.00 to 20.00
Plate, Cake 15.00
Plate, Compartment, 11 5/8 In. . 15.00
Plate, Deep, 8 In. 6.00
Plate, Good Luck Calendar, 10 In. 27.50
Plate, Grill, 10 1/2 In. 8.00
Plate, Grill, 11 1/2 In. 15.00
Plate, Ink Mark, 7 In. ... 2.00 to 7.00
Plate, Ink Mark, 10 In. .. 4.75 to 8.00
Plate, 6 In. .... .75 to 3.00
Plate, 12 In. 9.50
Plate, Luncheon, Ink Mark, 9 In. 4.00
Plate, 8 In. .... 6.00 to 7.50
Platter, Oval .... 6.00 to 10.00
Relish Side Insert 5.00
Relish, 4 Part 5.00
Salt & Pepper .... 4.00 to 7.00
Saucer, After Dinner 7.50
Saucer, Ink Mark .... .75 to 7.50
Shaker .... 2.00 to 6.50
Soup, Cream .... 5.00 to 10.00
Soup, Flat 6.25
Sugar & Creamer 5.75
Sugar, Covered .... 6.00 to 10.00
Sugar, Embossed Mark ... 5.00 to 6.50
Syrup 30.00
Teapot, Covered 20.00
Tray, Relish .... 40.00 to 35.00
Tray, Utility, 10 In. .... 5.00 to 10.00
Tumbler, Embossed Mark 10.00 to 14.00
Tumbler, Juice, 5 Oz. ... 9.00 to 10.00
Tumbler, 10 Oz. .... 9.00 to 12.00

Fuzz Ball

Fuzz Ball was made by Hall China Company, East Liverpool, Ohio.

Casserole, Covered 15.00
Drippings Jar 15.00

Shaker, Handle 5.00

Gingham

Gingham was made by Vernon Kilns, Vernon, California.

Bowl, Vegetable, 9 In. 4.00
Pitcher, 5 1/4 In. 5.00
Plate, 6 1/4 In. 2.50

Plate, 9 1/2 In. 3.00
Plate, 10 1/4 In. 3.50

Gold Label

Gold Label was made by Hall China Company, East Liverpool, Ohio, in the 1950s.

Cookie Jar, Gold Dots, Zeisel .. 20.00
Cookie Jar, Weave Design, Zeisel 18.00
Cookie Jar, Zeisel 20.00
Jug, Squiggle, 5 3/4 In., Sunshine 7.50

Hacienda

Hacienda was made first by Homer Laughlin China Company of Newell, West Virginia, in 1938.

Bowl, 5 1/2 In. 2.00
Plate, Salad, Homer Laughlin ... 1.50
Plate, 9 In. .... 1.50 to 2.50
Sugar & Creamer .... 5.00 to 8.00

Harlequin

Harlequin was made by Homer Laughlin Company, Newell, West Virginia, from 1938 to 1964. A reissue was offered for sale in 1979.

BLUE
Animal, Penguin, 2 1/2 In. 32.50
Bowl, 5 1/2 In. 1.50
Casserole, Covered .... 18.50 to 25.00
Cup .... 2.00 to 4.00
Dish, Nut .... 2.00 to 3.00
Eggcup 5.50
Lamp 69.50
Pie Baker, Oval, 9 In. 10.00
Plate, 6 In. .... .50 to 1.25
Plate, 7 In. .... 1.50 to 2.50
Plate, 8 1/4 In. 2.00
Plate, 9 In. .... 1.00 to 1.50
Platter, 11 In. .... 2.00 to 3.50
Platter, 13 In. 15.00
Saucer 1.00
Shaker .... 1.25 to 2.00
Soup, Bowl 2.00
Soup, Flat, 8 In. 8.00
Sugar & Creamer 11.00
Sugar, Open 1.50
Tumbler, Water 15.00
CHARTREUSE
Bowl, Cereal, 6 X 2 In. 15.00
Bowl, 5 In. 20.00

Cup .... 3.00 to 4.50
Cup & Saucer 10.00
Eggcup 14.00
Plate, 6 In. 3.00
Plate, 7 In. 4.00
Plate, 9 In. 8.00
Plate, 10 In. 10.00
Salt & Pepper 14.00
Saucer .... .50 to 1.25
Sugar, Open 1.50
GRAY
Bowl, Cereal, 6 X 2 In. 15.00
Bowl, Fruit, 5 1/2 In. ... 2.50 to 10.00
Cup .... 3.75 to 4.50
Plate, 7 In. .... 1.25 to 4.00
Plate, 10 In. .... 1.00 to 10.00
Eggcup 14.00
Gravy Boat 15.00
Saucer .... .75 to 1.25
Shaker 1.25
Soup, Flat, 8 In. 12.00
GREEN
Bowl, Cereal, 6 In. ..... 2.50 to 10.00
Bowl, Fruit, 5 1/2 In. ... 3.00 to 10.00
Bowl, Vegetable 3.50

Bowl, 9 In. 4.50
Creamer .... 2.00 to 12.00
Creamer, Novelty 4.50
Cup .... 3.00 to 3.75
Cup & Saucer .... 3.00 to 10.00
Eggcup 14.00
Pitcher, Miniature 4.00
Plate, 6 In. 3.00
Plate, 7 In. 1.50
Plate, 9 In. .... 1.00 to 2.50
Plate, 10 In. .... 1.50 to 15.00
Platter, 13 In. 8.00
Saucer .... .50 to 1.00
Shaker 1.25
Sugar & Creamer, Covered 9.50
Sugar, Covered .... 2.00 to 3.00
Syrup 55.00
Tumbler, Water 15.00
Water Jug 12.00

LIGHT GREEN
Bowl, Oatmeal, 6 1/2 In. 3.00
Cup 4.00
Cup, After Dinner 10.00
Plate, 6 In. 1.00
Platter, 13 In. 6.00

MAROON
Animal, Cat, 2 1/2 In. 45.00
Bowl, 5 1/2 In. 7.00
Cup .... 2.00 to 4.50
Cup & Saucer 10.00
Dish, Nut .... 2.00 to 6.00
Eggcup .... 14.00 to 15.00
Pie Baker, Oval, 9 In. 15.00
Plate, Deep, 8 In. ...... 4.50 to 12.00
Plate, 6 In. .... .50 to 3.00
Plate, 7 In. .... 1.25 to 4.00
Plate, 9 In. .... 1.75 to 8.00
Platter, 11 In. .... 4.00 to 12.00
Salt & Pepper 14.00
Saucer .... .50 to 1.25
Soup, Flat 3.00
Sugar, Covered 12.00
Tumbler, Water 17.00

MAUVE BLUE
Bowl, Fruit, 5 1/2 In. 2.50
Bowl, Salad 4.50
Bowl, Vegetable 4.00
Casserole, Covered 20.00
Creamer, Novelty 3.50
Cup .... 2.00 to 4.50
Cup & Saucer 3.00
Cup, After Dinner 10.00

Dish, Nut 6.00
Pepper Shaker 3.00
Pitcher, Miniature 15.00
Plate, Deep, 8 In. 4.50
Plate, 6 In. 1.00
Plate, 7 In. 1.25
Plate, 9 In. 1.75
Plate, 10 In. 1.50
Saucer 1.25
Sugar, Open 3.00
Teapot 10.00
Tumbler, Water 12.00

Harlequin

RED
Bowl, Fruit, 5 1/2 In. ... 7.00 to 10.00
Butter, Covered 32.00
Creamer .... 2.50 to 4.50
Creamer, Novelty 7.00
Cup .... 2.50 to 4.50
Cup & Saucer .... 2.50 to 10.00
Dish, Nut 6.00
Eggcup 14.00
Eggcup, Double 4.00
Nappy, 9 In. .... 6.00 to 8.00
Pitcher, Miniature ...... 5.00 to 15.00
Pitcher, Water 8.00
Plate, 6 In. .... .75 to 3.00
Plate, 7 In. 1.25
Plate, 9 In. .... 1.75 to 8.00
Platter, 13 X 11 In. ..... 6.50 to 10.00
Salt & Pepper 2.50

Saucer .... .75 to 1.00
Shaker 1.25
Soup, Cream 5.00
Soup, Flat, 8 In. 12.00
Sugar, Covered 6.00
Sugar, Open .... 1.75 to 2.00
Tumbler, Water 12.00
Water Jug 20.00
ROSE
Bowl, Cereal, 6 In. 15.00
Bowl, Salad 4.50
Bowl, 5 3/4 In. 3.00
Creamer .... 2.00 to 3.00
Cup .... 1.50 to 2.50
Cup & Saucer .... 3.00 to 10.00
Eggcup 14.00
Eggcup, Double 6.00
Fruit, 5 1/2 In. .... 1.50 to 10.00
Gravy Boat 4.00
Nappy, 9 In. 15.00
Pitcher, Milk 6.50
Plate, 6 In. .... .50 to 1.25
Plate, 7 In. .... .85 to 4.00
Plate, 9 In. .... 1.00 to 2.25
Plate, 10 In. 10.00
Platter .... 2.00 to 6.00
Salt & Pepper 14.00
Saucer .... .50 to 1.25
Shaker .... 2.00 to 2.50
Soup, Bowl, 8 1/2 In. .... 2.00 to 3.00
Soup, Cream .... 3.50 to 5.50
Soup, Flat, 8 In. .... 3.00 to 12.00
Sugar & Creamer, Covered 18.00
Sugar, Covered 2.50
Teapot 4.00
Tumbler, 4 1/4 In. 8.00
SPRUCE GREEN
Casserole, Covered 30.00
Creamer 2.00
Creamer, Novelty 3.50
Cup .... 1.50 to 4.50
Dish, Nut 6.00
Gravy Boat 5.50
Lamb, Animal 30.00
Plate, 6 In. .... 1.00 to 3.00
Plate, 9 In. 1.75
Saucer 1.25
Sugar & Creamer, Covered 18.00
Tumbler, Water 12.00
Water Jug 18.00
TURQUOISE
Ashtray 40.00

Bowl, Cereal, 6 X 2 In. 10.00
Bowl, Fruit, 5 1/2 In. .... 1.50 to 2.00
Bowl, 6 1/2 In. 10.00
Butter, Covered .... 27.00 to 40.00
Creamer .... 2.50 to 3.50
Creamer, Novelty .... 3.50 to 4.00
Cup .... 1.50 to 4.00
Cup & Saucer 3.00
Dish, Nut .... 3.00 to 6.00
Eggcup, Double 6.00
Gravy Boat .... 3.50 to 5.00
Pitcher, Miniature ...... 4.00 to 15.00
Plate, 6 In. .... .50 to 1.25
Plate, 7 In. .... 1.25 to 3.00
Plate, 9 In. .... 1.00 to 2.50
Plate, 10 In. .... 1.50 to 8.00
Platter, 13 In. 3.00
Salt & Pepper 6.00
Saltshaker 1.25
Saucer .... .50 to 4.00
Soup, Flat, 8 In. .... 3.00 to 8.00
Sugar 2.00
Sugar, Covered .... 3.00 to 5.00
Teapot 14.00
Tumbler, Water .... 12.00 to 15.00
WHITE & GOLD
Animal, Cat 20.00
YELLOW
Animal, Fish 29.75
Ashtray 15.00
Bowl, Cereal, 6 In. ..... 3.00 to 10.00
Bowl, Fruit, 5 1/2 In. ... 2.50 to 15.00
Bowl, Salad, 7 In. ...... 4.50 to 10.00
Bowl, 6 1/4 In. 2.00
Casserole, Covered 18.00
Creamer 3.50
Creamer, Novelty .... 7.00 to 8.00
Cup .... 1.25 to 4.50
Cup & Saucer .... 2.50 to 5.00
Cup, Coffee, After Dinner 10.00
Dish, Nut .... 3.00 to 6.00
Eggcup .... 4.00 to 15.00
Eggcup, Double 6.00
Gravy Boat 10.00
Marmalade, Covered 40.00
Nappy, 9 In. .... 6.00 to 12.00
Pie Plate, 10 In. 25.00
Pitcher, Water 10.00
Plate, Dinner, 10 In. 8.00
Plate, 6 In. .... .50 to 1.00
Plate, 7 In. .... 1.00 to 3.00
Plate, 9 In. .... 1.00 to 2.50

Platter, 11 In.	3.00 to 5.00	Soup, Flat, 8 In.	3.50
Platter, 13 In.	3.50 to 7.00	Sugar & Creamer, Covered	8.00
Salt & Pepper	5.00	Sugar, Covered	2.50 to 3.00
Saucer	.50 to 1.25	Sugar, Open	2.00
Shaker	1.25 to 3.00	Water Jug	12.00
Soup, Bowl	2.00 to 3.00	Water Jug, Ball Shape	9.00

Hawaiian Coral

Hawaiian Coral was made by Vernon Kilns, Vernon, California.

Plate, 10 In., Vernon Kilns 2.00

Hawaiian Flowers

Hawaiian Flowers was made by Vernon Kilns, Vernon, California, in 1939.

Plate, 10 In., Vernon Kilns 8.00

Holland, see Crocus

Holly

Holly was made by Stangl Pottery, Trenton, New Jersey, from 1967 to 1972.

Saucer, Stangl 1.00

Horseshoe

Horseshoe, maker unknown.

GREEN
Platter, 11 1/4 In. 5.50

YELLOW
Platter, 11 1/4 In. 6.00

Kitchen Kraft

Kitchen Kraft was made by Homer Laughlin China Company, Newell, West Virginia, from the 1930s. It was an oven-to-table line of serving pieces. The same ware was decorated with decals and is included under the decal name.

BLUE
- Casserole, Covered, 8 1/2 In. ... 30.00
- Spoon 30.00

GREEN
- Casserole, Covered 75.00
- Fork 30.00
- Pepper Shaker 30.00
- Plate, Cake 16.00

RED
- Casserole, Covered 75.00
- Pepper Shaker 35.00
- Saltshaker 35.00

YELLOW
- Casserole, Covered 75.00
- Fork 25.00

Lu-Ray

Lu-Ray was a solid color pattern made by Taylor-Smith-Taylor, Chester, West Virginia, after 1938.

BLUE
- Berry Bowl, 5 In. 1.75
- Bowl, Covered, Handle 15.00
- Bowl, 6 In. 1.50
- Bowl, 7 3/4 In. 2.00
- Creamer .... 3.00 to 5.00
- Cup 2.00
- Cup & Saucer .... 3.00 to 8.00
- Eggcup, Double 5.00
- Plate, Bread & Butter, 6 In. 7.00
- Plate, 7 1/2 In. .... 1.00 to 2.00
- Plate, 9 In. 2.00
- Plate, 10 In. 3.00
- Plate, 14 In. 5.50
- Platter, 11 3/4 In. .... 2.00 to 3.00
- Platter, 13 In. 4.00
- Platter, 14 In. 5.00
- Salt & Pepper 5.00
- Saucer .... .50 to 3.00
- Shaker .... 2.00 to 4.00
- Soup, Bowl, 8 In. 2.50
- Soup, Cream 3.00
- Sugar, Covered .... 3.00 to 3.50

CREAM
- Berry Bowl, 5 In. 1.75
- Bowl, Cereal 2.00
- Bowl, Salad 5.00
- Bowl, 4 1/4 In. 2.25
- Bowl, 6 In. 1.50
- Creamer 2.00
- Cup 2.00
- Cup & Saucer 3.00
- Gravy Boat 3.50
- Gravy Boat & Underplate 10.00
- Pitcher, Water, 6 Tumbler 39.50
- Plate, 6 In. .... 1.00 to 1.50

- Plate, 7 1/2 In. 1.00
- Plate, 9 In. 2.00
- Plate, 14 In. 5.50
- Plate, 8 In. 2.00
- Platter, 11 5/8 In. 3.50
- Platter, 13 In. .... 4.00 to 5.00
- Salt & Pepper 4.00
- Saltshaker .... 2.00 to 3.00
- Saucer .... .50 to 1.00
- Soup, Cream .... 3.00 to 4.00
- Water Jug, Ice Lip 15.00

GRAY
- Saucer 1.00
- Soup, Bowl 3.00

GREEN
- Bowl, Salad 1.50
- Bowl, Soup, Cream 4.00
- Bowl, Soup, Flat 1.50
- Bowl, Vegetable 4.50
- Bowl, 4 1/4 In. 2.25
- Bowl, 6 In. 1.50
- Creamer 2.53
- Cup 2.00
- Cup & Saucer 3.00
- Plate, 6 In. .... 1.00 to 1.50
- Plate, 7 1/2 In. 1.00
- Plate, 8 In. 2.00
- Plate, 9 In. 2.00
- Platter, 11 1/2 In. 2.00
- Saltshaker 2.00
- Saucer .... .50 to .75
- Shaker 2.50

PINK
- Berry Bowl, 5 In. 1.75
- Bowl, 4 1/4 In. 2.25
- Bowl, 6 In. 1.50

Bowl, 7 3/4 In.	2.00	Plate, 7 In.	1.00 to 1.50
Bowl, 8 1/2 In.	3.00	Plate, 8 In.	1.25 to 2.00
Bowl, 9 In.	5.00	Plate, 9 In.	2.00
Butter, Covered	8.00	Plate, 10 In.	3.00 to 4.00
Creamer	1.50 to 3.00	Plate, 14 In.	4.00
Cup	1.00 to 4.00	Platter, Oval, 11 3/4 In.	3.50
Cup & Saucer	3.00 to 8.00	Platter, 13 1/2 In.	3.00
Eggcup	7.50	Salt & Pepper	3.00
Gravy Boat	7.00	Saltshaker	2.00 to 3.00
Nappy, Oval, 10 In.	3.00	Saucer	.50 to 1.00
Nappy, 5 In.	2.00	Soup, Cream	2.00 to 5.00
Pitcher	12.00	Sugar, Covered	3.50 to 5.75
Plate, Cake	5.00	Water Jug	17.50
Plate, 6 In.	1.00 to 1.50		

Magnolia

Magnolia was made by Stangl Pottery, Trenton, New Jersey.

BROWN
Bookends, Stangl	45.00	Vase, 6 In., Stangl	16.00
Vase, 5 In., Stangl	16.00		

Mexicana

Mexicana was made by Homer Laughlin China Company, Newell, West Virginia, after 1938. It is a Kitchen Kraft ware with Mexican decal decoration.

Creamer	3.50	Platter, 2-Handled, 11 1/2 In.	12.50
Plate, 6 In.	4.00		

Modern California

Modern California was made by Vernon Kilns, Vernon, California, in the 1930s.

AZURE		**SAND**	
Plate, 9 1/2 In.	3.50	Plate, 9 1/2 In.	3.50

Morning Glory

Morning Glory was made by Hall China Company, East Liverpool, Ohio, from 1942 to 1949.

Bowl, Straight Side	8.00	Bowl, Straight Side, No.6	10.00
Bowl, Straight Side, No.4	8.00	Bowl, 7 1/2 In., Sunshine	10.00

Moss Rose

Moss Rose was made by Southern Potteries, Inc., Ervin, Tennessee, under the trade name Blue Ridge, from 1920 to 1957. It was hand-painted. Another pattern called Moss Rose was made by the Universal Potteries, Cambridge, Ohio, from 1953 to 1955. It had decal decorations.

Plate, 5 1/4 In., Blue Ridge 1.50

Orange Poppy, see Poppy

Organdie

Organdie was made by Vernon Kilns, Vernon, California, in the 1930s.

Creamer, Covered	3.00	Salt & Pepper	3.00
Cup	2.00	Server	10.00
Plate, 10 1/2 In.	5.00		

Peach Blossom

Peach Blossom, maker unknown.

Bowl, 5 3/4 In.	3.50	Platter	5.00
Bowl, 11 3/4 In.	12.00	Sugar & Creamer, Covered	7.50
Cup & Saucer	6.00		
Plate, 6 1/4 In.	1.50		
Plate, 8 1/2 In.	2.50		
Plate, 11 In.	4.50		
Plate, 15 In.	10.00		

Petitpoint

Petitpoint was made by Homer Laughlin China Company, Newell, West Virginia, in the 1960s.

Pitcher 25.00

Pink Cosmos

Pink Cosmos was made by Stangl Pottery, Trenton, New Jersey, in 1966.

Plate, 10 In., Stangl 5.50

Pink Mums

Pink Mums was made by Hall China Company, East Liverpool, Ohio, possibly in the 1930s.

Bowl, Sunshine .... 5.00 to 8.00   Saltshaker 5.00

Plaza

Plaza, maker unknown.

DARK GREEN   YELLOW
Water Jug, Covered .... 40.00   Water Jug, Covered 40.00

Poppy

Poppy was made by Hall China Company, East Liverpool, Ohio, fro 1933 through the 1950s. It is sometimes called Orange Poppy by collectors to differentiate it from another Hall pattern called Red Poppy.

Bean Pot, Handle ..... 22.00 to 45.00
Bean Pot, Individual 2.00
Bowl, Cereal, Rimmed, 6 In. 1.75
Bowl, Fruit, 5 1/4 In. 1.50
Bowl, Salad .... 8.00 to 15.00
Bowl, Vegetable, Round, 9 In. ... 7.00
Bowl, 6 In., Sunshine 6.50
Casserole 12.00
Casserole, Oval, 12 In. 25.00
Casserole, Sunshine 20.00
Coffeepot, Golden Key 18.00
Cookie Jar 22.00
Cookie Jar, Pretzel, Handled, Lid 35.00
Creamer 3.00
Custard 4.00
Drippings Jar, Covered 7.00
Fluted Baker, 3 Pt. .... 12.00 to 13.00
Jar, Pretzel 30.00

Mustard Pot 25.00
Pie Server 8.00
Pie, Baker, 10 In. 8.00
Plate, Cake .... 6.00 to 9.00
Plate, 6 In. 1.50
Plate, 10 In. 4.00
Platter, Oval, 11 In. 4.00
Platter, Oval, 13 In. 8.00
Salt & Pepper, Handle 9.00
Saucer .... 1.25 to 3.00
Shaker, Handle 7.50
Soup, Bowl, 2-Handled, 6 In. 2.00
Spoon 8.00
Sugar & Creamer, Lid, Golden Key 18.00
Water Jug, Ball 17.50
Water Jug, Lid, Refrigerator ... 25.00
Water Jug, Sunshine 30.00
Water Jug, Sunshine, No.5 ..... 14.00

Primrose

Primrose, maker unknown.

Bowl, 5 3/4 In.	3.50	Fluted Baker	7.00
Cup & Saucer	4.50	Plate, 9 1/8 In.	4.50

Priscilla

Priscilla was made by Homer Laughlin China Company, Newell, West Virginia.

Berry Bowl, 4 1/2 In.	1.25	Pie Plate, 10 In.	12.00
Bowl, Salad, 9 In.	12.00	Pitcher	12.00
Creamer	4.00	Plate, 6 In.	1.00
Cup & Saucer	3.00	Soup, Flat	3.00
Gravy Boat	5.00	Sugar, Covered	6.00
Pie Baker	5.00	Water Jug	8.00 to 8.75

Raisin

Raisin was made by Vernon Kilns, Vernon, California.

Creamer	5.00	Plate, 10 1/2 In.	2.50 to 10.00
Cup	1.00 to 3.00	Saucer	2.00
Plate, Chop, 14 In.	10.00 to 45.00	Shaker	6.00
Plate, 6 In.	2.00	Sugar & Creamer, Covered, Ring	10.00
Plate, 9 In.	2.00	Sugar, Covered	5.50
Plate, 10 In.	3.00		

Red Ivy

Red Ivy was made by Stangl Pottery, Trenton, New Jersey, after 1957.

Platter, Stangl 10.00

Red Poppy

Red Poppy was made by Hall China Company, East Liverpool, Ohio, from 1930 to the 1950s.

Bowl, Salad, 9 In.	6.50 to 7.00	Bowl, 7 1/2 In.	5.00
Bowl, Sunshine, 6 1/4 In.	10.00	Bowl, 9 In.	6.50

Cannister Set .... 9.00 to 30.00
Casserole, Covered .... 11.00 to 15.00
Coffeepot 16.00
Creamer .... 4.00 to 9.00
Cup 3.25
Drippings Jar, Covered 9.50
Fluted Baker 7.00
Jar, Grease, Covered 9.00
Mixing Bowl 6.00
Pie Plate 12.00
Pitcher, 6 In. 8.00
Plate, Cake 8.00
Plate, 9 In. 5.00
Platter, 11 In. 12.00
Platter, 13 In. 14.00
Salt & Pepper .... 7.50 to 9.00
Salt & Pepper, Handle .. 8.00 to 15.00
Soup Bowl, 8 In. 10.00
Sugar & Creamer, Covered 11.00

Red Poppy

Water Jug, Sunshine, No.5 ..... 16.00
Water Jug, 6 1/2 In. 10.00

Red Riding Hood

Red Riding Hood is a figural pattern made by Hull Pottery Company, Crooksville, Ohio.

Cookie Jar 24.90
Pitcher 35.00
Salt & Pepper 10.90

Shaker 10.00
Sugar & Creamer ..... 12.00 to 25.00

Rhythm Rose

Rhythm Rose was made by Homer Laughlin China Company, Newell, West Virginia.

Casserole, Covered 18.50
Coffeepot 25.00

Pitcher, Duck Bill 15.00
Plate, Cake, 11 In. 15.00

Ring

Ring, sometimes called Bee Hive, was made by J. A. Bauer Company, Los Angeles, California, from 1932 to 1962.

BROWN
   Coffee Server, Wooden Handle, Lid 10.00
HEMLOCK GREEN
   Pitcher, Milk, Beehive 6.00

MISTY GRAY
   Pitcher, Milk 6.00
TURQUOISE
   Coffee Server, Wooden Handle, Lid 10.00

Riviera

Riviera was made by Homer Laughlin China Company, Newell, West Virginia, from 1938 to 1950.

BLUE
Bowl, 5 In.	1.50 to 2.00
Bowl, 6 In.	3.00
Cup	4.00
Cup & Saucer	5.00
Gravy Boat	4.00
Nappy, 8 1/4 In.	4.00
Plate, 5 In.	1.50
Plate, 6 In.	1.00 to 4.00
Plate, 9 In.	8.00
Saucer	1.50
Soup, Flat, 8 In.	12.00
Tray, Batter	95.00

GREEN
Bowl, Fruit, 5 1/2 In.	2.50
Bowl, 5 In.	1.50
Bowl, 6 In.	3.00
Creamer	4.00
Cup	2.75 to 4.00
Cup & Saucer	6.50
Jug, Batter, Covered	60.00
Plate, 6 In.	1.00 to 2.00
Plate, 9 In.	2.50 to 4.00
Platter, Square, 12 In.	6.00 to 6.50
Saltshaker	2.00
Saucer	1.50
Soup, Flat, 8 In.	12.00
Sugar, Covered	4.00 to 6.00
Sugar, Open	2.00
Tumbler	40.00
Tumbler, Handle	30.00

LIGHT GREEN
Bowl, 5 1/4 In.	1.00
Plate, 6 In.	.60
Sugar & Creamer, Covered	4.50

MAROON
Bowl, 5 In.	2.00
Bowl, 6 In.	3.00
Cup	4.00
Nappy, 8 In.	3.00
Plate, 6 In.	1.00
Plate, 9 In.	3.00

MAUVE BLUE
Bowl, Fruit, 5 1/2 In.	2.50
Bowl, 5 1/4 In.	1.00
Cup & Saucer	6.50

Gravy Boat	4.00
Plate, 6 In.	2.00
Plate, 9 In.	4.00
Shaker	3.00
Tumbler, Handle	30.00
Tumbler, Juice	24.00

OLD IVORY
Bowl, 8 1/4 In.	4.50
Bowl, 9 In.	5.50
Cup	5.00
Plate, 6 In.	5.00
Plate, 7 In.	6.00
Plate, 9 In.	8.00
Platter, 12 In.	14.00
Soup, Flat, 8 In.	14.00
Tumbler, Juice	24.00

Riviera

RED
Bowl, Fruit, 5 1/2 In.	2.50
Bowl, 8 1/4 In.	4.50 to 6.50
Creamer, Covered	25.00
Cup	4.00
Plate, 6 In.	1.00 to 5.00
Saucer	1.00 to 2.00
Shaker	3.00

Soup, Flat, 8 In. 14.00
Tumbler, Juice 24.00
YELLOW
Berry Bowl 2.50
Bowl, Fruit, 5 1/2 In. 2.50
Bowl, 5 In. 1.50
Bowl, 8 1/4 In. 5.00
Butter 15.00
Creamer 3.00
Cup .... 2.50 to 4.00
Cup & Saucer 5.00
Plate, 6 In. .... .60 to 4.00

Plate, 9 In. .... 3.00 to 8.00
Platter, 11 1/4 In. 12.00
Platter, 13 1/2 In. 6.00
Platter, 2-Handled, 13 3/4 In. ... 5.00
Saucer .... 1.00 to 2.00
Soup, Flat, 8 In. 12.00
Sugar 4.00
Sugar, Covered 4.00
Tumbler 40.00
Tumbler, Handle 30.00
Tumbler, Juice 24.00

Rooster

Rooster was made by Stangl Pottery, Trenton, New Jersey, from 197 to 1974.

Plate, 6 In., Stangl 1.50

Rooster

Rose Parade

Rose Parade was made by Hall China Company, East Liverpool, Ohio, from 1941 through the 1950s.

Bean Pot 6.00
Bowl, Salad 5.00
Bowl, 9 In. .... 6.00 to 12.00

Casserole, Covered ..... 9.00 to 20.00
Coffeepot 15.00
Custard 4.50

Jar, Grease 7.00
Jug, 7 In., Sani-Grid 15.00
Shaker .... 7.50 to 10.00
Sugar & Creamer 8.00

Water Jug, Set Of 3 .... 35.00
Water Jug, 5 In., Sani-Grid 8.00
Water Jug, 5 1/8 In. 8.00

Rose White

Rose White was made by Hall China Company, East Liverpool, Ohio, after 1941.

Bowl, Mix, No.3 .... 6.00
Bowl, Mix, No.5 .... 10.00
Drippings Jar, Covered 7.00
Pitcher, 5 1/2 In. 7.00

Shaker 5.00
Sugar & Creamer ...... 8.00 to 10.00
Water Jug, 7 1/2 In. 12.00

Rosebud

Rosebud was made by Coors Pottery, Golden, Colorado, in the 1930s.

BLUE
  Plate, 10 In. 6.00
GREEN
  Planter, Rectangular, 8 In. 12.00
IVORY
  Plate, 10 In. 6.00

MAROON
  Plate, 10 In. 6.00
TURQUOISE
  Plate, 10 In. 6.00
YELLOW
  Plate, 10 In. 6.00

Royal Rose

Royal Rose was made by Hall China Company, East Liverpool, Ohio.

Bowl, 6 1/4 In. .... 3.50 to 6.00
Bowl, 7 1/2 In. .... 5.00 to 8.50
Bowl, 8 1/2 In. 10.00
Bowl, 8 3/4 In. .... 9.00 to 9.50
Casserole, Covered ..... 6.00 to 15.00

Drippings Jar, Covered, Big Lip . 7.00
Saltshaker 6.00
Shaker, Handle 10.00
Water Jug, Ball 18.00

Russel Wright

Russel Wright was a designer who made dinnerware in modern shapes for 4 companies. The Iroquois China Company, Harker China Company, Chester, West Virginia, Steubenville Pottery Company, Steubenville, Ohio, and Justin Therod and Sons all made dishes marked Russel Wright. The Steubenville wares, first made in 1938, are the most common today.

BLUE
    Cup 1.25
    Cup & Saucer 1.75
    Plate, 10 In. 1.75
BROWN
    Cup & Saucer 4.00
    Pitcher 10.00
GRAY
    Casserole 12.50
    Plate, 10 In. 3.00
    Shaker 3.00
    Sugar & Creamer .... 5.95 to 6.50
GREEN
    Pitcher 11.00
PINK
    Casserole, French, Covered 15.00
    Sugar & Creamer, Covered 10.00
WHITE
    Pitcher, Large 13.00

Russel Wright

Rustic Garden

Rustic Garden was made by Stangl Pottery, Trenton, New Jersey, from 1972 to 1974.

    Plate, 8 In., Stangl 2.75

Sani-Grid

Sani-Grid was made by Hall China Company, East Liverpool, Ohio, after 1941.

RED & WHITE
    Casserole, Covered 15.00
    Drippings Jar, Tab Handle & Lid 10.00
    Salt & Pepper 12.00

Shaker, Handle .... 5.00 to 8.00
Sugar & Creamer 12.00

Sevilla

Sevilla, maker unknown.

GREEN
    Bowl, Round, 9 3/4 In. 15.00

Silhouette

Silhouette was made by the Crooksville China Company, Crooksville, Ohio. The pattern is similar to Taverne but the silhouette included in this pattern has a dog, Taverne does not.

Bowl	7.50	Plate, 9 In.	4.00
Coffeepot	48.00	Platter, 13 In.	8.50
Creamer	4.50	Saucer	1.50
Pie Baker	10.00	Shaker, Ball	10.00
Plate, Square, 6 In.	1.00	Souffle, 3 Pt.	7.50

Tam O'Shanter

Tam O'Shanter was made by Vernon Kilns, Vernon, California.

Butter	15.00	Saucer	1.00
Gravy Boat	6.00	Soup, Bowl	4.00
Plate, 6 In.	1.00		

Taverne

Taverne was made by the Hall China Company, East Liverpool, Ohio, in the 1930s. It is similar to the pattern Silhouette, but Taverne does not show a dog.

Bowl, Salad	5.00 to 12.00
Bowl, Vegetable, Round	5.00
Bowl, 6 1/4 In.	6.50
Bowl, 8 1/2 In., Colonial	12.00
Casserole, Covered, Colonial	15.00
Casserole, Sunshine	20.00
Coffeepot, Banded	25.00
Coffeepot, Colonial	25.00
Cup & Saucer	8.00
Drippings Jar, Covered	9.50
Fluted Baker	9.00 to 15.00
Jar, Pretzel	20.00
Nappy	7.00
Plate, 7 1/2 In.	2.50
Shaker	10.50
Shaker, Pair	22.00
Sugar & Creamer	8.50
Water Jug, Classic	45.00

Taverne

Thistle

Thistle was made by Stangl Pottery, Trenton, New Jersey, from 1951 to 1973.

Bowl, 5 In., Stangl 2.00
Butter, Stangl 3.00
Cup, Stangl 4.00
Plate, Old Lady In Shoe, 9 In., Stangl
.... 5.00
Plate, 6 In., Stangl 1.50

Plate, 8 In., Stangl 4.50
Relish, 11 In., Stangl 7.00
Saucer, Stangl 2.00
Server, Center Handle, Stangl ... 7.50
Sugar, Covered, Stangl 6.00

Tulip

Tulip was made by Hall China Company, East Liverpool, Ohio, from the 1930s to the 1950s. Another similar pattern called Tulip was made by Universal Potteries, Cambridge, Ohio.

Bowl, Sunshine 5.00
Pitcher, 9 In. 8.00
Plate, 6 1/4 In. 1.50
Platter, 13 1/4 In. 6.00
Sugar & Creamer, Covered 7.50

Tulip

White Dogwood

White Dogwood was made by Stangl Pottery, Trenton, New Jersey, from 1965 to 1974.

Saucer, 6 In., Stangl 1.00

White Rose

White Rose was made by Harker China Company, Chester, West Virginia. The design is white and appears to be cut into the pink or the blue background.

CLEAR
Plate, 9 In. 5.00
Plate, 10 In. 6.50
BLUE
Basket, 12 In. 53.00

White Rose

Wild Rose

Wild Rose was a decal-decorated set made by the Homer Laughlin China Company, Newell, West Virginia. Another dinnerware set by the same name was made by Knowles, Taylor, Knowles, East Liverpool, Ohio, about 1933. Stangl Pottery, Trenton, New Jersey, made a hand-painted pottery dinnerware called Wild Rose from 1955 to 1973.

Bowl, Sunshine, No.5 .... 15.00
Bowl, 5 1/2 In. 3.00
Bowl, 8 In. 10.00
Butter, 6 1/4 In. 12.00
Casserole, Covered .... 15.00 to 18.00
Casserole, Open 5.00
Casserole, 8 In. 9.75
Creamer .... 5.00 to 8.00
Cup 5.00
Cup & Saucer 7.50
Custard 4.50
Drippings Jar 28.00
Fluted Baker, 3 Pt. .... 13.00 to 15.00

Pepper Shaker 8.00
Plate, 6 In. 2.00
Plate, 7 In. 3.00
Plate, 8 In. 1.50
Plate, 9 In. 4.50
Plate, 10 In. 7.50
Plate, 8 In., Stangl 1.50
Platter, 11 In. 6.00
Platter, 13 In. 7.50
Saltshaker 5.00
Shaker, Range, Pair 16.00
Sugar & Creamer, Covered 16.00

Wildfire

Wildfire was made by the Hall China Company, East Liverpool, Ohio, in the 1950s.

Bowl, Large 15.00
Bowl, Medium 8.00
Bowl, Straight Side 8.00
Bowl, Sunshine, No.3 .... 10.00
Bowl, Vegetable, Oval, 10 1/4 In. 10.00
Bowl, 8 1/2 In. .... 7.00 to 9.00
Casserole, Covered 12.00
Coffeepot 25.00
Coffeepot, S Lid 22.00

Cup 4.00
Custard 4.00
Drippings Jar, Covered 7.00
Plate, 7 In. 3.00
Plate, 10 In. 5.00
Platter, 11 In. 4.00
Platter, 11 1/2 In. 10.00
Sauce 3.00
Saucer 3.00

Shaker	10.00	Sugar & Creamer	10.00
Shaker, Egg Drop	10.00	Sugar & Creamer, Covered	14.00
Shaker, Sani-Grid	5.00		

Zeisel

Zeisel was made by the Hall China Company, East Liverpool, Ohio, in the 1950s.

Ashtray	3.00	Sugar & Creamer	7.00
Bowl, Salad	8.00	Vinegar & Oil Set	15.00
Cup & Saucer	5.00	PINK	
Demitasse, Cup & Saucer	7.00	Cookie Jar, Tab Handle	18.00
Plate, 10 In.	5.00		

Hall Teapots

(Colors listed are most commonly found for that pattern.)

Airflow, canary, 1940
Aladdin, camellia, 1939
Albany, emerald, 1930s
Automobile, Chinese red, 1938
Baltimore, emerald, 1930s
Basket, canary with silver, 1938
Basketball, Chinese red, 1938
Birdcage, maroon, 1939
Boston, warm yellow, early
Cleveland, emerald, 1930s
Doughnut, Chinese red, 1938
Football, delphinium, 1938
French, decorated, early
Globe, 1940s
Hollywood, maroon, late 1920s
Hook Cover, cadet, 1940

Illinois, cobalt, late 1920s early 1930s
Los Angeles, stock brown, 1926
Manhattan, stock brown
Melody, canary, 1939
Moderne, ivory, 1930s
Nautilus, canary, 1939
New York, blue turquoise
Parade, canary, 1942
Philadelphia, cadet, 1923
Rhythm, Chinese red, 1939
Saf-Handle, canary, 1938
Sani-Grid, cadet, 1941
Star, turquoise, 1940
Streamline, canary, 1940
Surfside, emerald, 1939
Windshield, camellia, 1941

Other Teapot Lines by Hall

Cube (made by other companies), red, green, cobalt
Disraeli, pink
Gladstone, pink/gold
Lipton, same shape as French, label on bottom, black lustre, warm yellow, daffodil
   cozy

McCormick, 1907, maroon, turquoise, green & silver
Miss Terry
T-Ball, designed for Bacharach, Inc., in 1948, maroon, daffodil, delphinium, round
& square
Tea for Two, angled top, undecorated, 1930s, sand dust, old rose
Teataster (oval), made for the Teamaster Co. late 1940s, still in production, cobalt,
lettuce, daffodil
Twinspout (round), made for the Teamaster Co. late 1940s, maroon
Twin-Tee, flat top, decorated in gold or decal, 1926, stock brown, cobalt, light
russet,
Victoria & Albert, 1940s, celadon/gold

Hall Coffeepots

Armory, warm yellow
Big Boy, maroon/silver
Blaine, cadet
Carraway, Chinese red
Coffee Queen, Chinese red

Deca-Flip, red & hi-white
Step-Down, red, black & green
(some decals)
Step-Round, ivory

Drip-O-Lator

(This is a line of pots made for the Enterprise Aluminum Company from 1930s
through the present. They ordered the pots from Hall, added an aluminum drip
section and marketed them under the name Drip-o-lator.)

Arch
Basketweave
Bell
Bricks 'n' ivy
Bullseye
Crest
Monarch

Panel
Petal
Sash
Step-Round (only one that had been
previously designed)
Sweep
Trellis

American Dinnerware Reissues

Harlequin. Put back into production in February of 1979. The Woolworth Company will be the sole distributor. Complete dinner sets are being made in the orginal colors. The only difference is that the salmon now being produced is a deeper color than the original. The sugar bowls are being made with closed handles.

Fiesta. Very similar ware produced in 1978 by Franciscan under the name "Kaleidoscope."

Harker Pottery Company, Chester,
West Virginia, 1840–1972

Coors, Golden, Colorado, c. 1900–1930s

Paden City Pottery, Paden City,
West Virginia, 1930–1956

Salem China Company, Salem, Ohio,
1898–present

Blue Ridge (Southern Potteries, Inc.)
Ervin, Tennessee, 1917–1957

Hall China Company, East Liverpool, Ohio,
1903–present

Hall China Company, East Liverpool,
Ohio, 1903–present

West Virginia, 1899–present
Taylor-Smith-Taylor, Chester,

Harker Pottery Company, Chester,
West Virginia, 1840–1972

Steubenville, Steubenville, Ohio, 1879–1959

Homer Laughlin China Company, East
Liverpool, Ohio and Newell, West Virginia,
1877–present

Stangl Pottery, Trenton, New Jersey,
1805–1978

Iroquois, Syracuse, New York, 1900–1970

Universal Potteries, Inc., Cambridge, Ohio, 1935–1956

Universal Potteries, Inc., Cambridge, Ohio, 1935–1956

Homer Laughlin China Company, East Liverpool, Ohio and Newell West Virginia, 1877–present

American Dinnerware Pattern List

Pattern	Shape	Maker	Date	Description
Acorn		Harmony House		Blue & pink Cameo Ware
Adam Antique		Steubenville		Ivory glaze
Adrian		Stangl	1972–74	
Adobestone	Ceramastone	Red Wing	1967	
Al Fresco	Al Fresco	Franciscan	1952	Hemlock green, coffee brown, lime green, olive green, misty gray
Alia Jane	Round	Taylor-Smith-Taylor	1933–34	Decal
Aloha		French-Saxon		
Amapila	Amapila	Franciscan		Hand-painted
Amber Glo		Stangl	1954–62	
Amberstone	Fiesta	Homer Laughlin	1967–	Solid colors
American Beauty		Stetson		
Anniversary		Salem China	1943	
Antiqua		Stangl	1972–74	
Anytime	Vernon Kilns			
Apple	Apple	Franciscan	1940	Hand-painted
Apple	Watt Ware	Watt Pottery	1922–60	Hand-painted
Apple Delight		Stangl	1965–74	
April (No. 4812)		Blue Ridge	1954	
Arabesque	Arabesque	Catalina	1935	Solid colors
Arcadia		Vernon Kilns	C. 1947	
	Argosy	W. S. George	1930	Ivory body
Ardennes	1941 Provincial	Red Wing	1941	Laurel leaf band

Pattern	Shape	Maker	Date	Description
Art Deco	Art Deco	Catalina	Early 1930s	Solid colors
Asbury	Pegasus	Sebring	1940s	
Aster	Ultra California	Vernon Kilns		
Autumn Apple (No. 3735)	Colonial	Blue Ridge	1941	
Autumn Fancy		Universal		Decals
Autumn Leaf		Crooksville China		Floral decals
Autumn Leaf		Hall China for Jewel T.	1933–present	Floral decals
Autumn Leaf		Harker Potteries		Floral decals
Autumn Leaf		Paden City		Floral decals
Aztec		Stangl	1967–68	
Aztec on Desert Sand	Citation	Steubenville		
Bachelor's Button		Stangl	1965	
Ballerina	Ballerina	Universal Potteries	1952–56	Forest green, burgundy, chartreuse, dove gray, sierra rust, moss rose, pine cone, solid colors
Banded	Banded	Hall		Floral decals, solid colors
Barkwood		Vernon Kilns		Beige and brown (like tree bark)
Basket Petitpoint	Victory	Salem		Decals

J. A. Bauer is a mark found on pottery by firm later using mark J. A. Brushe. Most pieces of Bauer are "Ring."

Bauer, see Ring

Pattern	Shape	Maker	Date	Description
Bee Hive, see Ring				
Bel Air		Vernon Kilns		3 lines crossing 3 lines
Bella Rosa		Stangl	1960–62	
Bermuda		Homer Laughlin	1977–78	
Berry		Blue Ridge (H.P.)	1920–57	
Bimini		Homer Laughlin	1977–78	
Bird in the Heart		Universal Cambridge		
Bird Pottery		Vernon Kilns		
Bit Series		Vernon Kilns		
Bittersweet		Universal Pottery	1949	Decals
Bittersweet		Hall		Flowers
Blossom Ring		Stangl	1967–78	
Blossom Time	Concord	Red Wing	1947	
Blue Bell		Stangl	19??–42	
Blueberry		Montgomery Ward	1921	Decals
Blue Blossom		Hall	c. 1939	Blue background, floral decals
Blue Bouquet	D-Line	Hall (Premium for Standard coffee)	1950–60s	Floral decals
Blue Daisy		Stangl	1963–74	
Blue Dresden	Virginia Rose	Homer Laughlin	1949	
Blue Garden		Hall	1939	Blue background, floral decals

Pattern	Shape	Maker	Date	Description
Blue Medallion		Homer Laughlin	1920	Decals
Blue Rhythm (Cameo)		Harker	1959	
Blue Shadows	True China	Red Wing	1964	
Blue Symphony		Homer Laughlin		
Blue Willow		Sebring-Limoges		
Blue Willow		Homer Laughlin	1942	Blue or pink
Bob White	Casual	Red Wing (H.P.)	1956	
Bolero		Homer Laughlin	1977–78	
Breakfast Nook	Lido	W. S. George		
Breeze	Bountiful	Salem China French-Saxon	1948	
Briar Rose		Homer Laughlin	1934	
Bridge	Tricorne	Salem		Decals
Bridle Rose		W. S. George		
Brittany	1941 Provincial	Red Wing	1941	Yellow rose
Brocade	True China	Red Wing	1964	
Brown-Eyed Susan		Vernon Kilns	1940s	Flower
Brown Satin		Stangl		
Bud	Concord	Red Wing	1947	
Buddah	Corinthian	Sebring		
Bunny Lunch	Kiddieware	Vernon Kilns		
Buttercup	Ultra California	Vernon Kilns	1947	

Pattern	Shape	Maker	Date	Description
Capistrano	Anniversary	Red Wing	1953–67	Swallow design
Capri	Rhythm Coupe	Homer Laughlin		
	Capri	Paden City	1933	
Carnation-Beauty		Homer Laughlin	1920	Decal
Carnival		Stangl	1954–57	
Caroline		Blue Ridge (H.P.)	1920–57	
Casa California		Vernon Kilns	1938	Blue, green leaves, pink flowers, yellow border
Cascade		Montgomery Ward	1936	White with red lines, Solid colors
Casual California	Casual California	Vernon Kilns		
Casualstone		Coventry	1970	Solid colors
Cat & the Fiddle	Kiddieware	Vernon Kilns		
Cat Tail		Universal for Sears, Roebuck, And Co.	1934–56	Decals
Chanticleer		Blue Ridge	1920–57	Hand-painted
Charstone Bleu	Ceramastone	Red Wing	1967	
Cabaret	Cabaret	Franciscan (H.P.)		
Cactus	Banded	Hall	1937–40s	Floral decals
Cactus		Homer Laughlin		Mexican decal
Call Rose	Century	Homer Laughlin		Floral decal

Pattern	Shape	Maker	Date	Description
Calico Fruit		Universal Potteries		Decals of fruit
Caliente		Paden City		Solid colors
California Provincial	Poppytrail	Metlox	1965	
California Shadows		Vernon Kilns		Colored edge
California Strawberry	Poppytrail	Metlox		
Cameo		Harker		White cameo design, blue, pink background
Cameo Rose, see White Rose				
Canton	Encanto	Franciscan	1953	
Chartreuse, Green Border		Montgomery Ward	1936	Decals
Chateau-France		Sebring-Limoges		
Cherry		Salem China	1951	
Chevron	Gypsy Trail	Red Wing	1935	Blue, ivory, turquoise, orange, yellow
Chicory		Stangl	1961	
Children's Plates: Duck, Teddy Bear, Dog		Harker		Blue & pink Cameo Ware
Chinese Red (color used by Hall)				
Chintz		Vernon Kilns	1940s	Floral design
Chrysan-themum	Concord	Red Wing	1947	

Pattern	Shape	Maker	Date	Description
Clio	Corinthian	Leigh Potters		Floral
Clover		Blue Ridge	1947–54	
Cock O'Walk		Blue Ridge	1948	
Cocolo	Cocolo	Franciscan		Hand-painted
	Colonial	Stangl	1926	Silver green, Persian yellow, colonial blue, tangerine, aqua blue, rust, brown, surf white, solid colors
Colonial Dogwood		Stangl		
Colonial Rose		Stangl	1970–74	
Colonial	Futura	Red Wing	1960	Pillars
Colonial Silver		Stangl	19??–70	
Colorado				Brown
Columbine		Homer Laughlin		Floral decal
Conchita		Homer Laughlin	1938	Mexican decal
Concord		Stangl	1957	
Contempo				
Contemps		Brusche	1952	Slate, champagne white, desert beige, indigo brown, spicy green, pumpkin
Coral Reef		Vernon Kilns	1939	
Cornflower Blue		G. M. Knowles	1930s	Decals
Corn Gold		Montgomery Ward	1921	Decals
Corn King	Corn King	Shawnee	1954	Yellow & green
Corn Queen	Corn Queen	Shawnee	1954–61	Lighter kernel, dark foliage

Pattern	Shape	Maker	Date	Description
	Corn	American Pottery		
	Corn	Brush McCoy		
	Corn	Brush Pottery		
	Corn	J. W. McCoy		
	Corn	Standard Pottery		
	Corn	Stanford Pottery	1945–61	
Coronado	Coronado	Franciscan	1940s	Hand-painted
Coronado	Coronado	Vernon Kilns (grocery promotion)	1939	Orange, turquoise, yellow, dark blue
Coronation	Ultra California	Vernon Kilns		Aster, buttercup, carnation, gardenia
Coronation Organdy		Vernon Kilns		Gray & rose plaid
Cosmos		Stangl		
Cosmos		Vernon Kilns		Allover floral
Country Garden		Stangl	1956–74	
Country Garden	Anniversary	Red Wing	1953	Floral
Country Life		Stangl	1956–67	
Country Road		Homer Laughlin	1977–78	
Crab Apple		Blue Ridge		
Cranberry		Stangl		
Crazy Quilt		Homer Laughlin	1977–78	
Crazy Rhythm	Futura	Red Wing	1960	Abstract, hand-painted
Crocus	True China	Red Wing	1960	Floral
Crocus		Stangl		

Pattern	Shape	Maker	Date	Description
Crocus		Hall	1950	Floral
Crocus	D-Line	Hall	1930s	Floral decal (called Holland by some collectors)
Cumberland		Blue Ridge	1948	
Cynthia		Blue Ridge	1949	
Dahlia		Stangl	1970–74	
Dainty		Vernon Kilns		
Daisy		Stangl	1936–42	
Daisy	Fiesta Casuals	Homer Laughlin	1962–68	Solid colors
Daisy Chain	True China	Red Wing	1960	Floral
Daisy Wreath	Daisy Wreath	Franciscan		Hand-painted
Damask	True China	Red Wing	1964	Hand-painted
Dahlia		Blue Ridge	1948	
Della Robbia	Vernonware	Metlox	1965	
Del Mar	Del Mar	Franciscan		Hand-painted
Delmar		Stangl	1972–74	
Delores		Vernon Kilns		
Delta Blue	Village Green	Red Wing	1954	Light blue with floral decor
Desert Bloom		Vernon Kiln		
Desert Rose	Desert Rose	Franciscan		Hand-painted
Desert Sun	New Shape	Red Wing	1962	Geometric
Diana		Stangl	1972–74	
Dixie Honest (No. 3913)	Pie Crust	Blue Ridge	1949	
	D-Line	Hall	1936	Plain, round, floral decals
Dogwood	Century	Homer Laughlin		Floral decals

Pattern	Shape	Maker	Date	Description
Dogwood		Stangl	1965	
Dogwood	Dogwood	Franciscan		Hand-painted
Dolly Petit Point	Victory	Salem	1950s	
Dolores		Vernon Kilns	1940s	Floral border
Dominion	Victory	Salem		Poppies, wheat, blue flowers, decals
Driftwood	Anniversary	Redwing	1953	Tree branch design
Ducky Dinner	Kiddieware	Vernon Kilns		
Dutch Petitpoint	Tricorne	Salem		Decals
Early American		Homer Laughlin	1960s	Floral
Early California	Early California	Vernon Kilns	1930s	Orange, turquoise, green, brown, blue, pink, yellow
Early Days		Vernon Kilns		
Ecstasy		Vernon Kilns		
Edmonton		Syracuse		
Eggshell Polka Dot		Hall	1934	Dots in: matte white, ivory glaze, red, green, blue, floral decals
Eggshell Theme		Homer Laughlin	1940s	"English" look, decals, floral border
Emerald		Montgomery Ward	1921	Decals
Emma Susan	Washington Square	Taylor-Smith-Taylor	1933–34	Decals
English Garden		Homer Laughlin	1934	

Pattern	Shape	Maker	Date	Description
Eureka Homewood		Hall (made for Eureka Co.)		Decal
Eureka Serenade	D-Line	Hall		
Evening Flower	Skyline	Blue Ridge	1950	
Eventide		Blue Ridge	1920–57	Hand-painted
Fairlawn		Stangl	1959–62	
Fantasy	Ball	Hall		(Teapot) decal
Fantasy	Concord	Red Wing	1947	Abstract
Fashion White		Montgomery Ward	1936	Decals
Federal		Sebring-Limoges	1942	
Festival		Stangl	1961–67	
Field Daisy		Stangl	1941–42	
Field Daisy		Stangl	1941–42	
Fiesta	Fiesta	Homer Laughlin	1936–72	Dark blue, old ivory, medium green
Fiesta Ironstone	Fiesta	Homer Laughlin	1969–72	Antique gold, turf green, mango red
Fiesta Kitchen Kraft		Homer Laughlin		
First Love		Stangl	1968–73	
Five Little Pigs	Kiddieware	Vernon Kilns		
Flamingo		Hall		
Fleur de Lis	Kitchen Kraft			Homer Laughlin

Pattern	Shape	Maker	Date	Description
Flight	New Shape	Red Wing	1962	Birds
Flight of the Swallows		Homer Laughlin	1941	
Flora		Stangl	1947–57	
Floral		Stangl	1941–42	
Floral	Floral	Franciscan		Hand-painted
Floral Birdsong	Sabina II	Sabin	c. 1946	
Floral Border		Montgomery Ward	1936	Decals
Floral Plaid		Stangl	1940–42	
Florence	Squared-Off Edges	E. M. Knowles	1933–34	Decals
Florentine		Stangl	1958	
Florette		Stangl	1961–62	
Flower Basket	Yorktown	E. M. Knowles		
Flower Fantasy		Blue Ridge	1954	
Flower Pot		Hall		Early decal
Flower Power		Homer Laughlin	1977–78	
Flying Bluebird	Empress	Homer Laughlin	1920	Decal
Fondoso	Gypsy Trail	Red Wing	1938	Blue, yellow, turquoise, pastels
Forest Fruits	Skyline	Blue Ridge	1950	
French Provincial				Silhouette decal
Frontenac	Futura	Red Wing	1960	Abstract flowers
Frosted Fruit		Stangl	1957	
Fruit	Concord	Red Wing	1947	
Fruit		Stangl	1942–74	

Pattern	Shape	Maker	Date	Description
Fruit Basket		Homer Laughlin	1977–78	
Fruit & Flowers		Stangl	1957–74	
Fruitdale		Vernon Kilns	c. 1945	Flower & fruit center
	Futura	Red Wing	1961	Hand-painted
Fuzz Ball		Hall		Early decal
Galaxy		Stangl	1963–70	
Garden Design		Salem China	1940s	
Garden Flower		Stangl	1947–57	
Garden Party	Garden Party	Franciscan		Hand-painted
Gardenia	Ultra California	Vernon Kilns		
Garland		Pickard		
Garland		Stangl	1957–67	
Ginger Cat	Kiddieware	Vernon Kilns		Hand-painted
Gingersnap	Gingersnap	Franciscan		Hand-painted
Gingham		Vernon Kilns		Green & yellow plaid
Glamour		Vernon Kilns		
Glenedon		Leigh Potteries		
Glenwood	Cavalier	Homer Laughlin	1961–68	
Gloria		Blue Ridge	1949	
Godey Print	Victory	Salem		Decals
Gold Band		Montgomery Ward	1920	Decals
Gold Band		Montgomery Ward	1936	Decals
Gold & Cobalt	Empress	Homer Laughlin	1920	Decals

Pattern	Shape	Maker	Date	Description
Gold Floral Band		Homer Laughlin	1920	Decal
Gold Garland		Homer Laughlin	1920	Decal
Gold Initial		Montgomery Ward	1921	Decal
Gold Label		Hall	1950s	Gold stamped decorations
Gold Lace		Homer Laughlin	1920	Decal on cobalt blue pieces
Gold Stripe		Montgomery Ward	1936	Decals
Golden Blossom		Stangl	1964–74	
Golden Crown	Queen Anne	Sabin		
Golden Grape		Stangl	1963–72	
Golden Harvest		Stangl	1953–73	
Golden Laurel		E. M. Knowles	1930s	Decals
Golden Viking	Futura	Red Wing	1960	Geometric-gold
Golden Wheat	Rhythm Coupe	Homer Laughlin	1953–58	
Golden Wheat	Yorktown	E. M. Knowles	1936	Decals
Good Luck		Lee Mfg. Co.	1926	
Granada		French-Saxon	1939–40	
Granada	True China	Red Wing	1960	Floral
Grape		Stangl	1973–74	
Green Grapes		Stangl		
Green Valley		Homer Laughlin	1977–78	
Green Wheat	Yorktown	E. M. Knowles		Decals
Greenwichstone	Ceramastone	Red Wing	1967	

Pattern	Shape	Maker	Data	Description
Hacienda	Hacienda	Franciscan		Hacienda green
Hacienda		Homer Laughlin	1938	Mexican decal
Harlequin	Harlequin	Homer Laughlin	1938–64 reissue 1979	Cobalt blue, yellow, red, tangerine, gray, turquoise, gold, rose, maroon, mauve blue, spruce green, solid colors
Harvest	Concord	Red Wing	1947	
Harvest	Ultra California	Vernon Kilns	1930s	Fruits in center
Harvest		Stangl		
Hawaii		Vernon Kilns		
Hawaiian Coral		Vernon Kilns		Spatter edge
Hawaiian Flowers		Vernon Kilns	1939	
Hawthorne	Hawthorne	Franciscan		Hand-painted
Hazelnut		Universal		Decals
Hearthstone Beige	Ceramastone	Red Wing	1967	
Hearthstone Orange	Ceramastone	Red Wing	1967	
Hearthstone	Casual	Red Wing	1961	Beige, orange, solid colors
Hearthstone	Ceramastone	Red Wing	1967	
Heavenly Days		Vernon Kilns		Blue
Heritage		Stangl		
Heyday		Vernon Kilns		
Hibiscus		Vernon Kilns		
Highland Ivy	Pie Crust	Blue Ridge	1949	

Pattern	Shape	Maker	Date	Description
Hilo		Vernon Kilns		
Holly		Stangl	1967–72	
Homespun		Vernon Kilns		Brown, yellow, green plaid
Horseshoe				Green, yellow
Hostess Pantry Ware		Pottery Guild	1954	Hand-painted
Indian Tree	Victory	Salem		Decals
Inspiration		Stangl	1967–68	
Isle of Palms	Common-wealth	James River Pottery		
Iris	Concord	Red Wing	1947	
Ivy	Ivy	Franciscan	1948	Hand-painted
Jacobean	Queen Anne	Sabin	c. 1946	
Jade Ware		Sebring	1940s	
Jamoca	Jamoca	Franciscan		Hand-painted
Jane Adams	Victory	Salem	1950s	
Jean	Nancy	Steubenville		
Joan of Arc	Diana	Sebring-Limoges		
Jonquil	Tricorne	Salem		Decals
Jonquil		Stangl		
	J-Sunshine	Hall		Floral decals
Jonquil		Stangl		
Jubilee		Homer Laughlin	1948–? 1977–78	Pastel: celadon green, shell pink, mist gray, cream beige, solid colors
Karen		Sebring-Limoges	1940	

Pattern	Shape	Maker	Date	Description
Kashmir	True China	Red Wing	1964	
Kitchen Bouquet	Century-Kitchen Kraft	Homer Laughlin		Floral decals
Kitchen Kraft	Kitchen Kraft	Homer Laughlin	1930s	Red, blue, also decals under pattern name
Kitten Capers	Kiddieware	Vernon Kilns		
Kumquat		Stangl		
Lady Greenbriar	Liberty	Homer Laughlin		Green border
Lady Stafford	Liberty	Homer Laughlin		Maroon border
Landscape		Salem China	1940s	
Lanterns	Concord	Red Wing	1947	Abstract
Laurel		Stangl	19??–42	
Lazybone		Frankoma		Solid color
Leilani		Vernon Kilns	1939	
Lenore	Monticello	Steubenville		
Lenore	Olivia	Steubenville		
Lexington	Concord	Red Wing	1947	Rose
Lido		Homer Laughlin	1977–78	
Lime		Stangl	1950	
Linda		Vernon Kilns	late 1930s	Burgundy border, pink & blue flowers
Little Quackers	Kiddieware	Vernon Kilns		
Lotus (cameo)		Harker	1959	
Louise	Virginia Rose	Homer Laughlin		

Pattern	Shape	Maker	Date	Description
Lotus	Concord	Red Wing	1947	
Luna		Blue Ridge	1920–57	Hand-painted
Lupine	Futura	Red Wing	1960	Floral
Lu-Ray	Laurel, 1932 or Empire, 1936	Taylor-Smith-Taylor	1938	Pastel: Windsor blue, Persian cream, Sharon pink, surf green, gray solids
Lute Song	True China	Red Wing	1960	Musical instruments
Lyric		Stangl	1954–57	
Madeira	Madeira	Franciscan		Hand-painted
Madison		Leigh Potteries		
Madrid		Homer Laughlin	1977–78	
Magnolia	Concord	Red Wing	1947	
Magnolia		Stangl	1952–62	
Magnolia	Liberty	Homer Laughlin		Decal
Majestic	True China	Red Wing	1960	White
Mango	Mango	Franciscan		Hand-painted
Maple Whirl		Stangl	1965–67	
Mar-Crest				
Mardi Gras		Blue Ridge	1943	
	Marylou (creamer & sugar)	Hall		Floral decals
May Flower		Vernon Kilns	1940s	Floral pattern
Mayan Aztec		Frankoma		Solid colors
Maypole	Maypole	Franciscan		Hand-painted
Meadow Flowers	Ball	Hall (Teapot)		Decal

Pattern	Shape	Maker	Date	Description
Meadow Rose	Meadow Rose	Franciscan	1977	Hand-painted
Mediterranean	True China	Red Wing	1960	Floral
Mediterranean		Stangl	1965–74	
Merrileaf	True China	Red Wing	1960	Floral
Mesa	Encanto	Franciscan		
Mexicana	Kitchen Kraft	Homer Laughlin	1938	Mexican decals, scenes with different colored bands
Midnight Rose	Anniversary	Red Wing	1953	Rose
Midsummer		Sebring-Limoges	1940	
Midsummer	Victory	Salem		Decals
Ming Tree		Blue Ridge	1920–57	Hand-painted
Mirador		Homer Laughlin	1977–78	
Mirasol	Mirasol	Franciscan		Hand-painted
Moby Dick		Vernon Kilns	1939	
Modern		J. A. Bauer	1935	Solid colors
Modern California	Modern California	Vernon Kilns	1930s	Azure, orchid, pistachio, straw, sand, gray
Modern Tulip	Plymouth	Harker	1930s	
Monticello	Granitone	Hall	1941	
Monterey		Stangl	1967–68–70	
Monterey		Vernon Kilns		
Monterey Moderne		J. A. Bauer	1948	Solid colors: olive green, gray, black, yellow, pink chartreuse, brown, burgundy

Pattern	Shape	Maker	Date	Description
Montmartre	Futura	Red Wing	1960	French street scene
Montgomery Ward	Refrigerator Sets			
Moon Flower		Salem		
Morning Blue		Stangl	1970	
Morning Glory		Hall	1942–49	Cadet blue body (floral decals), blue with decal
Morning Glory	Concord	Red Wing	1947	
Moss Rose		Blue Ridge	1920–57	Hand-painted
Moss Rose		Universal Pottery	1953–55	Decals
Mount Vernon	Graniteware	Hall	1941	
Mountain Cherry		Blue Ridge	1951	
Mountain Cherry		Blue Ridge	1920–57	Hand-painted
Mountain Ivy		Blue Ridge	1951	
Mountain Laurel		Stangl	1947–57	
Nautical	Candlewick	Blue Ridge		
Nautilus	Century	Homer Laughlin		Floral decals
Nassau	Concord	Red Wing	1947	
Native American		Vernon Kilns	1930s	Mexican scenes
Native California	Native California	Vernon Kilns	late 1930s	Pastels
Newport		Stangl	1940–42	
New Princess		Sebring-Limoges		
Night Flower	Skyline	Blue Ridge	1952	

Pattern	Shape	Maker	Date	Description
Nordic		Homer Laughlin	1977–78	
Norway Rose		Homer Laughlin		Floral decal
Normandy	1941 Provincial	Red Wing	1941	Blue & maroon bands, later apple blossoms added
Northern Lights	Futura	Red Wing	1960	Geometric blue
Nove Rose	Colonial	Blue Ridge		
Nut Tree	Nut Tree	Franciscan		Hand-painted
Octagon	Octagon	Catalina	1930s	Solid colors
October	October	Franciscan (H. P.)	1977	
Old English		Homer Laughlin		Floral decals
Old Dutch		Sebring-Limoges		
Old Orchard		Stangl	1941–42	
Old Provincial (also called oomph)		Red Wing	1943	Aqua, brown bottom
Orange Poppy	Ultra California	Vernon Kilns	late 1930s	Pink band, yellow band, pink flower, yellow pear
Orchard	Ultra California	Vernon Kilns		
Orchard Song		Stangl	1962–74	
Organdie		Vernon Kilns	1930s	Orange, brown, yellow plaid
Orleans	1941 Provincial	Red Wing	1941	Red rose
Our America		Vernon Kilns	1939	

Pattern	Shape	Maker	Date	Description
Our Barnyard Friends	Kiddieware	Vernon Kilns		
Paisley		Stangl	1963–67	
Palo Alto	Encanto	Franciscan		Hand-painted
Pantry Shelf	Yorktown	E. M. Knowles		
Paradise	Coupe	Homer Laughlin		
Parsley	Salem	Salem		
Pastel Garden	Sabina	Sabin		
Pastel Tulip		Harker		Floral decals
Patchwork		Homer Laughlin	1977–78	
Pate-sur-Pate	Shalimar	Steubenville		
Pauda (Freesia)	Pauda	Franciscan		Hand-painted
Pebble Beach	Pebble Beach	Franciscan		Hand-painted
Pear Turnpike		Vernon Kilns		Brown
Penthouse	Yorktown	E. M. Knowles		
Pepe	New Shape	Red Wing	1962	Geometric
Peter Rabbit	Kiddieware	Vernon Kilns		
Petitpoint		Homer Laughlin	1960s	Floral decals
Petit Point		Montgomery Ward	1936	Decals
Petit Point Basket		Salem		
Petit Point Leaf		Crooksville		Decals
Petite Flowers		Stangl	1970–74	
Picnic	Picnic	Franciscan		Hand-painted
Picardy	Village Green	Red Wing	1960	Yellow rose
Pie Crust		Stangl	1969	
Pink Cosmos		Stangl	1966	

Pattern	Shape	Maker	Date	Description
Pink Dogwood		Stangl		
Pink Lady	Vernon Ware	Metlox	1965	
Pink Lily		Stangl	1953–57	
Pink Morning Glory		Hall		Early decal
Pink Moss Rose		Homer Laughlin	1920	Decal
Pink Mums		Hall		Floral decals
Pink Print		Montgomery Ward	1936	Decals
Pink Rose		Homer Laughlin	1920	Decals
Pink Rose & Daisy	Plain Edge	Homer Laughlin	1920	Decals
Pink Spice	Anniversary	Red Wing (H.P.)	1953	Butterfly design
Plain	Gypsy Trail	Red Wing	1935	Solid colors: blue, yellow, ivory, orange, turquoise
Plainsman		Frankoma		Solid colors
Plantation Ivy	Skyline	Blue Ridge (H.P.)	1920–59	
Plantation Ivy	Skyline	Blue Ridge	1951	
Playful Pups	Kiddieware	Vernon Kilns		
Plaza				Water jugs
Plum	Candlewick	Blue Ridge		
Plum Blossom	Dynasty	Red Wing	1947	Yellow, green, pink, oriental motif, six-sided
Pocahontas	Common-wealth	James River Pottery		
Poinsetta	Colonial	Blue Ridge	1950	

Pattern	Shape	Maker	Date	Description
Polka Dot		Hall	1942	
Polo	Tricorne	Salem		Decals
Pompadour	Sabina	Sabin	c. 1946	
Pompeii	New Shape	Red Wing (H.P.)	1962	Geometric
Pony Trail	Kiddieware	Vernon Kilns		
Poppy	C-Line	Hall	1933–50	Floral decals
Poppy & Wheat		Hall	1933– c. 39	Floral decals
Posey Shop	Triumph	Sebring-Limoges	1944–45	
Posies		Stangl	1973–	
Prelude		Stangl	1949–57	
Pricilla Bakeware	Century-Kitchen Kraft	Homer Laughlin		Floral decals
Primrose				
Prince		Hall	c. 1952	Refrigerator sets
Priscilla		Homer Laughlin		
Provincial		Stangl	1957–67	
Provincial Blue	Poppytrail	Metlox	1951	
Provincial Fruit	Poppytrail	Metlox	1965	
Provincial Tulip		Harker	1959	Cameo Ware
Puppy-Flower	Floral Edge	E. M. Knowles	1933–34	Decals
		Purinton Pottery	1941–59	Hand-painted
Quaker Maid		Harker		
Quartette	Concord	Red Wing	1947	Four solid colors
Quilted Fruit		Blue Ridge	1920–57	Hand-painted

Pattern	Shape	Maker	Date	Description
Raffia		Vernon Kilns		Green & brown (like tree bark)
	Rainbow	Stangl	1935	Solid colors: silver green, Persian yellow, colonial blue, tangerine, aqua blue, rust, brown, surf white
Rainbow		Hall		Hall's radiant ware
Raisin	Ring	Vernon Kilns		Drip glaze, solid colors
Rambler Rose	Aristocrat	E. M. Knowles	1930s	Decals
Random Harvest	Futura	Red Wing	1955	Harvest colors
	Random Harvest	Red Wing	1961	Hand-painted
Ranger		Stangl		
Raymor		Roseville (Ben Siebel)	1952	White, brown, mottled green, dark green, blue, rust, brown
Raymor Contempora		Steubenville		Faun, mist gray, sand white, charcoal
Red & Gold		Montgomery Ward	1936	Decals
Red & Gold		Montgomery Ward	1936	Decals
Red Berry	Victory	Salem		Decals
Red Ivy		Stangl	1957	
Red Pony	D-Line	Hall	1930s–50s	Floral decals
Red Riding Hood	Figural	Hull		
Red Rooster Provincial	Poppytrail	Metlox	1965	
Red Tulip	Kitchen Kraft	Homer Laughlin		Decals

Pattern	Shape	Maker	Date	Description
Red Wing Rose	Futura	Red Wing	1960	Rose
Reed	Gypsytrail	Red Wing	1935	Blue, yellow, turquoise, ivory, orange
Regal Rings	Queen Anne	Sabin	c. 1946	
Remembrance	Citation	Steubenville		
Rend Leaf		Blue Ridge	1942–43	
Rhea	Trend	Steubenville		
Rhythm		Homer Laughlin	c. 1938–50s	Solid colors: yellow, chartreuse, gray, green, burgundy
Rhythm		Paden City	1936	
Rhythm Rose	Century	Homer Laughlin		Floral decals
Richmond	Graniteware	Hall	1941	
Ringles		Stangl	1973–74	
Ring or Bee Hive		J. A. Bauer	1932–62	Solid colors: orange, burnt orange, dark blue, yellow, green, ivory, maroon, black; pastel: turquoise, olive, green, gray, white, pale blue, light yellow, pink, chartreuse
Rio		Salem China	1943	
Riviera	Century	Homer Laughlin	1938–50	Mauve blue, red, yellow, light green, ivory, dark blue, solid colors
Rococo	Princess	Paden City	1933	
Romance	Cavalier	Homer Laughlin		

Pattern	Shape	Maker	Date	Description
Rooster		Harker		Blue & pink Cameo Ware
Rooster		Blue Ridge	1920–57	Hand-painted
Rooster		Stangl	1970–74	
Rope Edge	Rope Edge	Catalina	1936	Solid colors
Rose & Lattice	Plain Edge	Homer Laughlin	1920	Decals
Rose Bouquet	Floral Edge	E. M. Knowles	1933–34	
Rosebud	Horizon	Steubenville		
Rosebud		Coors, Golden, Colo.	1930s	Solid colors: green, turquoise, ivory, yellow, maroon, blue
Rose Garland Border		Homer Laughlin	1920	Decals
Rose Leaf		Syracuse		
Rose Marie		Sebring-Limoges		
Rose O'Day		Vernon Kilns		
Rose Parade		Hall	1941	Cadet blue body, floral decals, blue with decal
Rose Point		Pope-Gosser		Rose decal or plain
Rose White		Hall	1941	Hi-white, cadet blue body, floral decals
Round-Up	Casual	Red Wing	1958	
Roxanna		Universal		Decals
Roxanne		Stangl	1972–74	
Royal Harvest	Coupe	Homer Laughlin		
Royal Marina		Sebring-Limoges	1944–45	
Royal Rose		Hall		Blue with decal, silver trim, floral decals

Pattern	Shape	Maker	Date	Description
Royal Windsor		Salem	1950s	
Russel Wright	Casual	Iroquois China		Solid colors (modern shape)
Russel Wright		Harker		Solid colors (modern shape)
Russel Wright		Justin Therod & Sons		Spruce green (modern shape)
Russel Wright	American	Steubenville	1938	Chartreuse, pink, white, bean brown, gray, black chutney, seaform blue, spruce green (modern shape)
Rustic		Stangl	1965–74	
Rustic Garden		Stangl	1972–74	
Sailing	Tricorne	Salem		Decals
Salamina		Vernon Kilns	1939	
Sampler	Victory	Salem		Decals
Sandra		Salem	1950s	
	Sani-Grid	Hall		Chinese red
Santa Barbara		Vernon Kilns		
Saratoga	Skyline	Blue Ridge	1952	
Scenic America		Vernon Kilns		
Sculptured Daisy	Poppytail	Metlox	1965	
Sculptured Fruit		Stangl	1966–74	
Sculptured Grape	Poppytail	Metlox	1975	
Sculptured Zinnia	Poppytail	Metlox	1965	
Sears R.		Hall		Cadet blue, hi-white
Serenade		Homer Laughlin	1940s	Yellow, green, pink, blue, pastel, solid colors

Pattern	Shape	Maker	Date	Description
Sesame		Stangl	1972–74	
Seven Seas		Vernon Kilns		
Sevilla				Solid colors
Shadow Leaf				
Shalimar	Shalimar	Steubenville		
Shawnee				
Sheffield		Salem China	1943	
Sherwood		Vernon Kilns		
Sierra		Stangl	1967/68–70	
Silhouette (has dog)		Crooksville		Silhouette decal
Silver Rose		Homer Laughlin	1960s	Floral decals
Skiffs	Yorktown	E. M. Knowles		
Skyblue		Homer Laughlin	1977–78	
Skyline		Blue Ridge	1954	
Skytone	Liberty	Homer Laughlin		Light blue
Smart Set	Casual	Red Wing	1955	Hand-painted
Smooth		J. A. Bauer	1936–37	Solid colors
Snowflake		Homer Laughlin	1920	Decals
Snowflower		Montgomery Ward	1936	Decals
Sonesta		Homer Laughlin	1977–78	
Sorrento		Homer Laughlin	1977–78	
Southern Camellia	Pie Crust	Blue Ridge	1948	
Southern Dogwood		Blue Ridge	1920–57	Hand-painted

Pattern	Shape	Maker	Date	Description
Speck Ware		J. A. Bauer	1946	Tan, pink, gray, white
Spring	Trend	Steubenville		
Spring Bouquet		Montgomvery Ward	1936	Decals
Spring Song	Cavalier	Homer Laughlin		
Spring Song	Concord	Red Wing	1947	Birds
Springtime		Hall		
Spun Gold		Stangl	1965–67	
Stardust		Stangl	1967	
Starlight	Starlight	Catalina	1936	Solid colors
Star Flower		Stangl	1952–57	
		Stetson China Co.	c. 1959	Hand-painted
Streamline	Streamline			Modern
Suburbia		McCoy	1964	Brown, blue
Summer Days		Homer Laughlin	1977–78	
Sundance	Sundance	Franciscan		Hand-painted
Sunflower		Blue Ridge	1947	
Sun Gold		Homer Laughlin	1977–78	
Sunny Spray		Blue Ridge	1951	Hand-painted
Sun Pebbles		Stangl	1973–74	
Sun Ray	Elite	Paden City	1936	Red & black cross-stitch
Sunshine (No. 448)		Hall	1933	Floral decals, white with red decal flower
Sunshine		Stangl		
Susan		Blue Ridge		
Susan		Stangl	1972–74	

Pattern	Shape	Maker	Date	Description
Susan	Trend	Steubenville		
Tahiti	Triumph	Sebring-Limoges	1938	
Tahitian Gold	New Shape	Red Wing	1962	Gold
Tam O'Shanter		Vernon Kilns		Green, chartreuse, brown plaid, green border
Tampico (watermelon)	Futura	Red Wing	1955	Hand-painted
Tango		Homer Laughlin	1930s	Solid colors: blue, green, yellow, red
Taverne		Hall	c. 1930s	Silhouette decal
Taverne	Laurel	Taylor-Smith-Taylor		Silhouette decal
Terrace Ceramics	Corn Shape	Terrace Ceramics,		
Terra Rose		Stangl	1941–42	
Thistle		Blue Ridge	1954	
Thistle		Universal		Decals
Thistle		French-Saxon		
Tia Juana	Yorktown	E. M. Knowles		Decals
Tickled Pink		Vernon Kilns		Pink
Tiger Flower	Tiger Flower	Franciscan		Pink, hand-painted
Tiger Lily		Stangl	1957–62	Decal
Tip Toe	Casual	Red Wing	1958	
Toledo Delight	Trojan	Sebring	1941–42	
Town & Country		Red Wing	1946	Metallic brown, forest green, rust, sandy peach, blue, chartreuse
Tower		Leigh		

Pattern	Shape	Maker	Date	Description
	Tricorne	Salem	1934	Red orange, stripes
Trade Winds		Vernon Kilns		
Trailway		Blue Ridge	1954	
Traveler		Syracuse		Railroad china
Treasured		Stangl	1968	
Trinidad		Stangl	1972–74	
Trojan	Trojan	Catalina	pre-1935	Solid colors
Tropical		Blue Ridge	1920–57	Hand-painted
True Blue	Vernonware	Metlox	1965	
Tudor Rose	Sabina	Sabin		
Tulip	D-Line	Hall	1930-50s	Floral decals
Tulip		Universal		Decals
Tulip		Hall	1949	
Tulip: Blue & Yellow		Stangl	1942–73	
Tulips		Blue Ridge	1942–	
Tulips		Blue Ridge	1920–57	Hand-painted
Tulip Tree		Homer Laughlin	1977–78	
Tulip Wreath	Coupe	Homer Laughlin		
Turtle Dove	New Shape	Red Wing	1962	Two doves
Tweed		Vernon Kilns		Gray & blue plaid
Tweed Tex	Anniversary	Red Wing	1953	White
Twilight		Flintridge China Co.		
Two Step	Village Green	Red Wing	1960	Geometric design
Tyrol	Olivia	Steubenville		
Ugly Couple		Blue Ridge	1920–57	Hand-painted

Pattern	Shape	Maker	Date	Description
Ultra California		Vernon Kilns	1930s	Carnation, buttercup aster, gardenia
Vermillion Rose	Triumph	Sebring-Limoges		
Vernon 1860	Village Green	Vernon Kilns	1955	Brown
Vestal Rose		E. M. Knowles	1930s	Decals
Vienna	Victory	Salem China	1940s	
Village Brown	Village Green	Red Wing	1955	Brown
Village Green	Village Green	Red Wing	1953	Green
Vine Yard	Vernonware	Metlox	1965	
Vine Wrath	Laurel	Taylor-Smith-Taylor	1933–34	Decals
Vintage		Vernon Kilns		
Vintage	True China	Red Wing	1960	Floral
Vintage Pink	Poppytrail	Metlox	1965	
Violet		Blue Ridge		
Violet	Trend	Steubenville		
Violet Spray		Homer Laughlin	1920	Decals
Virginia Rose	Kitchen Kraft	Homer Laughlin		Floral decals
Vistosa		Taylor-Smith-Taylor		Solid colors
Vistosa		E. M. Knowles	1936	Solid colors: cadet blue, yellow, russet, burgundy, red
Vogue		Syracuse		
Wagon Wheels		Frankoma	1933–present	Solid colors: desert gold, prairie green
Waldorf		Sebring-Limoges	1939	

Pattern	Shape	Maker	Date	Description
Wards Garland		Montgomery Ward	1936	Decals
Water Lily	Yorktown	E. M. Knowles		
Water Lily		Stangl	1949–57	
Waverly		Homer Laughlin	1977–78	
Weather Bloom	Squared-Off Edges	E. M. Knowles	1933–34	Decals
Weathervane		Blue Ridge	1920–57	Hand-painted
Westwind		Frankoma		Solid colors
Wheatfield		Sebring-Limoges		
White & Embossed		Montgomery Ward	1920	Decals
Wheat		Harker	1961	Cameo Ware
White & Gold		Homer Laughlin	1920	Decals
White & Gold Carnation		Homer Laughlin	1920	Decals
White Gold Ware		Sebring	1940s	
White & Green Persian		Homer Laughlin	1920	Decals
White Dogwood		Stangl	1965–74	Decals
White Grape		Stangl	1967	
White Rose		Corncraft		
White Rose		Harker Potteries		Blue & pink Cameo Ware
Wild Bouquet		Homer Laughlin	1977–78	
Wild Flower	Floral Edge	E. M. Knowles	1933–34	Decals

Pattern	Shape	Maker	Date	Description
Wild Rose	Floral Edge	E. M. Knowles	1933–34	Decals
Wild Rose		Homer Laughlin		Floral decals
Wild Rose		Stangl	1955–73	
Wild Rose & Flower	Empress	Homer Laughlin	1920	Decals
Wildfire	D-Line	Hall	1950s	Hi-white floral decals
Wildwood		Stangl		
Willow	Willow	Franciscan		Hand-painted
Willow Wind	Concord	Red Wing	1947	Abstract
Windfall		Stangl	1955–57	
Windmill	Victory	Salem		Decals
Winged Streamliner		Homer Laughlin		Railroad china
Woodcrest		Blue Ridge	1954	
Woodfield		Steubenville		
Wood Rose		Stangl	1973–74	
Wrightwood	Rainbow	E. M. Knowles	1930s	Decals
Yellow Carnation	Fiesta Casuals	Homer Laughlin	1962–68	Solid colors
Yellow Flower		Stangl	1970	
Yellow Matte Gold		Homer Laughlin	1920	Decals
Yellow Matte Gold Band	Plain Edge	Homer Laughlin	1920	Decals
Yorktown	Yorktown	E. M. Knowles	1936	Maroon, terra-cotta, periwinkle blue, light yellow

Pattern	Shape	Maker	Date	Description
Zeisel		Hall	1950s	
Zinnia		Homer Laughlin	1977–78	
Zinnia	Concord	Red Wing	1947	

Glossary

Akro Agate: glass made in Clarksburg, West Virginia, from 1932 to 1951. The firm has been known for making marbles but started making children's dishes. The marbleized glassware is sometimes incorrectly referred to as Akro Agate, meaning a color.

Ball jug: round pitcher, Hall China Company shape introduced in 1938.

Bottom's-Up: drinking glass made so it cannot be put down because the bottom is rounded. Often made with the figure of a girl molded across the sides and bottom.

Butter dish: a covered dish used to hold butter on the table; or a covered storage dish used for butter in the refrigerator.

Chinese red: Hall China Company color.

Chinex: a pattern by MacBeth Evans Division of the Corning Glass Works from the late 1930s to the 1940s. This ivory-colored glass with scroll designed edges was made either with plain or with a colored decal decoration. Sometimes confused with Cremax.

Coupe soup: flat, shallow round bowl about seven or eight inches in diameter, no handles. Used to serve soup.

Cream soup: two-handled low bowl used for service of cream soup or bisque.

Cremax: an ivory colored glassware made by MacBeth Evans Division of the Corning Glass Works in the late 1930s and early 1940s. It is sometimes confused with Chinex but it has a ridged edge. Cremax is also used as a color name for a creamy opaque glass used in some other patterns such as American Sweetheart.

Delphite: opaque light blue colored glass, sometimes incorrectly called "blue milk glass."

Drip-o-lator or dripper: additional piece put between cover and coffeepot. Coffee is put in the top or spreader, hot water is poured in and drips through to the pot to make coffee.

Fired-on colors: color applied to glass then baked under high heat at the factory.

Flashed or flashed-on: color added over clear glass.

Flat soup or rimmed soup: similar to coupe shape but with a rim that makes it seem larger.

Fluted baker: sometimes called French flute. Dish with ridges and straight sides, of a type now called a souffle dish. Comes in various sizes.

French flute: see Fluted Baker.

Grill plate: round three-section plate used to serve meat and vegetables in the separate sections. Similar to a modern TV dinner tray.

Ice lip: specially shaped lip of a pitcher curved to keep the ice cubes from falling out with the water when the water is poured.

Iridescent: rainbowlike colors that appear on glassware when the light reflects.

Ivy ball: round glass vase, may or may not have a pedestal stem.

Jade-ite: opaque light green colored glass.

Jadite: opaque light green colored kitchenware made by Jeannette Glass Co.

Leftover: covered dish used to hold leftover food in a refrigerator—part of the refrigerator sets.

Monax: white colored glass made by MacBeth Evans Division of the Corning Glass Works, has "fire" on edge, a slightly iridescent coloring.

Opalescent: opaque white glass that appears to have colors at the edges.

Plate sizes: 6 in.–dessert
                          7 in.–bread & butter
                   7–7½ in.–salad
                      8–9 in.–luncheon
                          9 in.–breakfast
                        10 in.–dinner
                        13 in.–chop

Platonite: heat resistant white glass made by Hazel Atlas Glass Company.

Reamer: dish and pointed-top cone used to extract juice from lemons, oranges or grapefruits.

Sani-Grid: Hall China Company shape introduced in 1941.

Tilt jug: pitcher.

Tumble-Up: glass bottle with small tumbler turned upside down over the neck to serve as a top and a drinking glass.

Water server: covered pitcher kept filled with water in the refrigerator—part of refrigerator sets.